The Cinema of Satyajit Ray
Between Tradition and Modernity

Satyajit Ray is one of India's best-known filmmakers, and his importance in the international world of cinema has long been recognized. Darius Cooper's study of Ray is the first to examine his rich and varied work from a social and historical perspective and to situate it within Indian aesthetics. Providing analyses of selected films, including *Shatranj-ke-Khilari* (*The Chess Players*), *Jalsaghar* (*The Music Room*), the films of *The Apu Trilogy*, and others, Cooper outlines Western influences on Ray's work: the plight of women functioning within a patriarchal society, Ray's political vision of the "doubly colonized," and his attack and critique of the Bengali/Indian middle class of today. The most comprehensive treatment of Ray's work, *The Cinema of Satyajit Ray* makes accessible the oeuvre of this prolific and creative filmmaker.

Darius Cooper is Professor of Literature and Film at San Diego Mesa College.

Cambridge Studies in Film

General Editors
William Rothman, University of Miami
Dudley Andrew, University of Iowa

Selected Titles from the Series

Satyajit Ray: framing his universe through the lens of his vision. (Photo by Nemai Ghosh; gift of Ben Nyce)

The Cinema of Satyajit Ray
Between Tradition and Modernity

DARIUS COOPER

San Diego Mesa College

CAMBRIDGE
UNIVERSITY PRESS

PUBLISHED BY THE PRESS SYNDICATE OF THE UNIVERSITY OF CAMBRIDGE
The Pitt Building, Trumpington Street, Cambridge, United Kingdom

CAMBRIDGE UNIVERSITY PRESS
The Edinburgh Building, Cambridge CB2 2RU, UK   http://www.cup.cam.ac.uk
40 West 20th Street, New York, NY 10011-4211, USA   http://www.cup.org
10 Stamford Road, Oakleigh, Melbourne 3166, Australia
Ruiz de Alarcón 13, 28014 Madrid, Spain

First published 2000

Printed in the United States of America

Typeface Sabon 10/13 pt.   *System* QuarkXpress®   [MG]

A catalog record for this book is available from the British Library

Library of Congress Cataloging in Publication Data
Cooper, Darius, 1949–
The cinema of Satyajit Ray : between tradition and modernity / Darius Cooper
p.   cm. – (Cambridge studies in film)
Filmography: p.
Includes bibliographical references and index.
ISBN 0 521 62026 0 (hb). – ISBN 0 521 62980 2 (pb)
1. Ray, Satyajit, 1921–1992 – Criticism and interpretation.
I. Title.   II. Series
PN1998.3.R4C88   1999
791.43´0233´092 – dc21   99–24768
CIP

ISBN 0 521 62026 0 hardback
ISBN 0 521 62980 2 paperback

Contents

Illustrations

Acknowledgments

My *shukriya*/thanks are due to the following:

This study was first undertaken on the campus of the University of Southern California as a Ph.D. dissertation in the Department of English. It had a slightly different format, but nevertheless much of it was closely read and many valuable suggestions were made by Professors Leo Braudy and Ron Gottesman from the English Department and Allen Casebier from the School of Cinema's Department of Critical Studies. For their scrutiny I am very grateful. I must acknowledge the valuable support granted by Professors Peter Manning and Stephen Moore, who as rotating chairpersons continued my teaching assistantship and encouraged me to persevere with Ray at USC. Thanks are also due to the anonymous reader at the University of California Press, Berkeley, who carefully read the original dissertation and submitted a detailed report of how I could turn it into what this study finally became. More thanks are due to Professor Bill Rothman and the anonymous reader at Cambridge University Press who have shaped and honed this study.

I am very grateful to Ernest Callenbach and the editorial board of *Film Quarterly*, who were the first to publish my film criticisms on recent Indian cinema in general and the Ray essay on *Ghare-Baire* in particular in America. The same goes to Wimal Dissanayake and the editorial board of *The East–West Film Journal*, which published my essay on Ray's *Sadgati*. My essay on the representation of colonialism in Ray's *The Chess Players* was also included by Wimal Dissanayake in his anthology *Colonialism and Nationalism in Asian Cinema*. I extend my gratefulness to the editors of *Women's Studies: A Feminist Journal* from Claremont Graduate School for accepting for publication my study of *Charulata*.

Thanks are due to Professor Dilip Basu of the University of California at Santa Cruz for accepting my essays on *Mahanagar* and *Ghare-Baire*, which will appear in an anthology dedicated to *Women in Ray's Films* that he is editing for Oxford University Press, India. I am grateful to Professor Basu for inviting me to read my paper on *Mahanagar* at a Satyajit Ray conference organized by him at Santa Cruz in 1994, and for providing me with stills from the Ray Archives. I am grateful also to Sandip Ray for allowing me to use these stills in this study. Thanks are due as well to Professor Ben Nyce for generously gifting me with his unused collection of stills as photographed by Nemai Ghosh.

I am very grateful to Professors Gautam Kundu and Suranjan Ganguly for giving me the opportunity to present my paper on *Pratidwandi* at the Commonwealth Literature Conference held by the English Department at Georgia State University at Statesboro in 1993. I also acknowledge the opportunity given at the Ohio Film Conference, where I presented a paper on *Aranyer Din Ratri* in 1994. Thanks are also due to the Social Sciences Forum at San Diego Mesa College, where I presented a paper on *Shatranj-ke-Khilari* in 1992, and to the Tagore Conference at the University of Connecticut, where I read a paper on "The Postmaster" in 1998.

I am indebted to my wife, Pravina, who is my real teacher and guide in the exciting and complex world of contemporary criticism. It was under her tutelage that I was introduced to the superb knowledge of so many Western and Indian critical thinkers whose insights I have tried to incorporate in this study. I must also thank my father and two of my closest friends, Rafique Baghdadi and Rashid Irani, who patiently collected all kinds of materials that were published on Ray in Indian newspapers and journals and regularly sent them to me here in America. I would like to include Cuthbert Lethbridge in this group for sending me important critiques related to Ray's last three films; they helped a lot in the writing of the final chapter. My thanks also go to my fourteen-year-old son, Nikhil, whose perennial antics of wonder and mischief kept the Apu magic alive in all the tiny rooms where this manuscript slowly took shape. He and another dear friend, Kironmoy Raha, kept the sun shining, the ink flowing, and saw to it that all of these pages on Ray were properly filled.

Last, but not least, my thanks go to Michael Gnat for his superb editing skills, infinite patience, and the care and devotion he has given to this study, and to Beatrice Rehl at Cambridge University Press for graciously piloting this project to completion.

Introduction

In his very revealing 1963 "Calm Without, Fire Within" (from his collection of writing on films entitled *Our Films, Their Films*), Ray refers to his formative years at Rabindranath Tagore's university in Santinikitan. In order to learn the rudiments of Chinese calligraphy, Ray writes:

We rubbed our sticks of Chinese ink on porcelain palettes, dipped our bamboo-stemmed Japanese brushes in it and held them poised perpendicularly over mounted sheets of Nepalese-parchment. "Now draw a tree," our Professor Bose would say. (Bose was a famous Bengali painter who made pilgrimages to China and Japan). "Draw a tree, but not in the western fashion. Not from the top downwards. A tree grows up, not down. The strokes must be from the base upwards. . . ."[1]

The aim of this study is to situate and evaluate the cinema of Satyajit Ray from an Indian aesthetic as well as an Indian social and historical perspective. His rich and varied filmic oeuvre arises, I intend to show, from within the Indian tradition itself. He drew his cinematic tree along the very same lines as designated by his teacher, Professor Bose, in the above citation. Now, this does not mean that Ray deliberately shunned or avoided any influences derived from his profound knowledge of Western art forms. A closer look at his vast array of films confirms, in his own words, the parallel

existence of an art form, western in origin, but transplanted and taking roots in a new soil. The tools are the same, but the methods and attitudes in the best and most characteristic work are distinct and indigenous.[2]

Lest Ray be falsely accused of being self-congratulatory here, the above remarks were made by Ray in relation to Akira Kurosawa's *Rashomon*. This study, however, aims to single out both the Western and the Indian influences in his films, thereby laying bare a truly indigenous style and vision that makes his cinema receptive and accessible to the Western as well as the Indian spectator.

It was *The Apu Trilogy* (*Pather Panchali*, 1955; *Aparajito*, 1956; *Apur Sansar*, 1959) that established Ray on the international film scene. While many critics celebrated it as a eulogy of third-world culture, others criticized it for what they took to be its romanticization of such a culture. In the wake of modern critical theory emphasizing that artistic production be seen in its historicity and not be celebrated merely as an isolated phenomenon, Ray came in for some severe criticism. He was charged by critics like Robin Wood with being "less interested in expressing ideas than in communicating emotional experience."[3] They also singled out his apparently overriding "concern with nuances of character relationships and character development."[4]

In this study, I hope to provide a deeper understanding of Ray's nexus with Indian society and his own position as artist and spokesman in relation to it. One of my critical concerns is to show how, beneath the variety of narrative discourses that he develops, Ray is intent in telling us another story. In film after film, he investigates India's social institutions and the power structures to which they give rise, or vice versa. He works out, in concrete terms, the conflicts and issues of his times, both in his own state of Bengal and in the larger Indian nation. To quote Ashish Rajadhyaksha, from his excellent essay "Satyajit Ray, Ray's Films, and Ray-Movie":

[In] Ray's early realism of *The Apu Trilogy* . . . key characters are each assigned a highly idealized, even mystical, set of privileged spaces. . . . Those spaces are occupied by objects that for the characters resonate with primal emotional appeal; and a virtual rite of passage. . . .[5]

In *Jalsaghar* (*The Music Room*, 1958), Ray's concern shifts to the fading away of the feudal era in India. In the women's films, Ray establishes their sensitivity, integrity, and their triumph amid unjust patriarchal surroundings. He demystifies the revered Hindu ideals inscribed in their roles of mothers and wives and shows how they achieve their emancipation. In his portrayal of Indian men, on the other hand, he reveals to us their cowardice and shallowness as they take shelter in male-dominated social institutions and hegemonic structures. In *Shatranj-ke-Khilari* (*The Chess Players*, 1977), Ray depicts feudal irresponsibility and a self-obsessed nobility lost in its own mythic roles, and in *Sadgati* (*Deliverance*, 1981), he indicts religious spirituality by showing the antihuman doctrines of hierarchy and Untouchability on which a cruel and unjust Hindu caste system is based and run. Whereas the Brahmin priest's spiritual supremacy is ordained and ensured by religion, Ray shows us how he is materially dependent on the labor and donations of the Untouchables and how he uses the Hindu-assigned principles of exclusivity, pollution, and hierarchy to perpetuate the continuance of the caste system.

This book, apart from the Introduction, is divided into five chapters, which should be read as five distinct movements. Through these I intend to show how Ray's cinema comes not only to enunciate new and controversial themes but also to inscribe powerful meanings through the compelling and innovative fashioning of varied discourses that he forges out of Indian as well as Western forms of expressions and resources.

Ray's cinema began with children, nature, paddy fields, and a village. Geeta Kapur, in her excellent essay "Cultural Creativity in the First Decade: The Example of Satyajit Ray," alerts us to what could have been Ray's impetus in his very first film:

But then *Pather Panchali* and the *Apu Trilogy* as a cycle could also be seen as answering, in some unprecedented sense, a contemporary and most immediate need for a suitable visual solution to the question of representing everyday life in India. The perennial and the everyday. . . . Now, as a film-maker, he seemed to resolve with exemplary economy the question of image, iconography and pictorial narrative.[6]

In his 1957 essay "A Long Time on the Little Road," Ray maintains that when he "chose *Pather Panchali*, for the qualities that made it a great book: its humanism, its lyricism, and its ring of truth,"[7] considerations of "form, rhythm or movement did not worry me at this stage."[8] However, in the making of the film, he soon discovered the emotion-centered form of the *rasa* theory that enabled him to both represent and present what Kapur classified as "everyday life" in India in *The Apu Trilogy*. Hence, in Chapter 1, I begin my study of *The Apu Trilogy* and *Jalsaghar* (which he made in 1958, just prior to the trilogy's completion) by examining them through the intricate theories of *rasa* laid down by three Sanskrit theoreticians – Dandin (seventh century), Anandvardhana (ninth century), and the most important scholar of them all, Abhinavagupta (tenth century).

Bibhuithibhusan's novel *Pather Panchali* was cinematically translated by Ray along the lines of *rasa*, defined by A. K. Ramanujan as follows:

In each man's history there are feelings (*bhāva*) of all sorts, and the poeticians single out eight of these: love, mirth, grief, energy, terror, disgust, anger, and wonder. Each of these is, in the poetic context, transmuted into a corresponding mood (*rasa*). . . . They carry with them all the physical phases of their expression, their allied feelings, their dominants and their consequents in emotional behaviour. Each mood has a characteristic set of these, and it is on this fact that the whole analysis of dramatic performance is based. . . .[9]

Ray is quite aware of this when he tells us in his same essay:

I had my nucleus: the family . . . whose characters had been so conceived by the author that there was a *constant* and *subtle interplay between them.* I had my time span of one year. I had my *contrasts-pictorial* as well as *emotional:* the rich and the poor, the *laughter* and the *tears,* the *beauty* of the countryside and the *grimness* of poverty existing in it. Finally, I had the *two* natural halves of the story culminating in two poignant deaths. What more could a scenarist want?[10]

The italics, all mine, highlight words directly relate to *rasa*-conceived critical principles. More *rasa*-related concepts are offered by Ray as he continues with his meditations:

While far from being an adventure in the physical sense, these explorations into the village nevertheless opened up a new and fascinating world . . . you wanted to observe and probe, to catch the revealing details, the telling gestures, the particular turns of speech. You wanted to fathom the mysteries of atmosphere.[11]

Rasa's complicated doctrine centers predominantly on feelings experienced not only by the characters but also conveyed in a certain artistic way to the spectator. The duality of this kind of a *rasa* imbrication was not lost on Ray; indeed, Ray's awareness of it shows in his very first film. The following utterance bears eloquent testimony to it: "Experience tells us that the subtlest of emotional states affects a person's speech and behaviour and such revealing speech and behaviour is at the very heart of cinema's eloquence."[12]

At the end of *The Apu Trilogy* and *Jalsaghar,* Ray found himself at a critical crossroad. *Pather Panchali* had won Best Human Document at Cannes in 1956, the President's Gold and Silver Medals in India in 1955, and ten prestigious international awards. *Aparajito* walked away with the Golden Lion and Critics Award at Venice in 1957 and collected four additional international awards. *Apur Sansar* added five more international awards, and *Jalsaghar* completed the tally with two.[13] However, once his cinema left the paddy fields of *Pather Panchali* and the *zamindar*'s crumbling *haveli*/mansion of *Jalsaghar* and, after a brief sojourn to Benares, entered the city of Calcutta with *Aparajito* and *Apur Sansar,* the form and content of Ray's cinema changed dramatically. What became noticeable was a determined effort on Ray's part to move into more contemporary concerns and work more consistently in the realm of ideas rather than the framework of feelings. As Geeta Kapur accurately observes, in this new stage of Ray's cinematic unfolding:

[T]he wager on the contemporary surfaced as a vestigial presence in the reflective films [that followed]. The contemporary became a pressure on the cinematic figuration of his narratives; it left traces which allowed themselves to be read as secular. . . . He did this . . . , by handling directly and to his advantage, the relations between civilizational motives and historical affect. Letting the one and then the other outpace each other he filled the "ideal" role of an Indian artist within the progressive paradigm of the first decade.[14]

Ray's ideological stance, in fact, is spelled out very clearly in his 1958 essay "Problems of a Bengal Film Maker." Mapping out the kinds of films a truly serious and socially conscious Bengali/Indian filmmaker should *not* make (which he defines as the mythological, the devotional, and the social melodrama), Ray comes to the conclusion that the authentic Bengali/ Indian filmmaker "must face the challenge of contemporary reality, examine the facts, probe them, sift them, and select from them the material to be transformed into the stuff of cinema."[15]

The material he chose to transform into cinema, taking his filmmaking in new directions, dealt with two distinct ideological concerns. From 1960 to 1985, Ray embarked on a series of woman-centered films in which he traced, with a remarkable feminist sensitivity and historical insight, the troublesome *yatra* or journey the trapped Bengali/Indian woman had to make under the patriarchal gazes and threat of a conspicuously Bengali/ Indian masculinity. This forms the central thesis of Chapter 2. Since any worthwhile examination of women and their struggle must include a parallel investigation of men and their problems, Ray shifted his critical focus, especially in his films of the seventies and eighties, to male trauma and problems of a divided *purush* (male) subjectivity. This is explored in Chapter 3. His ideological period climaxed, it seems to me, with his political and historical examination of Indian bourgeois nationalism and British colonialism in his 1977 film *Shatranj-ke-Khilari* (*The Chess Players*) and the evils of the Hindu caste system in his 1981 film *Sadgati* (*Deliverance*). These were his only two non-Bengali films, and they are scrutinized in their relevant political historical context in Chapter 4. Chapter 5 deals with Ray's final trilogy: *Ganashatru* (*An Enemy of the People*, 1989), *Shakha Proshaka* (*Branches of the Tree*, 1990), and *Agantuk* (*The Stranger*, 1991). There I try to show how Ray partitions (to use Ashis Nandy's terminology) his *bhadralok* (middle-class Bengali sensibility) self and tries to create new "marginal" selves who can, on his behalf, assault the bastions of the middle-class Bengali "center" in an attempt to bring it to its knees. Although the first attempt, *Ganashatru*, in my opinion fails, confidence is regained rapidly with *Shakha Proshaka*, and by the time he arrives at

Agantuk, Ray is all set to demolish the cultured Bengali gentry through a nomadic vagabond whose tribalized weapons both wound and enlighten his victims and show them the folly of their insular ways.

Ray's choice of filmic material was to a large extent also determined by what was happening in India at the time. In his perceptive review of Chidananda Das Gupta's study *The Cinema of Satyajit Ray,* Professor Gautam Kundu points out:

From *Pather Panchali* to *Jana Aranya,* Ray's films record, sometimes ruefully and sometimes dispassionately, the inevitability of change ("progress") and all that it entails. But even if there is nostalgia for the past, there is no sentimentality in Ray's rendition of the gradual movement of one era into another. If over the years, Ray's vision of life has progressively darkened, it is because the realities that he confronts in post-Tagore, post-colonial India are harsh and unsettling.[16]

Ashish Rajadhyaksha indicates how the changes in Ray's cinema were directly inspired and instigated by the political changes erupting in India from the 1950s to the 1980s. He points out how Bibhuti Bhusan Banerjee, author of *Pather Panchali* (1929), showed

a whole trend of pre–World War II fiction working with a realism of minute description of the everyday, but inventing simultaneously the scale of an epic, of changing season and vast landscape, death and the struggle to live. . . .

It was this novel, then, that Ray updated [in the 1950s] through his formal and technical apparatus. It was as if he looked back on the novel, and through the novel its prewar world, and through that to India's near-century-old history of encountering the modern. Now, finally, the fumbling, the anticipation [of Ray's 1950 filmic efforts] could find contemporary form – and ideological stability.[17]

In the 1960s and 1970s, Rajadhyaksha tells us that Ray, along with most Indian artists of his generation,

shared the classic liberal nationalist discomfort . . . when the "Naxalite" Communist Party of India (Marxist–Leninist) appropriated for itself the voice of radical change. Its student agitations and consequent state brutality informed his Calcutta films (*Pratidwandi/The Adversary,* 1970; *Seemabaddha/Company Limited,* 1971).[18]

Indira Gandhi, reelected Indian Prime Minister in 1972, openly declared a state of emergency in 1975 at the center in Delhi. With the state capitals "demanding an increasingly fascist state intervention," Ray, "having no sympathy for the Indira regime" – and almost in retaliation – "set out on a politically determined critique that he spelled out in his adaption of the two Premchand stories, *Shantranj-Ke-Khilari/The Chess Players* and *Sadgati/Deliverance*, 1981."[19] So disgusted was Ray, Rajadhyaksha continues, that

in indirect response, Ray quit making films set in the contemporary for the next fourteen years, withdrawing into children's stories (at least one of which, *Hirok Rajar Deshe/The Kingdom of Diamonds*, 1980, made veiled allusions to the Emergency) and period movies including his trusty Tagore (*Ghare-Baire/The Home and the World*, 1984).[20]

There is currently a surprising paucity of critical scholarship on the cinema of Satyajit Ray. Eric Rhode's study of *The Apu Trilogy*, published in *Sight and Sound* in the summer of 1961, is the earliest. In 1963, Erik Barnouw and S. Krishnaswamy included a long chapter on Ray in their book *Indian Film*. Eight years later, Marie Seton's biocritical monograph, *Portrait of a Director*, and Robin Wood's auteurist monograph, *The Apu Trilogy*, followed. Another nine years were to pass before an Indian film critic, Chidananda Das Gupta, was to publish a hurriedly written critical book on *The Cinema of Satyajit Ray* to mark the twenty-fifth anniversary of the release of *Pather Panchali* (*Song of the Little Road*) at the Indian film festival Filmotsav 80. Henri Micciollo came out in 1981 with the first French full-length study, *Satyajit Ray*. Recent additions have been Professor Ben Nyce's *Satyajit Ray: A Study of His Films*, released in 1988, and yet another biocritical effort, *Satyajit Ray: The Inner Eye* by Andrew Robinson, published in 1989.

Part of my desire to undertake this study arose from numerous lapses I discerned in the works of these critics. In order to demonstrate the pitfalls into which Ray scholarship appears regularly and repeatedly to fall, I would like to dwell briefly on some critical insights offered by a few of these critics. With all due respect to their efforts, I have to maintain that most Western readings of Ray's films seem to suffer from a very serious lack of critical understanding of the social, historical, and cultural traditions of India within which Ray's films predominantly function. Wood, Rhode, and Nyce, for example, often tend to cover up this ignorance by lapsing into hazy, almost mystical notions, like India's "spirituality." Such notions as spirituality are nothing less, it seems to me, than convenient labels arbitrarily imposed by Western theoreticians to explain many of the differences in a culture totally unfamiliar to them. When Rhode examines, for instance, Apu as an avatar of Krishna in *Apur Sansar* (*The World of Apu*), he makes the following misleading statements:

Krishna, you will remember, was allowed for a brief time to love a milkmaid Radha; and so for a brief time Apu is allowed to love Aparna, his wife. . . . After Aparna's death Apu descends into the underworld, where he is imprisoned with his own echo in a landscape of salt.[21]

Since Krishna is the supreme God, responsible for the creation of the universe – man, woman, nature, and everything else in it – the idea that he could be "allowed" to love Radha is completely misconceived. No force or destiny controls Krishna. There is no descent by Apu into the underworld either: His retreat from the outside world into his garret is because of his timidity. He has the Krishna attributes but fails to use them in his relations with women.

In the early sections of this study on Ray, Nyce seems to come up with similar "spiritual" attributes that he heaps on Apu. As an Indian myself, I am rather tired of seeing this word "spiritual" uttered so carelessly and freely by Western critics and commentators. Ray never puts halos around his characters; it is his Western critics who persist in doing so. In Nyce's review of *Apur Sansar*, he tends to explain the Apu/Krishna fusing in the following way:

It doesn't seem too farfetched to suggest that Apu himself has elements of the God Krishna within him and that he himself is going through stages of regeneration which can be likened to incarnations. Ray's need to use different actors to play the growing Apu even makes a contribution here. As Apu's spirit moves through its various growths, his body takes different forms. He is both single and multiple. He is the same Apu throughout the trilogy, and yet he is in the process of becoming different from his prior selves – or, more accurately, of becoming more and more himself.[22]

This is completely erroneous and adds a metaphysical dimension to the film that is never there in the first place. Apu's Krishnacity is seen only on the level of his physical attractiveness. Women are attracted to him, but his shyness always makes him fail to take advantage of his resemblances to Krishna. By insisting on all this redundant business of incarnations and regeneration, Nyce seems to promote an exotic third-world looked-at-ness for Ray's presentation of Bengali culture. My study wishes to free Ray's cinema from such unnecessary contextualizations. Ray is not a great user of myths in his films, but when he does use them, it is for a specific aesthetic purpose (like the death scenes in *The Apu Trilogy*) or to highlight a specific "flaw" in a character (as in the case of Apu's timidity).

A close reading of Wood's *The Apu Trilogy*, while often stimulating and rigorous (especially in his treatment of the psychology of the child's vision of the universe, or the use of the train as a recurring thematic motif, to cite only a few examples), is often marred by arbitrary references to the music of Mozart, the films of Renoir and Bergman, and the nature poetry of Wordsworth. Wood does not critically elaborate these references, nor does he indicate their purpose. He doesn't even in the Forsterian dialectic "connect" them. What is one to make of the link that Wood tries to establish, for instance, between Apu's flinging of the stolen necklace into the pond in *Pather Panchali* and Johan's hiding of the old waiter's funeral photographs under the carpet in Bergman's *The Silence*?

But no sooner has one made the comparison than important differences spring to mind: the associations of the necklace are much more present and personal to Apu then those of the photographs to Johan, and are consequently felt as closer to conscious formulation; and the more conscious the associations the less explainable the actions in terms of blind instinct.[23]

Surely a more detailed explanation, especially of Johan's conduct, is required here to make such a comparison work. After all, these are two *boys* performing similar actions but under different circumstances and in two entirely different cultures. Wood, however, offers no explanations. Instead, he plunges into the proverbial "metaphysical" side of Ray, which by *not* accounting for Apu's motivation in this scene "seems to me a strength in the film rather than a weakness. . . . Ray is representing the essential mystery and integrity of the individual psyche. The effect is of psychological density not thinness."[24] Since the reference is never developed, one wonders why Wood uses it at all.

Another disconcerting characteristic I often find in Ray's Western critics is a reckless kind of hyperbolization that fails to give any redeeming insight into either Ray or his cinema. Pauline Kael, for example, ends her review of *Ghare-Baire* (*The Home and the World*) by claiming: "When it comes to truthfulness about women's lives, the great Indian moviemaker Satyajit Ray shames the American and European directors of both sexes."[25] From Kael's narrow perspective, Western filmmakers like Michelangelo Antonioni, Krzysztof Zanussi, Marta Mazoras, Agnès Varda, John Cassavetes, Robert Altman, Woody Allen – all seem to have toiled in vain to establish the truthfulness of their European and American womens' lives.

Hyperbole and eulogy of this kind is what mars Marie Seton's book on Ray as well. It concentrates, by and large, on the biographical aspect of Ray, commemorating him as the most accomplished Indian Renaissance man of his time, but offers little critical evaluation of his achievements in

Indian cinema. The second part of Seton's book very often deals with mere summary sketches of plot narratives. In her analysis of *Jalsaghar* (*The Music Room*), for instance, she observes:

This first performance [of the *jalsa*] establishes the music room as the dominant central focus of Roy's [the *zamindar*, or feudal landlord] inherited way of life in which he is petrified. The vast room itself is the microcosm of the enclosed, leisured, luxurious society of inherited privilege which Ganguly is determined to blast his way into as his lorries [trucks] hint the ruthless energies of his activities in the distance.[26]

Such a reading implies that while a music performance is about to be enacted in the music room, Ganguly's trucks are planning some mischief outside. There *is* a scene with a lorry in the film, but it takes place elsewhere and has really nothing to do with the music room. The scene to which Seton alludes occurs earlier in the film, where first we see the *zamindar* watching his feudal possessions, his horse and elephant, as they graze in the distance. The next shot shows one of Ganguly's clattering trucks bursting upon the scene and destroying the nostalgic mood of our protagonist by swirling dust all over the scene. By simplistically juxtaposing Ganguly's truck with Roy's music room, Seton is offering us an incorrect pair of cultural signifiers to delineate the conflict between the feudal *zamindar* and the nouveau-riche industrialist Ganguly. Although one anticipates that Seton will next critically discuss how Ray's mise-en-scène establishes the music room as the dominant focus of Roy's inherited way of life, on the screen itself, we get instead an account of all the *problems* that Ray had to overcome behind the scenes while this particular shot was being filmed. She describes the furniture of his set and how various objects had to be loaned by a member of the Tagore family because the production had run out of money, and so on. We learn a lot about Ray's working habits, his family ancestry, and his tastes in art, music, and literature. What we don't learn is how all this is reflected in his films. My study intends to do just the opposite: to explain the artist *through* the evidence of his art and what one can critically discern in it.

Andrew Robinson's critical eyes fail to open any inner eyes on Ray's filmcraft. Not only does he perpetuate Seton's gushing approach to Ray; he progressively worsens it by constantly offering us someone else's confirmation of Ray's genius. Thus, Akira Kurosawa's praise of *Pather Panchali* is lavishly inscribed on page 91:

I can never forget the excitement in my mind after seeing it. I have had several more opportunities to see the film since then and each time I feel more overwhelmed. It is the kind of cinema that flows with the serenity and nobility of a big river. . . .[27]

Robinson erects this adulatory scaffolding over Ray and gets so carried away with its imposition that the one person constantly referred to in a self-congratulatory vein is none other than Satyajit Ray himself! On page 118, for example, he cites the following remark by Ray in reference to *Jalsaghar*:

The idea of the candles going out one by one was devised on location while we were shooting. I was working like I usually do; every evening I was sitting with the script and thinking in case any fresh ideas might come for the next day's shooting. And this suddenly came to me in a flash and I described it to him (Chhabi Biswas, who plays the central role of the *zamindar*). He was terribly excited; he said, "I have never come across such a brilliant and fresh and expressive idea."[28]

The book is full of such narcissistic utterances, often attributed to Ray. This is how Robinson scrutinizes the sweet-seller scene in *Pather Panchali*:

. . . the tripping sweet-seller yolked to his swaying, bobbing pots, pursued with eager innocence by the children and their canine accomplice. This brief wordless interlude of lyrical happiness belongs uniquely to the cinema; it is the kind of peak in Ray's work that prompted Kurosawa to say: "Not to have seen the cinema of Ray means existing in the world without seeing the sun or the moon."[29]

Nothing of any critical value is offered by this kind of an adulatory approach. Robinson seems to have inherited this nagging and reverberative corroboration method of what Ray said/wrote/told me not only from Seton but also from earlier Ray commentators like Barnouw and Krishnaswamy. Their chapter on Ray, entitled "Wide World," indulges in a lot of this. Ray's statement of "Villains bore me," for example, immediately produces from the authors a grocery list of "many figures of Indian Society [in Ray's films] representing power and privilege, and those who willingly or unwillingly accepted the dominance."[30] But this list displays a lot of misinformation. According to the authors, Ray scrutinizes the world of the husband in *Charulata* (*The Lonely Wife*, 1964) as one of these figures. Had he done so, Bhupati would emerge as a willing or unwilling chauvinist to Charulata, which he, most decidedly, is not. Ray depicts him as someone who loves his wife in spite of neglecting her. In *Aranyer Din Ratri* (*Days and Nights in the Forest*, 1970), they feel Ray takes a hard look at businessmen. There are no tradesmen in the film, however: Ashim is a corporate executive, Sanjoy is a Labour Officer in a jute mill, Hari is a sportsman, and Shekar is a jobless parasite. They also pick out only Ray's scrutiny, in *Shantranj-ke-Khilari,* of the colonial commander (i.e., General Outram). Why are the two Lucknowi landlords and Wajid Ali Shah, the ruler of Oudh, not mentioned? Didn't these people represent and practice the twin doctrines of power and privilege as well?

What is very conspicuous in Barnouw and Krishnaswamy is that they first indulge in long passages of impressionistic description alluding to important moments in Ray's films and then quickly offer us a one- or two-line critical summation. For instance, they give us in eighteen lines what the eponymous wife sees and does in the silent opening tableau of *Charulata* and then proclaim in the end: "Via such suggestions" (which, please note, have all been descriptive and completely devoid of any evaluation) "a *Charulata* world takes shape around her." No commentary is forthcoming, however, as to how this world is shaped by Ray's mise-en-scène, camera movement, editing, and so on. What follows breathlessly is the usual adulatory coronation: "Few film-makers have matched Ray in this building of evocative detail."[31]

Chidananda Das Gupta's study of Ray's cinema is the first by an Indian critic, and although it offers very interesting background material on "the Bengali Renaissance and the Tagorian Synthesis" and the influence both had in shaping Ray's liberal-humanist values and in molding his craft, it disappoints when it actually concentrates on particular films. In his perceptive review of the book, Professor Gautam Kundu suggests its scope very accurately. According to him, Das Gupta divides Ray's cinema into two distinct periods. The first begins with *Pather Panchali* (1955) and ends with *Charulata* (1964). Das Gupta calls this Ray's "searching and finding phase" where, according to him, Ray seems to have made his most artistic and aesthetically satisfying films. The second period commences from *Kapurush-o-Mahapurush (The Coward and the Holy Man,* 1965) and seems to be, in Das Gupta's estimation, characterized by "an emptiness and spiritual exhaustion."[32] There are, Kundu continues, exceptions in this second period: notably, *Aranyer Din Ratri* and *Seemabaddha.* Such an evaluation, however, exhibits an unwillingness on Das Gupta's part to accept Ray's new concerns and very clearly demonstrates his preference for the aesthetic vision and classical style of the earlier Ray. Kundu is very right when he concludes that

There is one aspect of Ray's work that Das Gupta does not discuss at all: his politics. . . . To ignore the class question and the fact that Ray's cinema expresses itself in the forms of bourgeois culture is to attempt a "purely aesthetic appreciation" of his films, an approach that Das Gupta wants to avoid; at least, that is what he says in the introduction.[33]

Though Das Gupta is eloquent and penetrating in his analysis of the classical Ray films, he is ill at ease and often misleading when dealing with the filmmaker's more innovative cinematic expressions. In his analysis of *Pratidwandi* (*The Adversary*), for example, he dismisses most of Ray's newly acquired cinematic vocabulary in the film as "gimmicks," concluding, "It is as if Ray is out to prove that when it comes to gimmicks, he can invent them just as well as anyone else, perhaps better."[34]

Ray deliberately jettisons his classical style in *Pratidwandi*, however, because the nature of his film's central protagonist dictates a fragmented style of filmmaking. The switch to negatives, the dream sequences, the abrupt flashbacks and the playful flash-forwards – all express very suggestively and accurately Siddhartha's hesitant and inarticulate character. The conflicts, doubts, and problems that continually assail him find their most relevant cinematic expressions through such a style.

One gets the impression that Das Gupta does not want Ray to abandon the artistic conservatism of his earlier films. This is why a film like *Aranyer Din Ratri* appeals to Das Gupta: "In every way so different from *Charulata*, it has the same perfection of structure and a musical rhythm with melodic themes, varied repetitions, exactness of proportion."[35] But this film is one of Ray's most critical attacks on the contemporary Indian middle class, and its strength lies not in its classical structure alone. Ray's later work, in fact, has been increasingly drawn to concerns such as the middle class, the status of Indian woman, the paralysis of Indian men, and caste and class divisions – concerns that Das Gupta pointedly chooses to ignore.

In the final analysis, Das Gupta fails to express critically what his introduction had promised:

In a tradition that equates the beautiful with the good and the true, the relationship of the sociological to the artistic plays a vital role. This saddles Indian critics with a duty they have so far done little to perform.[36]

The relationship of the sociological to the artistic is what the present study of Ray is largely about.

Finally, let me mention one predominant area in the Ray oeuvre that I would have wanted but have not been able to evaluate in this study. It involves Ray's retreat into children's stories, namely:

Goopy Gyne Bagha Byne (*The Adventures of Goopy and Bagha*, 1968)
Sonar Kella (*The Golden Fortress*, 1974)
Joi Baba Felunath (*The Elephant God*, 1979)
Hirok Rajar Deshe (*The Kingdom of Diamonds*, 1980)
Pikoo (*Pikoo's Day*, 1981)

I have not been able to see any of these films as they are very rarely shown abroad or, for that matter, even outside Bengal. It would have been worthwhile to examine how different these films are reported to be and find an adequate theoretical framework to see what interesting insights they have to offer about Bengal and India, both through their mythical recreation of history as well as all the veiled allusions made to contemporary India.

Ray's final triad marks his return to the India of the 1990s, namely:

Ganashatru (*The Enemy of the People,* 1989)
Shakha Proshaka (*The Branches of a Tree,* 1990)
Agantuk (*The Stranger,* 1990)

Ray's last films prompted widely disparate critical reactions. Amaresh Misra, on the one hand, felt that Ray had become

an armchair liberal functioning as a simple humanist who now viewed social reality in terms of a naïve individual-versus-society conflict and placed his hopes and disillusionment either in some grassroots cultural activity or the travails of innocent children, sensitive, but mentally retarded figures and maverick outsiders.[37]

On the other hand, despite Ray's being old-fashioned in his understanding of Indian society, could one still discern in these films what another critical voice defines as

the inner health and durable values he stood for and his unique distillation of Indian and western values and forms [which] continues to overwhelm one with their balance of breadth and power (as for instance, in the ending of *Ganashatru*).[38]

Through a close examination of these three films in my last chapter, I attempt to arrive at a clearer understanding of who Ray finally was and where his extraordinary vision was taking him.

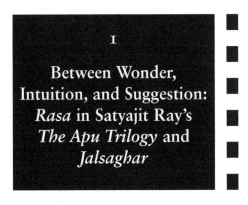

Between Wonder, Intuition, and Suggestion: *Rasa* in Satyajit Ray's *The Apu Trilogy* and *Jalsaghar*

To my
"Hari" and "Sarbojaya" –
my father and mother;
my "Durga" – my sister
and her family; and
my "Apu" of fourteen years,
Nikhil, who many times
behaves like a zamindar

Rasa Theory: An Overview

Although Satyajit Ray had a Western education and was deeply influenced by occidental modes of filmmaking – namely, Hollywood, the French cinema, and Italian neorealism – it is very important to remember that he was equally influenced by Indian culture and the various art forms, especially during his prolonged studies at Tagore's Fine Arts Academy at Santiniketan. As Ray describes it, such a fusion between the East and West should be considered

as a strength all along. But you have to have the backing of your own culture very much. Even when I made my first film the awareness was there. I had a western education. I studied English, but more and more over the last ten years I have been going back to the history of my own country, my people, my past, my culture. . . .[1]

Ray's early films provide us with a rich evidence of this, especially in his handling of the elaborate and often intricate theories of *rasa* as laid down by classical Sanskrit theoreticians like Dandin (seventh century), Anandvardhana (ninth century), and Abhinavagupta (tenth century). As Edwin Gerow writes:

It can be argued, that certain contemporary literary and cultural modes of expression, notably the novel and Indian film, can better be understood in their aesthetic impact by reference to well developed, indigenous, classical traditions of aesthetic criticism; they can be better understood, that is, than they often are when treated primarily as derivative resonances to, and in the context of recent Western literacy and cultural modes.[2]

My aim in this chapter is to show precisely how the aesthetic mode of *rasa* informs the early films of Satyajit Ray, notably *Pather Panchali* (*Song of the Little Road*, 1955), *Aparajito* (*The Unvanquished*, 1956), *Apur Sansar* (*The World of Apu*, 1959), and *Jalsaghar* (*The Music Room*, 1958.[3] The validity of *rasa* as a theoretical concept is best expressed by Professor V. K. Chari:

A properly evaluative judgment of a work of literature will, in terms of the *rasa* theory, consist of explaining how the work achieves success as a presentation of an emotive situation, whether it is consistent with the logic governing that kind of discourse, what the elements in it are that make for its coherence as an emotive utterance, whether the language employed is right for the kind of utterance it aims to be. . . .[4]

The same validity is reaffirmed by Rosie Thomas in her essay on "pleasure and popularity" in Indian cinema, where she says:

What seems to emerge in Hindi [by extension, Indian] cinema is an emphasis on emotion and spectacle rather than tight narrative, on *how* things will happen rather than *what* will happen next. . . .
   The spectator is addressed and moved through the films primarily via *affect*. . . . The theory of *rasas* (flavors/moods) is concerned with moving the spectator through the text in an ordered succession of *modes of affect* (*rasa*) by means of highly stylized devices. All Indian classical drama, dance, and music draw on this asthetic.[5]

In the Western critical canon, Susanne Langer immediately comes to mind as the foremost aesthetician valorizing the importance of *feeling* in art. She refers most pointedly to *rasa* as "vital feeling" in *Feeling and Form* when she states "*rasa* is, indeed, that comprehension of the directly experienced or 'inward life' that all art conveys." In *Problems of Art* Langer categorically defines "feeling" as

everything that can be felt, from physical sensation, pain and comfort, excitement and repose, to the most complex emotions, intellectual tensions, or the steady feeling tones of a conscious human life.[6]

The oldest known, available, Indian work on literary theory is Bharata's *Natyasastra,* most probably written in the third century A.D. Although the work refers specifically to *natya* (drama), its influence on Indian literary criticism – like that of its famous Western counterpart, Aristotle's *Poetics* – was and still is considerable. The most important chapter in the *Natyasastra* is the sixth, on *rasa* or the aesthetic and imaginative experiencing of the drama. The commentary on Bharata's treatise was undertaken by a Kashmiri-Brahmin aesthetician, Abhinavagupta, in the eleventh century. His remarks on the *rasa* theories constitute the most important part of his commentary *Abhinavabharati*.

The essence of *rasa,* as defined by Bharata, became a very critical subject of study and debate for many classical rhetoricians and thinkers. The earliest of these was Dandin in the seventh century, who in his *Kavyadarshana* spelled out sustained *intuition* as one very important aspect of the *rasa* theory. Another important aesthetician was Anandvardhana in the ninth century, who conceived of *rasa* as *dhvani* or suggestion. The contributions of both were accepted and further elaborated by Abhinavagupta. This is how Raniero Gnoli defines *rasa* in his introductory commentary on Abhinavagupta:

Drama is considered as a form of synthesis between the visual and aural arts. In it both collaborate at arousing in the spectator more easily and forcibly than by any other form of art a state of consciousness *sui generis* conceived intuitively and concretely as a juice or flavour called *Rasa*.[7]

According to Bharata, *rasa* consists in the *active creation* of one of eight defined *emotional* states that figure as the theme or subject of an artistic work. The four positive emotional states that Bharata singles out are *rati* (love), *hasa* (mirth/laughter), *utsaha* (dynamic energy), and *vismaya* (wonder/astonishment). The four negative emotions, in their turn, are *soka* (sorrow/grief), *bhaya* (fear/terror), *krodha* (anger), and *jugupsa* (disgust). Later speculation includes in this pantheon the ninth positive emotion of *sama* (serenity/calmness).

The portrayal of *sringara* (erotic love) can evoke pleasurable emotions in everyone; but what about a painful experience with which one is confronted in a work of art? Can we leave a play or film in which a tragedy has been dramatized and say that we *enjoyed* the subsequent *rasa* of *karuna* (sorrow) arising out of the *soka* (grief) we have just witnessed? For Bharata, the sorrowful *karuna rasa* is not painful at all, since

[w]hat the spectator sees is divorced from time and space. No kind of intellectual thinking bears any parallel to what happens in the theater. The spectator is so rapt in what he sees, so carried away by a mysterious delight, that he identifies completely with the original character and sees the whole world as he saw it. The whole fairy world of the play is now deeply embedded in his heart and can never be extracted, nor can it lose its original power for it has now become a part of his innermost experience.[8]

The aesthetic experience of *karuna* or sorrow, as many commentators of *rasa* have noted, is therefore not to be confused with the actual experience of day-to-day living. What the spectator is being offered in this artistic experience is not the real world (in which such a painful experience is shown as taking place) but a world transformed by the machinery of art and by the artist's *prathibha* or imagination. As a result, while witnessing such a transformation, the spectator experiences the bliss of *rasa* and is paradoxically able to *enjoy* the presentation of an extremely painful experience. This completes the crucial step in the *rasa* experience which, according to Bharata, should now bring about the mutual absorption of the artist and the audience in the emotional state so created.

This view is also endorsed by Langer when she maintains that what an artwork expresses is not "feeling or emotion experienced in response to real events" but "an imagined feeling or imaginary affect." The former is created by the author and the latter is experienced by the spectator. The emphasis on the "imagined" and "imagery" make them twice removed from reality. From this thesis Langer distinguishes between "the emotion presented in the work" by the characters and "the emotion presented by the work" which refers to the unfolding of the composition of the work in its entirety.[9] Professor Chari accurately links Langer's critical observations on feeling to the *rasa* theory when he asserts that

> The *rasa* theory too distinguishes between the symptomatic emotions occurring within the work (*bhāvas*), presented descriptively through their objective correlates, which the persons in the work are shown as suffering, and the emergent emotional quality or dominant feeling tone of the whole (*rasa*) which we savor. . . . It is an emotion of a particular description – tragic, comic, marvelous, heroic, serene or other – and it is firmly anchored in the concrete emotive situation presented in the work.[10]

Aestheticians like Abhinavagupta, Dandin, and Anandvardhana attempted to explain the complicated process by which *bhāvas* (raw emotions) extracted from life are transformed by the *prathibha* or poetic imagination of the artist into *rasa* or aesthetic emotion and presented through the vehicle of art – be it a play, novel, poem, or film. According to these classical theorists, the *sara* or essence of *rasa* is determined by the following principles: (1) *camatkara*, the element of wonder; (2) *prathibha*, the artist's intuition or imagination; and (3) *dhvani* or suggestion.

It was Abhinavagupta who introduced the concept of *camatkara*. The term means aesthetic experience, or the state of fruition of the *rasa*. Gnoli defines *camatkara* as being

> compounded of the *camat* and *kara*. *Camat*, which occurs only in this expression, is no more than an interjection expressing surprise or wonder, whereas *kara* means the act of emitting such an interjection or finding oneself in this state

of consciousness. This sense of wonder or surprise at the presence of something which suddenly invades our field of consciousness is never absent from the word *camatkara*.[11]

In the following poem, for instance, Ksemendra, a pupil of Abhinava-gupta, sketches the faculty of wonder that a good poet must possess and present in his poetry:

> A poet should learn with his eyes
>   the forms of leaves
> he should know how to make
>   people laugh when they are together
> he should get to see
>   what they are really like
> he should know about oceans and mountains
>   in themselves
> and the sun and the moon and the stars
> his mind should enter into the seasons
> he should go
>   among many people
>   in many places
> and learn their languages.[12]

According to Dandin, *prathibha* as "[s]ustained intuition is the basis for the successful execution of a poetic composition. . . . If intuition at any level fails, or does not satisfy, then the whole composition is in danger of crashing to the ground."[13]

As the artist's intuition/imagination, *prathibha* is best defined by Gnoli, who states:

The chief thinkers to study the nature of the birth of a work of poetry were Anandvardhana and Bhatta Tota and later Abhinavagupta. . . . Writes Anand-vardhana: "the poet is the true sole creator and as it pleases him to create so the world grows and is transformed." The poet is at once who sees [the seer] and who is able to express what he sees. *Rasa,* the aesthetic state of conscious-ness belongs, in reality to the poet alone; it is nothing but his generalized con-sciousness. . . . In other words, artistic creation is the direct or unconventional expression of a feeling of passion "generalized," that is, freed from all distinc-tions in time and space and therefore from all individual relationships and prac-tical interests by an inner force within the poet himself, the creative or artistic tuition [*prathibha*].[14]

Dhvani or suggestion is a very important concept of Indian aesthet-ics developed initially by Anandvardhana in *The Dhvanyāloka* and later modified by Abhinavagupta. In Anandvardhana's definition, *dhvani* assigns critical importance to the concept of suggestion in a work of art over the normal expression of something merely depicted or explicitly stated.

Abhinavagupta improved upon Anandvardhana's reasoning by focusing on the difference that lies between the "suggestion" and the "denotative/connotative" use of language. For Abhinavagupta, "suggestion" could not be intellectually articulated. Meaning, he claimed, should be divorced from its literal sense and should not be allowed to indicate or yield any kind of certainty. Through *dhvani,* meaning should be able to maintain a mystery. For Abhinavagupta, it was the *aniyata* or *unfixed* meaning that enabled the reader to go deeper and deeper into a poem (or any work of art), whereas the *niyata* or *fixed* meaning limited the scope of a work and merely gave us the intellectual function, which was not the aesthetic purpose of a good poem or work of art.[15]

Professor Chari points out that all Sanskrit aestheticians were very careful to indicate that

[t]he *rasa* theory does not believe that poetry is merely an emotional discharge of the poet; it firmly asserts that poetic creation involves the shaping of the materials of experience into the controlled expression of the poem.[16]

Wadiyar Bahadur explains this aspect very evocatively in his monograph on Indian aesthetics:

Rasa or aesthetic delight is brought about by *artistic creation....* This is illustrated by the *imaginative powers* of the first poet Valmiki. Valmiki saw the Crauncha bird crying piteously. [It was mourning for its mate killed by the cruel arrows of hunters.] This was his *perceptional experience.* Later, he had the *experience* transferred to his *imagination.* This in its turn stirred within him his instinct for pathos; and, in such a moment of intense feeling, he burst out into *spontaneous* verse. Later he used this verse to write the *Ramayana* in which he depicted the sentiment of pathos.[17]

As I have tried to point out earlier, the principle of *rasa*

does not eliminate considerations of metaphor, suggestion, formal organization ... but works in co-operation with such elements.... All such formal or stylistic elements are only a means to the primary end of *rasa* evocation. This is also Langer's position. Commenting on Eliot's theory of poetic expression, she writes: "Sound and structure, imagery and statement all go into the making of a vehicle for the poet's idea, the developed feeling he means to present."[18]

Thus it is easy to conclude that the *rasa* theory deals with emotions and their presentation in an entirely objective way. To sum up:

1. The emotions treated in poetry are neither the projections of the reader's own mental states nor the private feelings of the poet; rather they are the objective situations abiding in the poem.

2. *Rasa* is apprehended as residing in the work, in the situational factors presented in an appropriate language . . . and the emotions are apprehended from the language that describes them.

It would therefore be wrong to bring the charge of naïve emotionalism against the *rasa* theory.[19]

In order to understand and enjoy aesthetically the early films of Satyajit Ray, namely *The Apu Trilogy* and *Jalsaghar* (*The Music Room*), we must at this juncture displace some familiar Aristotelian categories that are the foundations of Western literary criticism. Let us begin with "character," "action," and "plot." For Aristotle, the "plot" was the heart and soul of the play, and "character" was fully realized and actualized only when it was seen in "action." "Character," according to Aristotle, gave us "qualities," but it was in our "actions" that we were really seen as happy or sad. In classical Sanskrit drama and in these early Ray films, what is represented is a *dominant state of emotion,* and the actions performed by the characters are subordinated to this prevalent emotional tone. The plot's importance lies in consciously organizing all the dramatic factors, which as an ensemble creatively suggest the dominant emotion. Their purpose is to present the spectator with the various *rasas* or flavors that the dominant emotion is capable of producing. The "plot" and the "actions" performed by the "characters" become mere vehicles for this activity. The spectator, in turn, is asked to savor each scene, determine the emotional nuance executed there, and "taste" its quality in order to experience and enjoy the *rasa* completely.

Another Aristotelian category with which we have to come to terms is that of "mimesis" or "imitation." According to the *rasa* theory, art is a kind of mimesis, but as Eliot Deutsch convincingly points out:

[R]*asa* does not initiate things and actions in their particularity, in their actuality, but rather in their universality, their potentiality. This theory would agree with Aristotle that history has the task of relating what actually happens, while poetry (art) of what may happen; that history records the activities of particular things and beings while art expresses the possibilities of man and nature and gods.[20]

In his discussion of mimesis, R. A. Scott-James points out that Aristotle, in his evaluation of the epic, indicates how that form affords wider scope not merely for the marvelous, but even the irrational. Hector pursued by Achilles [in Homer's *The Iliad*] round the walls of Troy whilst the Greeks stand still and look on would be ludicrous if realistically presented, but the absurdity is not noticed in Homer.[21]

A similar moment of the *marvelous* can be placed alongside Homer's from Kalidasa's celebrated Sanskrit play *Sakuntala*. King Dushanta's nobility of character is established right from the beginning of the play, where he is introduced as a great hunter chasing a deer. Instead of portraying him as a man in a state of bloodthirsty excitement (which the sport of hunting is normally supposed to arouse), Kalidasa presents him in his opening speech as a man profoundly moved by the exquisite grace exhibited by his small prey in eluding his deathly arrows. Dushanta tells his charioteer:

> His neck in beauty bends
> As backward looks he sends.
> At my pursuing car that threatens
>   death from far.
> Fear shrinks to half the body small;
> See how he fears the arrow's fall!
> The path he takes is strewed
> With blades of grass half-chewed
> From jaws wide with the stress
> Of fevered weariness
> He leaps so often and so high,
> He does not seem to run, but fly.[22]

When a hermit intervenes and pleads with the king to desist from this cruel sport since the deer belongs to this sacred hermitage, the king instantly obeys, gaining accolades of praise from the hermit. What we perceive in this passage is the principle of *camatkara* or wonder (the marvelous) and how the spectator is made to relish the *rasa* of *bhayanaka* or fear. What becomes important to us is not the painful particularity of what is happening to this deer, but the tasting of the *rasa* of fear itself. This *rasa* is delineated by the king's utterances describing the trembling physical exertions of the deer: the way it bends its neck gracefully; the way in which it shrinks its body to make it a difficult target for the king's arrows; as well as the series of accompanying emotions like its fevered weariness, its flight over the earth, the stressing of its jaws, and so on. The spectator, enmeshed in a *camatkara* state, finds himself completely absorbed in this aesthetic dance of the deer, and the *rasa* of fear thereby enters his being directly to be enjoyed.

Finally, the most important distinction is between Aristotle's theory of "catharsis" – which also deals with the *arousal* of two emotions, "pity and fear," that a good work of art is expected to produce – and the arousal of emotion in the *rasa* theory itself. Aristotle's description of "catharsis" occurs in Chapter XIII of the *Poetics*, where he says: "Pity is occasioned by undeserved misfortune, and fear by that of one like ourselves [i.e., by the misfortune of one like ourselves]."23 Humphrey House, in his lecture on "Catharsis and Emotions," points out that pity and fear in Aristotle's theory are very closely linked:

There is no pity, in his view, where there is not also fear. Both pity and fear are derived from the self-regarding instinct, and pity springs from the feeling that a similar suffering might happen to ourselves.24

Citing the passage that he thinks expresses Aristotle's concept of catharsis most clearly (*Nicomachean Ethics*, II.vi), House points out that

both *fear* and confidence and appetite and anger and *pity* and in general pleasure and pain may be felt both too much and too little, and in both cases not well; but to feel them at the right times, with reference to the right objects, towards the right people, with the right motive, and in the right way, is what is both intermediate and best, and this is characteristic of virtue.25

House, therefore, comes to the conclusion that "the result of the catharsis [as Aristotle perceived it] is an *emotional balance and equilibrium*; and it may well be called a strategy of emotional health."26

Ludovico Castelvetro, however, gives Aristotle's "catharsis" a different interpretation, one that many critics seem to favor.

Now I have no doubt that Aristotle meant by the word [cathartic] "pleasure" *the purgation and expulsion* of fear and pity from the human soul. . . . And it occurs when, feeling pain from the misery which comes unjustly to another, we recognize that we are good. . . . And added to this pleasure is another which is not in the least trivial . . . when we see tribulations beyond reason which have come upon others and which might possibly come upon us . . . we realize . . . that we are subject to the same fortune and that we cannot trust in the tranquil course of worldly things.27

Aristotle's theory of catharsis involves two emotions, pity and fear. However, neither House nor Castelvetro seem to make any distinction between the two: They are either linked together or always function as a single unit. Bharata's most original contribution to the aesthetic of emotions in the *rasa* theory lies precisely in "the distinction [he makes] between basic or durable emotions and transient or fleeting emotions."28

The durable emotion, in Professor Chari's excellent explanation of both the *Natyasastra* and the *Dasarupaka*, is defined as

the emotion which is not swallowed up by other emotions whether friendly with it or unfriendly; which quickly dissolves the others into its own condition; which endures continuously in the mind and which, in conjunction with other feelings and circumstances, attains its fullest expression as *rasa*.[29]

"We have," Professor Chari continues, "a basic emotion that is developed as the dominant and on which the poem [or a work of art] rests. Other emotions congruent with the basic emotion come in as its accessories."[30] *Rasa*, therefore, requires a work of art to have only a single predominant emotion. It rules out the possibility of two or more dominant emotions functioning as a unit or being balanced to produce any kind of pleasure or relish. Applying this important doctrine to Aristotle's "catharsis," Professor Chari concludes:

Although as Aristotle said, most tragedies are wrought out of both pity and fear, pity alone is the essential element of tragedy and its dominant tone; fear, whenever it enters, is subordinated to it as its accessory. If fear were treated as the principal theme, it would become a horror drama like the Gothic romance. Even if pity and fear were treated with equal emphasis [as House maintains], fear would still swallow up pity and become the principal theme. . . . At any rate, the *rasa* theory argues that aesthetic poise results, not from an unresolved tension of feeling tones, but from their resolution into a single tone.[31]

The Excellence Implicit in the Classical Aesthetic Form of *Rasa*: Three Principles

Rasa theory involves certain specific principles of aesthetic organization. Let us categorize three important ones, which will be critically applied to *The Apu Trilogy* and *Jalsaghar*: (1) the epiphany of wonder, (2) constancy of character, and (3) constancy of gesture.

The Epiphany of Wonder

The epiphany of wonder, or *camatkara*, is defined by Abhinavagupta in the *Abhinavabharati* as follows:

That is to say what is called *camatkara* is an uninterrupted (*acchina*) state of immersion (*avesa*) in an enjoyment characterized by the presence of a sensation of inner fullness (*trpti*). It might be said indeed that *camatkara* is the action proper to a tasting (*cam*) or enjoying subject, i.e., to a person immersed in the inner movement (*trpti*) of a magical (*adbhuta*) enjoyment. This may be presented under the aspect of a form of mental cognition (*manasadhyavasaya*) consisting of a direct perception (*saksatkara*), or of imagination (*samkalpa*), or of a form of memory, which, nevertheless, is manifested in a different manner to its ordinary nature. . . . In fact we might say that its nature is that of direct perception, i.e., of the form of direct perception known as intuition.[32]

In *Pather Panchali*, Ray chooses a child, Apu, as his main protagonist through whom the universe is revealed. To Apu is given the dominant quality of *camatkara,* and it is through this sense of wonder that Apu is made to discover and enjoy not only the world that constantly surrounds him but also that other world created by his *prathibha* or imagination. All his actions embody Apu's sense of wonder as an "uninterrupted (*acchina*) state of immersion (*avesa*)." Throughout the film, we never see Apu abandon this sense of wonder: It remains with him as a *constant* factor. It is present when Apu goes about his daily tasks in the narrow familiar world of the village, his parents, and the dusty paths on which he plays. We see Apu using his imaginative *camatkara* faculties even when he creates his other world, fed as it is by the stories and songs that his grandaunt Indir (henceforth called Granny) tells him and his sister Durga. ("Granny" is a term of endearment used to facilitate her identification.)

Constancy of Character

The second Indian aesthetic principle refers to the quality of *constancy* in the main character and how this is to be depicted in him or her. As Gerow explains it, the character must in some sense remain

constant, for the play clarifies that constancy as a means to generalizing the apprehension of the character. A character such as Hamlet, who is unsure of himself and "wind-tossed on the sea of fate" gives no scope to the development of *rasa,* for we do not know what he *is.* The *rasa* is developed, not monotonously, by iterative statement, but by essential contrasts that set the generalized character in opposition to contrary characters and events, viewed as subordinate; and they thus reaffirm and rediscover that character. In fact no *rasa* can be developed "denotatively" by statement, but only as its inherent contrasts are continually clarified and refined.[33]

In *Pather Panchali*, Apu's constancy of character is developed and maintained through his essential contrast with his elder sister, Durga. After her death in *Pather Panchali* and that of his father, Harihar, in *Aparajito,* it is Apu's mother, Sarbojaya, who serves as the opposing character against whom Apu's identity is constantly reaffirmed. After Sarbojaya's death later in *Aparajito*, Apu is contrasted in *Apur Sansar,* the next part of the trilogy, with the two people who exert their strongest influences on him: his best friend, Pulu, who protects and guides Apu like an elder brother, and his wife, Aparna, who briefly brings order, stability, and love to Apu's life.

Constancy of Gesture

The third Indian aesthetic principle deals with the theory of action and *abhinaya,* or gesture. In Gerow's definition,

[t]he theory of action is reduced to *abhinaya,* look or gesture: actions are signs, as it were, stylized gestures that do not so much express the inner, the concrete man, his commitment and passions as they convey, through a general theory of appropriateness (*aucitya*), important aspects of the latent emotional tone. They signify and are understood.[34]

V. Raghavan, in his informative paper on Sanskrit drama, provides the following crucial components of *abhinaya* along traditional performative strategies demanded by such drama:

The word *abhinaya* means that which brings the thing to the spectator, or, the different ways in which the play, with its meanings and feelings, is brought by the actor to the spectator. . . .
Abhinaya in its fullest meaning encompasses four components. The first is make-up (*āharyā*), so called because it is external to the actor, to be put on and taken off. The other three are more intimate to the actor: the spoken word (*vā-cika*), which is what the poet has given in his play (if a song is sung, that too would come under *vācika*), voluntary actions of the various parts of the body (*āngika*), and involuntary reactions (*sātvika*) that manifest themselves in the body when one is under emotional stress.[35]

Rasa in *Pather Panchali* (1955)

Ray introduces Apu to us in *Pather Panchali* as a wondrous eye, peering at a strange universe through a torn blanket. Whether he is watching a *jatra* (folk-play) performance, a train for the very first time, his mother viciously beating Durga, or the larvae slowly choking the pond's surface during the monsoon months, it is his face with the *camatkara* element constantly shining in his eyes that becomes the concomitant image of the various emotions of his childhood. Apu's witnessing of the *jatra* performance and the train become the two pivotal scenes in the film through which Ray establishes Apu's uninterrupted state of immersion and the sheer enjoyment gained from both these experiences.

Accustomed as he is to the familiar domestic dramas played out every-day in his family courtyard, Apu is thrilled to witness the *jatra* world of folk drama. Ray constantly focuses on Apu's *camatkara* gaze as it follows the mythologized fortunes of these actors indulging in all sorts of theat-rical passions: fighting, invoking love, trembling with fury or epilepsy, or using all the *abhinayas* or gestures of their craft to convey the embedded meanings of the play being performed for these simple villagers. The *ad-bhuta* or magical enjoyment that Apu gains from this kind of performance not only familiarizes him with a spectacle so distinctly remote and differ-ent from what he is daily confronted with, but also creates in him the mi-metic desire to adopt a *jatra* persona, thereby adding a sensation of *trpti* or inner fullness to his childhood as well. The *jatra* drama that Apu wit-nesses is shown by Ray alternately in long shot (an objective perspective) and close-up (from Apu's subjective perspective). In the long-shot presen-tation, the electric lamps that throw light on the improvised stage and the mass of eager faces surrounding it are very prominently displayed in the frame. Ray's editing unites the arrival of each *āharya* (madeup actor) in his persona (in close-up) as the consuming object of Apu's gaze. Then Ray punctuates his pace by pulling back to enlarge the frame, thereby enun-ciating the precious world for Apu within the mundane real one. Thus, when Ray shows Apu putting on a tin-foil moustache and a crown cut-out, we see the effort made by Apu's *prathibha* or imagination to become like one of those fabulous creatures whose antics he had savored and en-joyed at the *jatra* the previous evening. As pointed out by Indian psycho-analyst Sudhir Kakar:

Compared with western children an Indian child is encouraged to continue to live in a mythical world for a long time. In this world, objects, events and other persons do not have an existence of their own, but are intimately related to the self and its mysterious moods.[36]

In Apu's world, objects, events, and people are intimately related to his *camatkara* self and all its mysterious moods. It is in the sequence of Apu's wondrous discovery of the train that Ray categorically establishes this for us. As Apu runs through the tall grass toward the railway line, we see how he responds to each object. With his tin-foil crown, Apu puts his head against the pylon and listens to the strange, electric hum of the wires. We see him responding to the pylon in an intense *adbhuta* or magical way, as though he wants it to yield some of its mysterious secrets to him. Earlier, as Ray pans upward to the same pylon seen from Durga's point of view, two sounds proliferate on the sound track: The splash Durga makes as she wades through the surrounding paddy field and the hum emanating from the electric wires. Durga soon loses interest and wanders off, but not Apu. As he follows his sister, he repeatedly asks Durga about the pylon but receives no answer. Finally, when the train (which we have seen crossing the horizon near the top of the frame as Apu runs toward the embankment) does arrive, it is not presented subjectively, as a mere object of wonder for Apu, but instead revealed as an epiphany aesthetically captured by Apu's *camatkara* faculties. Ray does not cut traditionally from a close-up of the passing train to a close-up of Apu's awestruck face to register this wonder. We had seen the train enter the frame from the right side; holding the train in long shot, Ray pans from right to left. He then cuts to a reverse pan, this time from left to right, and the train suddenly passes very close to us. The compartments of the passing train fill up the entire film frame, and through the passing wheels we glimpse a crouching Apu on the other side of the tracks facing the camera, savoring the entire experience.

In James Joyce's *Portrait of the Artist as a Young Man*, Stephen Daedalus's explanations of the epiphany theory to his friend Lynch reflects very accurately, it seems to me, the Indian aesthetic principle of *camatkara* or wonder as utilized by Ray in this train sequence:

Stephen pointed to a basket which a butcher's boy had slung inverted on his head. "In order to see the basket," said Stephen, "your mind first of all separates the basket from the rest of the visible universe which is not the basket. . . . An aesthetic image is presented to us either in space or in time. . . . But temporal or spatial, the aesthetic image is first luminously apprehended as self bounded and self contained upon the immeasurable background of space and time which is not it. You apprehend it as *one* thing. You see it as one whole. You apprehend its wholeness. That is *integritas*."[37]

For Apu, the train is perceived as *one* integral object. Although moving visibly in space and audibly in time when Apu experiences it, the train is luminously perceived as a *whole* filling up the entire film frame. It is self-bounded and self-contained within not only the film frame but Apu's *camatkara* essence itself, which views it as a whole. Then, says Stephen:

". . . you feel the rhythm of its structure. . . . Having first felt that it is one thing you feel now that it is a *thing*. You apprehend it as complex, multiple, divisible, separable, made up of its parts, the results of its parts and their sum, harmonious. That is *consonantia*."[38]

Seeing the linked compartments of the train thundering past him as he crouches, Apu's *saksatkara* or intuitive faculties makes him taste this *thing* called "train" through the pulsating sounds and furious rhythms of its structure and all those various mechanical parts that make it a harmonious whole. In Stephen's words, "the synthesis of immediate perception," which occurs in Apu's *integritas* stage, "is followed by the analysis of apprehension," which now takes place in Apu's *consonantia* stage. Further:

"When you have apprehended that basket as one thing and have then analysed it according to its form and apprehended it as a thing you make the only synthesis which is logically and aesthetically permissible. You see that it is that thing which it is and no other thing. The radiance of which he [Aquinas] speaks is the scholastic *quidditas,* the whatness of a thing."[39]

For Apu, the train's soul, its whatness, leaps at him from the way its appearance totally engulfs him. Its radiance (*claritas*) lies in its whatness (*quidditas*). The instant when this supreme quality of the train's beauty is apprehended luminously by Apu's *camatkara* mind, the state of epiphany is achieved.

In order to realize the emotional awareness of *rasa,* a proper portrayal of events and a consistency of characterization become vital aesthetic principles for the artist to develop. Ray consistently reaffirms the constancy of Apu's character through the actions he shows him performing. The *rasa* is developed through the essential contrasts that Ray sets up between Apu and contrary characters, like his sister Durga and the other members of his family, especially in crucial incidents like the stealing of the necklace. This incident is especially important in revealing Ray's artistic *prathibha* by demonstrating his skillful development of the *rasa* of *rudra* or anger.

   According to Bharata, the *rasa* of *rudra* has anger as its predominant emotion. It arises from such *vibhavas* or sources as *krodha* (anger), *adharsana* (provocative actions), *adhiksipa* (insult), *upaghata* (assault), harsh words, and so on. The *anubhavas* (physical indices) of anger are beating and *samprahara* (hitting savagely). Its *vyabhicharibhavas* or accompanying emotions are panic, resentment, rashness, violence, pride, sweat, and trembling.[40]

   In Ray's mise-en-scène of the necklace-stealing incident, we are first made to feel the acute humiliation of Sarbojaya and Durga *before* they can be contrasted with Apu. It is the crushing insult or *adhiksipa* of being labeled as a "thief" by the wealthy neighbor Sejo-*thakrun* that causes Sarbojaya to target her wrath on her poor daughter, thereby making Durga the recipient of this humiliation. Sarbojaya is confronted in the mise-en-scène by the wrathful Sejo-*thakrun* and her two daughters through the wash that is drying on the clothesline. Ray pans to the right to reveal Apu who, on hearing the commotion, has retreated to one of the holes in the wall of the courtyard. Durga, who is about to enter the courtyard from the other side, is warned by Apu not to. We cut to a close-up of Durga's toy box, which is brought by one of the *thakrun*'s daughters to see if the stolen necklace is hidden there or not. Not finding it there, the accusers leave, and from a top shot we see the *thakrun* assailing poor Sarbojaya as the mother of a daughter, who in reality is nothing but a thief. She stalks off concluding to a passerby, "like mother, like daughter. They are all a bunch of thieves!"

Sarbojaya reacts to this accusation by throwing away all of Durga's "treasures" from her toy box, an action stemming from the *thakrun*'s implied accusation of a mother who has not properly brought up her own "treasure," her child. Sarbojaya retaliates by thrashing Durga, thereby trying to play role of the reformed mother. The two witnesses to her violence are Apu and Granny, with Ray's camera favoring the former's reactions over the latter's. Every blow delivered by the enraged mother on her frightened daughter is signaled by a cut to the small boy as he palpably winces with his sister in a collective recognition of pain. The dominant *rasa* of *rudra* is intensely manifested here. After the wailing Durga is dragged by her hair and thrown out of the courtyard, however, Ray's camera slowly pulls back to reveal the effect of this expulsion from Apu's point of view. Through Apu's eyes we now see the broken courtyard wall occupy the entire screen. On its western side and outside its periphery, we see the crumpled figure of Durga weeping. Inside its environs on the eastern side, we see Sarbojaya's reflexive collapse into uncontrollable tears. In between the two, we see Granny slowly gathering up Durga's strewn treasures. Now Ray changes the point of view. In midshot we see Apu slowly emerge from his hiding place, walk determinedly across the courtyard, rinse his mouth loudly with water, and quickly go back and pick up his schoolbooks. We see him squatting in the corner loudly memorizing a math problem in which "apples" prominently figure. From here begins the development of the *karuna* as compassionate *rasa*. So far we have observed Apu only as a witness. Now from all these *abhinayas* or symbolic actions we have just seen him perform we are instinctively made aware of a particular strategy adopted by this little boy in an effort, not only to obliterate the pain caused by this violent spectacle, but also to resolve it. When he suggestively rinses his mouth with water, it is not only to remove the acrid taste of fear but also to find some means by which he can extinguish the fires of anger, shame, and humiliation he sees simmering in the trembling *vyabhicharibhavas* of his mother and sister. He begins by reemphasizing his usual day-to-day actions and feelings of normality within the family courtyard itself. This is underlined by the recitation of the multiplication tables in which the "apples" (like Durga's stolen "mangoes") are boldly and loudly intoned. If she was expelled from the family Eden because of a stolen necklace (for which she has been adequately punished), her reentry into Eden can be effectively managed by the subtle *dhvanis* or suggestions of stolen fruits, like "apples and mangoes," for which Durga was *never* punished by her mother. When Sarbojaya does ask Apu to go fetch Durga for dinner a few minutes later, the little boy's plan seems to have worked – as confirmed by his radiant smile.

In the film (and in consonance with Indian society and tradition), Apu as the son is clearly shown to be the favored child, whereas Durga as the daughter always occupies a back seat. This kind of favoritism helps Apu to develop and retain his prevalent *camatkara* faculties, whereas poor Durga is denied this constancy. The patriarchal Indian tradition forces her to play what it deems as the appropriate roles of daughter and sister within the narrow and harsh confines of the family structure. Indian psychologist Sudhir Kakar observes:

The preference for a son when a child is born is as old as Indian society itself. Vedic rituals pray that sons will be followed by still more male offspring, never by females. A prayer in the *Atharveda* adds a touch of malice: "The birth of a girl, grant it elsewhere, here grant a son. . . ." At the birth of a son drums are beaten in some parts of the country, conch-shells blow in others . . . while no such spontaneous rejoicing accompanies the birth of a daughter. Women's folk songs reveal the painful awareness of this inferiority – of this discrepancy, at birth, between the celebration of sons and the mere tolerance of daughters. Thus in a North Indian song the women complain:

Vidya said, "Listen, O Sukhma, what a tradition has started! Drums are played upon the birth of a boy. But at my birth, only a brass plate was beaten."[41]

Durga, even as a child, is shown by Ray to be painfully aware of this inferiority. Sarbojaya, for instance, always takes Apu's side whenever the two children quarrel; and it is always Apu who is sent by Durga to receive pocket money from their father. While Apu is allowed to wander in nature, where we see his *camatkara* faculties blossoming, poor Durga is expected to abandon all her imaginary games with her toys and help her mother with domestic and religious chores. As a result, Durga's imaginative life is crushed at a very early stage, whereas no such obstacles hinder Apu's, which continues to thrive and prosper. Durga's fears are very well captured in the scene when a neighbor's daughter is about to get married.

Ray zooms in on Durga's excited face as she watches her friend being prepared by her household for the impending marriage. The shy bride looks
up and catches Durga's gaze. They smile. We then cut to the actual moment of the marriage ritual. Now the ornamentally decked bride is regarded more sadly by Durga. By focusing on her sad face Ray enunciates Durga's fear of one day having to leave her own family and going off with a
total stranger, as her friend was doing. Durga's fear stems from what Kakar defines as

"valid" ritual and economic reasons. . . . The presence of a son is absolutely necessary for the proper performance of many sacraments, especially those carried
out upon the death of parents. [Ray will indicate this in *Aparajito* when Apu
has to perform the last rites over his father's body at Benares.] In addition to
her negligible ritual significance, a daughter normally is an unmitigated expense,
someone who will never contribute to the family income, and who, upon marriage, will take away a considerable part of the family fortune as dowry.[42]

Every time Durga is scolded or beaten she is constantly reminded of
what she will take *away* from the family. The only one who tries very hard
to *give* her significance in the family and establish a bond with her is her
younger brother Apu; but because of their social and familial upbringing,
their personalities are entirely different. Moreover, since the authorial gaze
of Ray is directed primarily on the young Apu, it is his imaginative character that is constantly depicted and set in opposition to Durga's more
practical and impoverished one.

Durga's entire world is, in a way, devoid of any kind of *rasa*. This is
indicated to us by what she collects in her toy box. When Sarbojaya destroys this collection during the stolen necklace scene, she really destroys
Durga's entire world. Ray, emphasizing the contents of Durga's collection
as they lie strewn on the floor, is very faithful to the following catalog provided by Bibhuti Bhusan Banerjee in his novel *Pather Panchali*:

Durga was speechless. The doll's box was her life. Ten times a day she tidied it,
and now all the treasures it contained were scattered about the yard. Her doll,
a few bits of tin foil, some pieces of printed cloth, her *alta* (red dye used to paint
the edges of the feet for *sringara* or decoration), the *nataphul* (a hard marble-
like smooth fruit), she had been at such pains to collect, her mirror which was
mounted on a piece of tin, and a bird's nest; and they were all lying there in the
dark.[43]

Whereas Durga merely collects objects and stores them, Apu transforms
those objects he steals from Durga's box to suit the vicarious personae he
adopts and tastes the *rasa*s enjoyed from such recurrent metamorphoses.

Ray captures this quality very well when he shows Apu stealing Durga's tin foil and making a crown and moustache out of it to resemble one of the heroes he had recently witnessed at the *jatra* performance. When Durga catches him and is about to beat him, Sarbojaya intervenes and rebukes her strongly for being a bully; poor Durga runs off into the sugarcane fields to cry in secret. The ensuing reconciliation between brother and sister culminates in their first glimpse of the train.

The first *abhinaya* or gesture is made by Durga, who offers Apu the cane on which she has been munching – a sign indicating her pardon of Apu. This happens just after Apu asks Durga, "What is a pylon?" Her inability to answer him is compensated by the offering of this cane instead. Durga's mind extends only as far as her sugarcane and the sweet sticky juice she can extract from it. What lies just *beyond* the cane – the pylons, the electric wires, the strange humming sounds, the glistening railway tracks, and the impending arrival of the train – does not interest her. The *rasas* that all of these objects could convey are left for Apu to experience. When finally the train does arrive, Ray focuses only on Apu's encounter with it. Durga is clearly excluded, having been shown as uninterested in the train or the epiphany that, for Apu, results from such a vision. Unlike her brother, Durga is merely the devotee of tactile tastes like the one she is shown enjoying from the sugarcane.

Another scene that sharply defines the difference in their characters is the one that portrays the reactions of Durga and Apu to Granny's sudden death in the woods, which takes place just after their reconciliation and first glimpse of the train. Intercut with their reconciliation, Ray juxtaposes scenes of Sarbojaya and Granny quarreling. Sarbojaya's cruel *abhinaya* of refusing to pour water into Granny's water tumbler [Fig. 1] forces the older woman to sulk in a patch of woods. Now Durga, carrying a water pot and chattering happily with Apu, who laughs and prances as he leads the family calf home from pasture, sees Granny sitting all by herself in the distance amid the woods' splendid foliage. In midshot we see the girl slowly creeping toward the old woman, who sits motionless, clutching at a water tumbler. A subtle parallel thus emerges between the Sarbojaya–Granny conflict and the arrival of Durga carrying the water pot, connoting the difference between the two quarrels: one resolved on the level of *hasya* (laughter) and a welcoming of life, the other on the level of *soka* (grief) and impending death.

We see Durga approach Granny; cut to Apu intently watching. Ray then reverts to Durga shaking the bent old woman, who falls back lifeless with an agonizing bump. Cut to Durga bending over her prostrate body.

Figure 1. Granny's (Chunibala Devi) thirst for water (and more) rejected by Sarbo-jaya's (Karuna Banerjee) abhinaya of refusal in Pather Panchali *(Song of the Little Road, 1955). (Photo courtesy the Ray Archives, University of California at Santa Cruz)*

She then stands up, drops her pot, and runs. As the pot rolls and tumbles into the stream below, Ray focuses on this object rather than on the girl's reactions. The thirst for attention and affection that Granny sought and never got from Apu's parents, especially Sarbojaya, is painfully rearticulated here. Durga was the only one who gave the old woman some love and care, and hence is the only one who feels her loss so materially [Fig. 2]. Apu, on the other hand, does not run after Durga. Ray films him staring at this old woman's dead body, intrigued and mystified by it. For him, her death holds no sense of loss or terror. Like the train that he has just witnessed, it is registered as an epiphany. Apu perceives her as a whole vision, self-bound and self-contained, an object of wonder; and the sustaining presence of nature in which it occurs seems to transform Granny's death, from Apu's *camatkara* perspective, into a harmonious thing made luminous (rather than ominous) by the lush forest vegetation, the calf straining on the leash, and the beams of sunlight playing with the shad-

Figure 2. Granny's (Chunibala Devi) hunger for food (and more) fulfilled by Dur-ga's (Uma Das Gupta) fruitful abhinaya *in* Pather Panchali (Song of the Little Road, *1955). (Photo courtesy the Ray Archives, University of California at Santa Cruz)*

ows. The whatness of her death leaps at him from this radiance, and Apu, true to his character, relishes the *rasa* arising from such a vision.

Ray's dramatic presentation of *abhinaya* in his very first film is established by his camera's constant attention to the human face. The conflict often unfolds when we are forced to observe what a particular face is doing; how it is framed; how it reacts to or with another face; what strategies or solutions it is shown contemplating; what problems or solutions it is shown confronting, solving, or obliterating. When Granny, for example, sinks her toothless mouth into a globe of soggy rice, Ray's unflinching camera suggests through that face stark poverty itself ravenously satisfy-ing its hunger. When this same face sings a lullaby for a newborn baby in the family, however, the poverty with which it was previously associated is banished both visually and aurally: As Ray's camera frames the old woman's wizened features, we see her face radiating a marvelous, pristine beauty. Even the bickerings between Harihar and Sarbojaya cease to have any nagging presence on the sound track once Granny's toothless song establishes through *vacikas* – instances of the evocative power of speech – a determined will to welcome Apu into this bare and poor courtyard and lull him to sleep over his parents' quarrels and under a canopy of stars.

The importance of *abhinaya* is demonstrated repeatedly by Ray, especially in the expression of different "moods" that characters, carefully grouped, are shown displaying at the same time. Take the following sequence, for instance:

The night is resonant with the noise of crickets. Apu and Harihar (his father) sit on the veranda in the light of a hurricane lamp. Harihar has a small wooden table in front of him, and glasses on his nose. His lips move silently as he reads to himself what he has just written. Apu sits by him, writing something on his slate with deep concentration. In the dim light Sarbojaya can be seen moving around in the room behind. . . . She comes out of the room as Durga reaches the veranda. She slaps Durga and draws her down to the floor. . . . Sarbojaya starts combing Durga's hair. On her own veranda Granny tries to thread a needle, holding it near a flame.

SARBOJAYA: When do you think you will do your hair? Sit down.
DURGA: *(After a pause)* Mother – can you make a plait with four strands?
SARBOJAYA: Uh! Don't move your head.
DURGA: Ranu-di knows how to.
SARBOJAYA: Look at the state your hair is in. No oil. Nothing. And you want a plait with four strands.
DURGA: Mother, did you know, they are coming to see Ranu-di.
APU: Who are coming?

But no one explains this to Apu. Harihar turns a page. Granny still struggles with the needle. The whistle of a distant train breaks the stillness of the night. Apu looks up from his slate once more, this time to listen to the fading noise of the train. . . .

HARIHAR: Let me see what you have written.
(Apu hands him the slate.)
Lovely! Now write. *(dramatically)* A ghost! Help!

Harihar smiles at Apu as he hands back the slate, then picks up his pen again. Sarbohaya has almost finished plaiting Durga's hair.[44]

In this sequence, Ray's mise-en-scène very distinctly establishes the receptive pairings of father–son sitting a little behind to the left of the frame and mother–daughter sitting closer to the camera, with Granny isolated and completely excluded from the family pantheon. Harihar, priest and failed realist, is writing yet another useless play and is shown completely lost in his creative efforts. When he asks Apu to write about "a ghost," prefacing it with a cry of "help," the dramatic *vacika* utterance through which he pronounces the words "ghost" and "help" ironically comments on his failure to see what is happening inside his own family courtyard. Harihar is so wrapped up in the creation of his own theatrical world of "ghosts" that he fails to hear his wife's frustrated and ominous comments about the family's actual impoverished conditions. The paucity of "No oil. Nothing" is communicated by the *angika* or hand movements of Sarbojaya trying to comb Durga's dry and stubborn hair in the best manner possible. At the same time Durga's concern with the impending marriage of one of her friends gets verbally braided with her mother's concern about Durga's future. When will her Durga get married? Sarbojaya would like to invoke "help" from some "ghost" too to accomplish this feat. Will she and Harihar be able to provide a dowry? Will any family come to see their daughter in this miserable house? All these *dhvanis* get stressed through the repeated *abhinayas* of Sarbojaya trying to comb Durga's undernourished hair. Apu, a dreamer like his father, is on the other hand shown totally immersed in the magic and mystery suggested by a train's whistle in the dark: The camera advances and frames his face in a wistful close-up when the whistle is heard. Amid them all sits Granny, trying to thread a needle and refusing to admit failure at this task of her *angika*. She is trying to mend all the tears in her "old shawl" since the family refuses to buy her a new one in spite of all the hints she has given them. Thus, we see how each character's world, obsession, and concerns get individually established through the *abhinayas* each is made to perform. What they signify is understood by us, and we can enjoy the various *rasa*s through the latent emotional tones underlying each of these actions as the camera pulls back and slowly tracks away from this family portrait.

The "look" occupies a very central place in the dramatic representation of *abhinaya* in Sanskrit drama, and Ray uses the "look" very significantly in *Pather Panchali*. In the film, when Ray frames Harihar and Sarbojaya, we notice that Sarbojaya never *looks* directly at her husband in public, usually when others are present, either when he speaks to her or when she replies to him. There are no action–reaction shots when the two converse in a public space like the veranda or the kitchen. Ray constantly shows both *within* the same frame, usually with the husband speaking *to* her and she replying with her face (generally hidden behind her *sari,* or draped garment) tilted *away* from his gaze. In similar scenes between the children, however, we are always shown them responding to each other through typical action–reaction shots.

In a Hindu family, the wife is never expected to speak to her husband except from a position of subservience. That is her social standing. She *must* have her *sari* over her head, and her face *has* to be partially covered in her husband's presence. The gazes of the traditional Hindu wife and husband can never meet because Hindu orientation always conditions the wife's gaze to be *lower* than her husband's. The children, of course, are not yet aware of this distinction: Their spontaneity has not yet been overtaken and obliterated by this strict Hindu code. Young Durga, who quite often looks her younger brother in the eye and, as the elder sister, at times even looks down on him, will not be able to do so once she gets married. Ray's method of *abhinaya* in this film can best be personified by the village grocer-cum-schoolmaster, whose one eye glares angrily at his brood of young pupils while the other eye is engaged in lively conversation and gossip with his regular customers.

It is once again *abhinaya* that emblematizes the event of Durga's death on two levels: the realistic and the symbolic. In India, especially rural India, the spectacle of death is accepted and understood on these two levels. In order to bring out the full relish of the *karuna rasa* as compassion, Ray brilliantly makes use of the *abhinayas* of *angika* or bodily movements and *vacika* or speech in Harihar's and Sarbojaya's reactions to Durga's death. Durga runs in the lush Bengali landscape to welcome Indra, the thunder/rain god. From Apu's sheltered perspective Ray frames Durga in medium shot as she bends forward, allowing the heavy downpour to clean her dirty hair. In the next shot, we see her slowly turn a complete circle, her hair swinging beneath her. As a result of her inundation she catches cold and falls critically ill with pneumonia. Her subsequent death, resulting from this kind of baptism, negates all the positive connotations of the Indian monsoon that Ray had built up so evocatively in earlier scenes, depicting the eagerly awaited welcome of the first rains. A rain god who offers so much can also take away the very little these people have – *that* is the god's enactment of a dual *abhinaya* too. This is a fact of life accepted and endured by the villagers. As lotus leaves flutter seductively in the wet wind and lily pads flap welcoming signs in the sudden torrents of gale outside, a young girl slowly breathes her last on her grieving mother's storm-tossed lap.

As Sarbojaya nurses the pneumonic Durga, a raging storm outside their house is shown slowly trying to force itself in. Ray conveys this through the *uddipanavibhava* or setting: Everything inside that weakly protected house is shown to be in a state of precarious imbalance. Harihar, who has left home to find better job prospects, has not written for a long time, and no one knows his whereabouts. All the food jars in the kitchen are empty. From Sarbojaya's point of view, Ray pans toward the rags serving as improvised curtains, which struggle to keep the rain and wind away from her and her feverish child. Sarbojaya turns, and we pan to the straining door bolt being pounded by the rain. While the lamp wick flickers its last gasp in the few remaining drops of oil and Durga's *sātvika* state of involuntary trembling increases, the image of the family deity – the elephant god, Ganesha (god of wisdom and *remover* of all of life's obstacles for the family that adopts him) – ironically totters on its seat on the shelf above. Lightning flickers successively over anxious mother, dying daughter, and impassive deity. There is a resounding flash. The tattered rags are blown away. The door bursts open. Cut to Apu knocking for help on a friendly neighbor's door. As the kind woman enters and observes Sarbojaya's stoic face, she knows that Durga is dead. There is no lament on Sarbojaya's part, just the *vyabhicharibhava* or accompanying emotion of her weariness confronting yet another calamity. The neighbor quietly pulls Sarbojaya toward her and rocks her gently. The stance of the two women ennobles the emotion of grief and takes it to a higher level. After the neighbor comforts Sarbojaya, Ray cuts to a close-up of a tree, then pans down to Apu. The boy is cleaning his teeth, and there is a faraway look in his eye. Cut to Sarbojaya drawing water from the well. Cut back to Apu, who goes into his room, comes out with a shawl wrapped around him, and begins combing his hair. He picks up an empty kerosene bottle, looks up at the sky, goes inside and fetches an umbrella. Ray frames him walking slowly down the familiar path, a little boy holding an enormous umbrella and an empty bottle. For Sarbojaya and Apu it seems as if the door, forced open by the storm, now points to a future for the family that lies *outside* this ruined house, this broken courtyard, and this constricted village. Having dealt with Sarbojaya's and Apu's responses, Ray next turns to Harihar's as he returns from his trip loaded with goods, not knowing he has been deprived of a daughter.

The storm has abated. Harihar enters the frame from the left in the foreground, encountering a wrecked yard, a broken home, and a calf wandering without shelter. He exits the frame at right and enters the remains of his home, this time facing us from the background. He calls out to the children, but no one appears. Sarbojaya comes out and quietly brings him his wooden slippers and a bucket of water. She is strangely withdrawn and silent. Harihar, on the other hand, armed with presents and flushed with news of his trip is talkative and gay. Sarbojaya is positioned close to the camera, while Harihar is placed squatting behind her. By concentrating on Harihar's *vacika* or continuous prattle of utterances and Sarbojaya's continuous silence, Ray keeps the rising *karuna rasa* of compassion firmly in check. "Our worries are over," Harihar tells his silent wife and proceeds to lay at her feet all the gifts he has purchased for his family. "Look at this. It's a *sari* for Durga. She'll wear it on her marriage day. How pretty she'll look. Why, don't you like it?" Cut to a close-up of the *sari* Harihar is shown forcing on Sarbojaya. Her silence breaks at this moment. Clutching that *sari* she breaks down and slowly crumbles on the floor. Her grief over Durga's loss is effectively conveyed to her husband through this *abhinaya* of her *sātvika* or trembling state. Ray frames Harihar now bending over her. The camera tracks toward his trembling fingers trying to comfort her. Then as the full impact of Durga's demise hits him, he tries to rise and falls back again. Resting *his sātvika* state against Sarbojaya's shaking shoulders, he wails, "Durga! DURGAA MA – !" Cut to Apu returning with the oil, listening to Harihar's anguished cry. The Durga–Ma juxtaposition evoked through Harihar's *abhinaya* of the *vacika* or spoken word is addressed not only to his dead daughter but *also* to the fierce patron Bengali goddess Durga, who, in Indian mythology, possesses the dual *shakti* or strength of one who can protect and kill, heal and maim, create and destroy. Since the mortal Durga's death has been willed by a higher *shakti*, Harihar is shown accepting it on that higher level too. Thus, the emotion of *karuna* is ennobled. It ceases to be Harihar's subjective loss. It has now become, through Ray's presentation of *abhinaya*, objectified and universalized.

Rasa in *Aparajito* (1956)

Pather Panchali ends with Apu, Harihar, and Sarbojaya's departure for Benares. In the bullock cart, while the mother bows her head and weeps silently and the father stares blankly ahead, Apu's *camatkara* eyes widely scrutinize this unknown future that now lies ahead of him in that strange new city of Benares.

Aparajito, part two of the trilogy, opens with the camera adopting Apu's subjective gaze as it gets its first glimpse of Benares. As the train carrying the family rumbles across a bridge, the bridge's steel girders flash past Apu's eyes. He sees brief glimpses of a wide river, the Ganges (the holy Ganga), for the first time. A whole new world is suddenly opened up

Figure 3. Apu's (Pinaki Sen Gupta) consistently displayed camatkara *vision in* Aparajito (The Unvanquished, *1956*). *(Photo courtesy the Ray Archives, University of California at Santa Cruz)*

for Apu, and we are made to observe this wonderful world through his consistently displayed *camatkara* vision. As in *Pather Panchali*, Apu is introduced to us in *Aparajito* as a face suddenly peeping out from behind a house wall [Fig. 3]. He is playing hide and seek with his friends in the lanes near his home. The boys scamper all over the narrow winding paths of the lanes. When a passing cow blocks their way, they crawl under her to get to the other side. On the steps of the Benares *ghats* (bathing places), Ray frames Harihar sitting under an umbrella surrounded by widows. He is a *kathak* (religious storyteller), chanting and interpreting verses from the Hindu holy text. Cut to a brass plate with a few coins which lies in front of him. In long shot, Ray focuses on Apu wandering all over the *ghats*. We see him playing with a paper pinwheel; sometimes we see him rushing down the steps with his pinwheel spinning crazily in his hands. At other times he goes past the other *kathaks* down to the river, where he hops onto one of the boats. Later we see him in a pensive mood, taking a quiet walk along the river bank and pausing at an open-air gymnasium, where one of the men is exercising with a heavy club. Apu is enchanted by this man's performance but declines to participate in it when asked by the athlete. As dusk slowly envelops the *ghats,* this opening tableau ends and Apu's uninterrupted immersion in all the sights and sounds of the city is complete. Benares becomes, for Apu, a marvelous spectacle ready to be savored once again with the coming dawn.

Two incidents in the first half of the film reaffirm and reinforce Apu's *camatkara* involvement with Benares: the scene with the alcoholic Nanda-*babu,* who lives alone in a room on the terrace just above Apu; and Har-ihar's death during the festival of Diwali. In the first, Apu is sent by his mother to Nanda-*babu* to get some matchsticks. When Apu goes up, the door is half open, and Apu sees Nanda-*babu* taking off his shirt, hum-ming a tune, picking up a paper bag, and taking out a bottle. The camera is behind Apu and adopts his perspective to heighten the moment con-siderably. Apu is soon transfixed by the image of this strange fat man who has always been so excessively friendly with his parents, especially his mother. Once inside his room, Apu's *camatkara* gaze, duplicated by Ray's camera movement, pans with wonder from the man's furtive actions at hiding the bottle to his trembling fingers clumsily tearing a box of matches from a brand new carton and giving it to Apu. We feel Apu's *adbhuta* (magical) enjoyment as he relishes not only the *abhinayas* of Nanda-*babu* but also the accompanying sights of his untidy room, which fills the mise-en-scène with a calendar on which all the holy days are marked, upturned *tablas* (little drums), stacked-up pillows, a picture cutout of a beautiful woman smelling a rose that has been hastily immersed into a dirty glass frame, blackened walls, and Nanda-*babu* himself with his bloodshot eyes, disheveled curly hair, and sweaty appearance. Like the exercising athlete Apu had seen practicing with his club on the *ghat* steps, Nanda-*babu* with his bottle in this room becomes yet another wondrous sight this city has to offer the boy.

Hari's death, the other crucial incident in *Aparajito* presented to us as a *camatkara* event, cinematically takes the form of memory: Several of the signifiers that figured in Granny's and Durga's death in *Pather Panchali* are deliberately repeated by Ray and then reflected through Apu's predict-able reaction in which grief *and* wonder are movingly juxtaposed. The overwhelming presence of nature that surrounded Granny's death in the woods is replaced by the festival of Diwali, the traditional Hindu festival of lights and sounds, in Benares. (Diwali was inaugurated by the citizens of Ayodhya, who, by lighting lamps and exploding firecrackers, welcomed the return of their noble king Rama after his fourteen-year exile in the forest.) Hari, sick in his dark narrow room, is surrounded by the lights and firecrackers of Diwali exploding outside in the city. Small oil lamps burn brightly on the threshold of all Hindu doors; but the lamps flicker weakly in Hari's room, reminding us of Durga's death and how it had been heralded by a similar image. Sarbojaya sits by the sick Hari as she did with the sick Durga. Instead of the sound of thunder there are the sounds of firecrackers and smoke rockets. In the early hours of the morning, as the dying Hari cries out for holy Ganga water, a sleepy Apu is asked by Sarbojaya to quickly run down the *ghats* and fetch it in a "tumbler." Again, this takes us back to Granny's quarrel with Sarbojaya over the tumbler of water and the water pot falling from Durga's frightened hands at the discovery of Granny's dead body. As Apu runs down the steps of the *ghat*, the temple bells from the Vishwanath temple begin to ring. Now, as he fills the tumbler and is about to hasten back, Apu's eyes linger a moment over a man exercising vigorously in the coming Benares dawn. It is a wonderful cinematic moment, in which we witness Apu's *camatkara* faculties acknowledging at the *same* moment not only *death* taking away his weakened, sick father but also *life* being vigorously embraced by this unknown athlete. Then we see Apu running into the room and helping Sarbojaya raise the dying Harihar so that he may drink the holy river. However, as the water touches his throat, Harihar gasps for air and life, his head falls back limp, and Ray abruptly cuts to a flock of pigeons suddenly rising into the air and covering the early morning sky with their outstretched wings.

Confronted by this startling juxtaposition, we wonder if Ray is not indulging in a *pathetic fallacy* here, where the false appearances of the pigeons are being used to suggest Harihar's soul ascending to heaven under the powerful *dhvani* (suggestive) fancy of the author. Although the pigeons' flight *does* suggest the soul's ascent, as many Indian and Western critics seem to have noticed, Ray reaffirms the Hindu essence stressed here by prefacing Hari's death with a deliberate cut to the priests in the Vishwanath temple performing their elaborate prayers, in which life and death are both celebrated as part of the Hindu cosmic process. Hari's impending death thus is commemorated as a part of this *puja* (act of worship), and Apu's lingering at the *ghat* to watch the exercising athlete at the same moment that death stalks his father also corroborates the life–death cosmic process. The aesthetic distance created by Ray's presentation evokes the *karuna rasa* as compassion and enables us to enjoy it on a higher, ennobled level.

In *Pather Panchali,* Durga's death and the destruction of their home in the village propelled Hari, Sarbojaya, and little Apu to move to Benares in hope of a better future. In *Aparajito,* Hari's death and Sarbojaya's temporary job as a servant in a wealthy family, where she sees Apu performing humiliating tasks like picking gray hairs from her employer-master's head, reverse the process. The scene in which Sarbojaya makes up her mind to return to her uncle's village is memorably executed by Ray. We see her coming toward the camera from her mistress's room. She stops and watches Apu trying to take a puff from his master's recently prepared hookah. On the sound track we hear a shrill train whistle. In the next shot, Ray whip-pans to the right, where we see a train thundering past the frame. We cut to Sarbojaya, her uncle, and Apu inside the train compartment. The next cut reveals the steel girders of a bridge passing by the window. Since the bridge girders are seen by Sarbojaya, they complete the Benares segment that had been prefaced by bridge girders seen by Apu (who is now sleeping). In marvelously edited shots, the urban landscape is left behind and successively replaced by the familiar village. They have returned to the world of *Pather Panchali.* Ray's camera now zooms to a close-up of Sarbojaya's smiling face. She will go back to her village with her uncle; there she hopes to have the time to become a proper mother for Apu all over again.

Whereas Sarbojaya returns to the village expectantly, Apu is still a child and has not yet developed his own expectations. As an obedient son, he learns all the priestly duties his granduncle teaches him. Both Sarbojaya and his uncle want Apu to become a priest like Harihar, in keeping with the family tradition. In keeping with the transcendental constancy of his character, however, Apu's attentions, as he grows, begin to wander. His face increasingly turns away from the temple (the familiar) where he sits and learns age-old rituals and toward the little village school (the unfamiliar) where the other children go. When he finally expresses to his mother his desire to go to school, the camera slowly zooms toward Sarbojaya's face, which for the first time registers pangs of estrangement. She agrees, but the look on her face clearly indicates her unease with the possibility that Apu may *not* follow in his father's footsteps.

When Apu starts going to school, the world of education to which he is introduced opens up for him a whole new and different world of *camatkara.* The tin-foil, bow-and-arrow *camatkara* of the *Pather Panchali*

Apu is now replaced by the *camatkara* of books on famous explorers, travel, stories of invention and science, and the lure of the dark continent of Africa for the eager and brilliant pupil Apurba Ray in *Aparajito*. This wonder is poured into Apu, like the water of the holy Ganga, by the headmaster of his small village school. In one scene, the headmaster turns to a cupboard in his office and starts removing dusty volumes, which he places on the table before his pupil. Apu is shown taking each book from the old teacher, who lovingly describes its contents, and clutching it eagerly to his chest. The headmaster, through his *abhinaya* of *vacika* (speech), powerfully instigates the *camatkara* that is embedded in each book as a discovery for Apu, and he wants to see its fruition in the mind of his most brilliant student:

In this cupboard I have many such books. If you don't read books like these you cannot broaden your mind. We may live in a remote corner of Bengal, but that does not mean our outlook should be narrow. Now, this book is about the North Pole. . . . This is about Livingstone's travels. You can learn about Africa from this one, this is the story of inventions. This contains biographies of famous scientists: Galileo, Archimedes, Newton, Faraday. . . .[45]

The books give Apu all sorts of *adbhuta* (magical) experiences, and we see him, with his *camatkara* faculties, step into various roles. As a scientist, he explains to his poor ignorant mother the mysteries of a lunar eclipse with the help of two fruits, one big, one small, and the light of the lantern signifying the sun. In another scene when Sarbojaya comes home from the pond, the door opens with a bang, and out jumps Apu as a Zulu warrior, dressed in a grass skirt and armed with a spear (he has made these toys himself), streaks of white emblazoned all over his blackened hands and face, yelling and screaming "Africa! Africa!"

Once Sarbojaya sees her adolescent son completely and delightfully immersed in the world of "Galileo, Archimedes, Newton, Faraday" that education has opened up for him, she knows that the path he wants to tread does not lead back to her family courtyard. Having lost her husband and daughter she is now faced with the *soka* (grief) of losing her son too. The manifestation of the *karuna rasa* as sorrowful begins from this point, with mother and son shown going their separate ways.

Apu first gets his opportunity to assert the choice that will free him from his mother and his life in this village when he wins a small scholarship to study in a college in the large city of Calcutta (the unfamiliar again). When he mentions this to Sarbojaya, her immediate reaction reveals most conspicuously the threatened break in the all-important bond between mother and son. "Who will look after me?" she shouts at him. Apu tells her most emphatically that he does not "want to be a priest" all his life. His response compounds the threat for Sarbojaya, as it implies the breaking of the bond between *father* and son too. "Your father was a priest," she responds in a rage, and slaps his face.

As the furious Apu stalks out of the house, Ray cuts to a shot of the room suddenly bereft of human presence, and he holds onto this "emptiness" shot before allowing Sarbojaya to enter. The emptiness that looms before her, once Apu leaves for Calcutta, is registered visually and very poignantly here. The scene that follows immediately evokes familiar signifiers from the thrashing Sarbojaya had given Durga in *Pather Panchali*. In that film Sarbojaya had thrown Durga out of their courtyard and asked Apu to bring her back. In *Aparajito*, after being slapped by Sarbojaya, Apu throws *himself* out of the courtyard; Sarbojaya has to venture out in the darkness and bring her sulking son back with a promise that she will send him to Calcutta. The scene fades out with Apu's *vacika* utterance of "hurray!"

For the first time Sarbojaya sees an altogether different Apu. He is no longer her naughty child shooting tiny bows and arrows at the dog (as we saw him do in *Pather Panchali*) while she laughingly runs behind to feed him. The arrows now are of another kind, and they are aimed at her, his dead father Harihar, this equally dead village life, this parched family courtyard, and all the effete priestly tools that Apu has not once touched since the day he started going to school. Apu has deliberately and very openly abandoned these old attachments before his mother. Now he astonishes her with new ones, like the sundial he has made in the courtyard, or the globe on which he constantly points out to her the city of Calcutta, or the phenomenon of the eclipse he patiently tries to explain to her – completely unaware of the shadows he is going to cast on his mother's threadbare and lonely existence once he leaves her and becomes, according to *his* great expectations, the sophisticated and educated urbanite.

On the day he leaves her, Apu, we notice, has a globe in his hand. He is all set to conquer the world. This little object has more fascination for him than the sadness in his mother's eyes and the trembling in her fingers as she dips them in curds and puts an auspicious mark on his forehead, omens for a safe journey. He displays excitement only for the world he is about to enter; he is completely indifferent to the old world and the grieving mother he is leaving behind.

Apu's migration to urban Calcutta further intensifies his *camatkara*. As he commences his college career, Calcutta in the second half of *Aparajito* offers him new spectacles of wonder balancing the wondrous spectacles offered by the city of Benares in the first half of the film. The little Apu of *Pather Panchali* had once found wonder in the birds, leaves, fruits, and ponds of his village; but once the older Apu tastes the urbanized *camatkaras* of the big city, he soon gets bored by these. His vacations in the village now fill the urbanite Apu with ennui. Local village amusements like the band, the boy acrobat, and the man singing a Hindi film song in a cracked voice no longer amuse him. In midshot Ray frames a bored Apu listlessly binding the branch of a tree. He longs for the city and all its memorable sights like the "Victoria Memorial, Whiteway Laidlaw, Hogg Market, the zoo, Fort William," which he describes to his mother with great excitement on his first visit home. In Calcutta, Apu's favorite spot is the grassy bank near the Hooghly River where he lies down watching the boats leaving the small harbor. He yearns for the boat that will take him away to another shore. Like Tennyson's Ulysses, he wants to sail beyond the sunset, but he cannot. Because of his mother, Apu feels, in the words of his friend Shbunath, trapped "like a frog in the well." In fact Apu now dislikes trains very much because they always take him *back* to his mother and a village that has been suddenly emptied of all its previously cherished sights of wonder. The *camatkara* that he once felt in a train's whistle in the dark (in *Pather Panchali*) is now transferred (in *Aparajito*) to the fog horns he hears from his favorite spot as boats ply the Hooghly River.

Ray movingly conveys the growing mother–son alienation for us in one marvelous scene. On one of his trips home, when Sarbojaya requests Apu to stay two days more after his vacation ends, the impatient Apu condescendingly answers that he cannot because it will interfere with his studies, as he'll have to miss two days of college. Sarbojaya's answer reveals a wonderfully worked-out scheme of logic: "If you could arrive two days late for your holidays, why can't you leave two days late for your mother's sake?" When Apu does realize his callous treatment of his mother and returns from the railway station to spend one more day with her, Ray zooms in toward Sarbojaya's grateful face breaking into a rare and beautiful smile. This *abhinaya* immediately reminds us of Granny's wonderful and memorable *abhinaya*-smiles in *Pather Panchali* in response to unexpected acts of kindness by members of her family.

Apu's final return to the village comes as a response to a letter informing him of his mother's "grave illness." Through a semicircular pan from left to right, Ray frames Apu coming up the well-worn path to the open door of his mother's courtyard. Ray's camera now observes him through the door as Apu frantically searches for his absent mother. Then as Apu exits the frame, Ray slowly tracks along the courtyard wall and picks up Apu heading toward his mother's favorite tree, by which we had earlier seen her sitting as she waited in vain for his return. As he stops near it, he confronts his granduncle. No words are exchanged: The look on the old man's face conveys the sad news of Sarbojaya's permanent absence. Apu sits by the tree and weeps. Ray keeps the emotion of *karuna* (sorrow) firmly in check by slowly tracking *away* from Apu, *back* toward the spectator – a camera movement that makes us identify quite strongly with Apu's previous emotional distancing from his mother. However, this kind of discourse opens up other interesting *dhvanis* (suggestions) as well: While stressing Apu's *orphaned state* and *sense of guilt*, it also potentially makes him transcend *both* by clearly indicating the opportunities that are now available for him to explore. He has no family responsibilities or dependents now. There are no "nets" to imprison him in this village, though his granduncle, in the scenes that follow, unsuccessfully flings a few in an attempt to snare Apu. He insists, for example, that Apu perform his mother's last rites then and there in accordance with her last wishes that he continue the priestly tradition of his father. Apu's response, however, is to start packing his belongings for Calcutta. "I've got my exams," he tells his granduncle. "I'll perform mother's rites in Calcutta." This remark indicates that he has transcended his grief and his guilt. Nothing can hold him back now. Only the future in Calcutta matters.

Two particularly noteworthy *abhinayas* (gestures) in *Aparijito* remain unmentioned. The first originates in the opening sequence: As Ray's camera travels across the *ghats* of Benares, it picks out Harihar carrying the holy Ganga water in a little brass pot up the steps of the *ghat*. He then stops to collect his glasses from another *kathak* who sits under a neighboring sunshade on the *ghat*. This seemingly casual *abhinaya* of friendliness between two *kathaks* takes on a different meaning when, in a parallel scene later in the film, a very ill Harihar, after bathing in the river, is called back by the other *kathak* because he has *forgotten* to take his glasses from him. The incident, rendered totally on the level of Harihar's *angika* (hand movement) and that of the *kathak,* not only points suggestively to Harihar's encroaching weakness but reasserts very strongly his predominant quality, which lies precisely in his complete lack of vision and inability to see the world as it actually exists around him.

In another scene, a single utterance of Apu's, spelled out through the *abhinaya* of *vacika* (speech) in English, delineates his desire to embrace another language and consequently another culture. This significant moment occurs when Apu has gone out to buy some firecrackers and sparklers for Diwali. His father lies sick and spent in the gloomy apartment smelling of herbal medicines and the strong, overwhelming odor of ginger and honey-paste that Sarbojaya is applying to his congested chest. Apu, who returns with the Diwali paraphernalia, is asked to sit with his ailing father. A neighbor's boy calls for Apu to come witness the spectacle of fireworks taking place outside. When Apu tells his father that this boy is teaching him English and is not a Bengali, Hari asks his son to translate "Apu bhalo chey." When Apu triumphantly succeeds by uttering in English "Apu is a good boy," the father rewards him by freeing him from his task of playing the nurse, and Apu runs off with the boy to enjoy the fireworks. Through this single *vacika* of Apu's, Hari is made to realize sadly and proudly that he cannot compete with Apu's newfound instructor or the new language his son is learning. He is too sick and hopelessly out of step with the newer forces being felt even here in one of India's most traditional cities, Benares. Apu, in fact, has gone far beyond Harihar's "ghosts" and "multiplication tables," with which we had seen him educating Apu in *Pather Panchali*. The "good boy" obedience suggested by the *vacika* utterance is directed not so much toward the father as toward another language and culture that lies beyond the walls of this temple city. One could easily imagine how Apu and his non-Bengali friend would have conversed in English throughout that evening while watching a very traditional Indian festival with fireworks taking place in Benares. In fact, the development of Apu's first taste of Westernization is revealed through this *abhinaya* of a *vacika* spoken in the English tongue.

Later in the film, Ray uses the *vacika* of another English utterance in relation to Apu to inscribe quite suggestively his estrangement from his mother. A college lecturer is teaching figures of speech to an English class in which Apu, tired and sleepy after nightly stints working in a printing house, is shown dozing. After defining categorically that "synecdoche is a figure of speech based on association," the teacher rouses Apu from his slumber and demands sarcastically in his precise and clipped English if "this strange word on the blackboard" conveys anything to him. As Apu is expelled from the class for failing to come up with the right answer, we immediately grasp the synecdochic references to Apu's own family situation in which his mother, the only other remaining member, figures. As a "son," a significant *part* of the family, who is drifting further and further away from his "mother," he portends the complete collapse of the *whole family*. The reference does not stop there, however: It also points forward to Apu's marriage in the third part of the trilogy, *Apu Sansar*. Once Aparna enters his life as his wife (to whom Apu also once speaks in English, as we shall see), the *wholeness* of family is temporarily restored, only to be broken with her untimely death at her pregnancy and Apu's stubborn refusal to accept fatherly responsibility toward his son, Kajal. All these *associations* are aroused from this single spoken synecdoche *abhinaya*, testifying to Ray's *pratibha* in making it relate to Apu's past, present, and future.

Rasa in *Apur Sansar* (1959)

In keeping with the dictates of his *camatkara* faculties, the Apu of *Apur Sansar* is introduced to us as a gifted, literary young man who constantly refuses to immerse himself in the world of workaday reality. He would rather write a short story and get it published for a pittance in a prestigious Bengali literary magazine than take up a salaried nine-to-five job monotonously labeling bottles. Anything that will interfere with his literary potential he avoids. What transpires from such a stance is a determination on Apu's part to indulge in a solipsism endorsed stubbornly by his *camatkara* aesthetic.

Ray depicts this solipsistic imperative in the film's early scenes. The most conspicuous objects in Apu's impoverished, garretlike room near the railway yard are his books, sheaves of paper scattered all over his untidy bed, pens and bottles of ink, his globe, atlases, maps, and a bamboo flute. He entertains no one here. We see only one person entering his room before his best friend, Pulu: his landlord, who has come to collect his three-months-overdue rent. The only other brief exchange we see Apu having is with the man downstairs, who has the same last name and receives one of Apu's letters by mistake. Apu has cut himself off from even Pulu, having left no forwarding address at his last lodging.

In the opening scenes of *camatkara*, a string of associative signifiers in the mise-en-scène function as *dhvanis*, suggesting links with the previous two films of the trilogy. As Apu gets up, it is raining. Like Durga in *Pather Panchali* he goes out to the terrace and enjoys getting completely drenched; then, like the athlete in *Aparajito* he bends down and does a series of exercises. The landlord teases Apu by deliberately switching off the light under which Apu is shaving. In retaliation, Apu not only switches that light on again, but he even goes and switches on the light for the staircase. Apu's *abhinayas* are more than just those of a defaulting tenant. They also remind us of Apu's first *abhinaya* in *Aparajito*: Entering for the first time his room above his patron's "Royal Press" in the city of Calcutta, Apu goes quickly toward the switch and turns on the light – having spent the better part of his childhood with lanterns and candles in a village bereft of electricity.

It is Pulu, his close college friend, who forces Apu out of his isolation by bursting into his garret and inviting him to accompany him to the marriage of his cousin, Aparna, taking place in the remote village of Khulna. By deliberately depicting a mock-poetic picture of the spectacle of nature he hopes Apu will find in Khulna, Pulu not only makes fun of Apu's urbanite sensibilities and his having abandoned the *camatkara* sights of nature, but also evokes in Apu the nostalgia for that wondrous childhood he had once experienced in his *own* village. Ray's mise-en-scène has the two friends chatting in a noisy, crowded restaurant full of smoke, dirty dishes, and the din of circulating conversation – a world far removed from Pulu's wondrous description of nature. However, as Pulu talks of "a river, with boats on it, [and] endless fields of grass and paddy, mango orchards, bamboo groves . . . trees full of birds . . . the songs of crickets . . . kerosene lamps – no electricity," the entire *camatkara* world of *Pather Panchali* is resurrected for Apu, who joyfully agrees to go. Later that night, as the two friends return from a play, Apu confirms this rekindling of wonder by dramatically reciting lines from Tagore's poem *Basundhara* (The Universe):

Take me back, O mother earth,
Take thy son to thy lap, wrap him in thy flowing veil,
Let me be one with the soil, and spread myself
Far and wide, like the joys of Spring.
Let me burst open the heart's narrow edge,
Break down the hard stone walls,
The dark and cheerless prison of my mind
To rush forth in a rapture of delight
Surging, billowing, tossing, rolling on . . .

So wonderful is this imaginative return to nature that when a passing policeman threatens to interrupt, an undaunted Apu refuses to be brought back to reality even by such an authorized agent of the law.

When Pulu cautions him to come to his senses at last and take up a regular job, Apu counters in the true romantic idiom of the authentic free man: "Why should I become a clerk? Why? There's no reason why I should. I am a free man. No ties, no responsibilities, no problems, no one to worry about. Why should I suddenly become a clerk?" Once again he avows that he will not allow his *camatkara* to be hemmed in by any practical responsibilities. He wants his life to flow freely like the river on which he and Pulu are next seen proceeding to Khulna in a small open boat. Freed from the narrow confines of his room and the constant smog of smoke and charcoal drifting in from the neighboring railway yard, Apu blossoms in nature's idyllic presence. He plays his flute as the boat slowly takes him past paddy fields where the sun shines, the cattle graze, and the village women wash their clothes in the shallows. He delights in the boatman's oar splashing a soothing rhythm in the water. Again his *camatkara* manifests itself through the recitation of a Tagore poem, *Nirrudesh Jatra* [Destination Unknown]:

> How much further will thou lead me,
> O Fair One?
> Tell me what shore
> thy golden boat will touch.
> Whenever I ask thee,
> O thou from distant lands,
> Thou only smilest in thine own sweet way.

Through Ray's playful editing, the boatman, thinking that he is being referred to, gives Apu a toothless grin. The irony, however, made manifest by the poem and hidden from Apu, is that this river is propelling him toward his future bride, Aparna. When he returns, *she* will in actuality be the "Fair One" beside him as personified by the poem.

The other character who endorses the *camatkara* for Apu is Aparna herself [Fig. 4]. It is she who transforms the *solipsistic* quality of Apu's sense of wonder into one of a *shared* bliss.

The love scenes between the two show the moving presentation of the *sringara* or erotic *rasa* through the evocative use of *dhvani* in which the physical idyll of shared intimacy between Apu and Aparna is never directly stated but tenderly and poetically suggested. The love scene in Apu's garretlike room begins with Ray panning down the newly decorated curtain window, then continuing over their sleeping faces. The alarm rings, and Aparna gets up. As she tries to leave the bed she realizes she cannot; Apu has knotted the end of her *sari* to his *dhoti* (pajamas). She smiles as she bends down to untie the knot. This "knot" is not merely naughty: It refers to an important emblematic moment in the Hindu wedding ritual when the ends of the bride and bridegroom's garments are tied to register symbolically their "union" as they take their seven turns around the sacred fire. The "sexual union" of the previous night also gets immediately invoked by this suggestively playful prank of Apu's. Then in midshot we

Figure 4. Aparna (Sharmila Tagore) endorsing Apu's (Soumitra Chatterjee) camat-kara in Apu Sansar *(The World of Apu, 1959). (Photo courtesy the Ray Archives, University of California at Santa Cruz)*

see Apu opening his eyes. Groping under his pillow, he is delighted to discover her hairpin. He stares at it and lovingly starts to play with it.

This *abhinaya* of Apu's intensifies the sexual suggestiveness of the previous night's fulfilling connubial union, conjuring up for us the wonderful image of Aparna's slowly removing most of her hairpins to loosen her hair before the actual act of lovemaking. Apu then looks at her as she prepares the cooking fire. As she becomes the consuming object of Apu's gaze, we see her returning his looks and scolding him for staring at her so brazenly.

Ray's editing intensifies the intimacy in their repeatedly exchanged glances, which display their complete delight in each other's presence. Even simple actions like her attempts at starting the cooking fire suggest not only the fond memory of the previous night's passion but also her pleasure at being looked at by her husband, since it can kindle in him an identical fire of passion. The *abhinayas* with which each responds to the other maintain the *camatkara* that each feels for the other, while at the same time strengthening the manifestation in us of the *sringara rasa* being created so suggestively by Ray's cinematic language out of every new gesture, action, and reaction.

We cut back to Apu as he pulls out his cigarette packet. On its inner flap Aparna has written, "Remember – one after each meal." As he looks delightedly at her now appreciating *her* prank, she smiles, swats a wandering cockroach, and gets to work, clumsily breaking coal with her bare hands for the cooking stove. Coming from a wealthy family (where such domestic chores would be strictly performed by servants), her clumsiness at once makes it apparent she has never done a task like this. Within that clumsiness, however, there is also very visible a lot of love. She does this labor willingly for Apu, who soon strolls up to her and starts serenading her with his flute.

While his flute gradually gains ascendancy on the sound track over the whistles and shunting engines of the trains nearby, Ray's camera lingers over the smoke from Aparna's cooking stove as it floats and mingles with the smoke coming from the engines' funnels in the railway yard below. Through such juxtapositions we see how Ray asserts the intimacy of this attractive couple's connubial space over the ordinary daily occurrences in the space outside their dwelling. Lost in their love for each other they grow and blossom with every new *abhinaya* and movement, making the whole experience of the *sringara rasa* more enjoyable and worthwhile for all of us who are witnessing this very intimate spectacle.

Another scene that commemorates this shared *camatkara* is the one in which Ray shows Apu and Aparna watching a crude commercial Indian film, a run-of-the-mill "mythological." Ray dissolves from the film frame (in which wee see the pious little child of God, Dhruva, surrounded by a protective cordon of fire and Lord Vishnu's sacred weapon – the *sudarshana chakra,* or sacred wheel) to the back window of a carriage (through which we glimpse the electric lights of the passing streetlamps) taking them home. We are given no sense of anything going on outside of this frame; we are privileged only to witness the private, internal drama of *camatkara* enacted within this frame between a loved husband and an adored wife.

Aparna, we learn in this scene, is going to her *mahike* (her parents' house) to have their first baby (in keeping with traditional Hindu mores). Apu will now have all the time to create his own baby, namely his novel, which he has not "once touched" since experiencing the new wonders of connubial bliss. He tells her dreamily that he will dedicate his first novel "to my wife" (said by him in English). Although Aparna does not know English, she exclaims proudly that she knows what the word "wife" means. Apu, who has been teaching her the English alphabet, beams at her and whispers that *she* doesn't – *he* does! Here, Ray very movingly isolates and frames Aparna's face in close-up as she lights his cigarette and watches the match burn down.

In the entire scene, the use of space consolidates the prevalent *camatkara*. The space inside the carriage becomes the appropriate embryonic metaphor of their mutual love and adoration. It makes them reject even the fantasy of the cinema, which they don't need because they are so totally absorbed in each other's presence. Each, in fact, becomes for the other a window through which their shared happiness can be framed. When Ray makes Aparna the lingering object of Apu's gaze, however, we immediately sense how dependent Apu has become upon her. He has even suspended his life's greatest ambition – the writing of his novel – because of her. The fact that very soon he is going to lose her will completely shatter not only his sense of space but his *camatkara* universe as well. It will make him renounce *camatkara* until his son Kajal, after reconciling with his wayward father, finally ushers in again this sense of wonder and delight.

In *Apur Sansar, rasa* is also developed by an essential contrast that sets Apu's character in opposition to a contrary character like Pulu. The constancy of Apu's character is reaffirmed through the various challenges and trials Pulu forces him to confront and experience. Through Pulu, we rediscover Apu's characteristic qualities and are made to enjoy the wholeness of his character, especially in light of his evolution in the previous two films. When, for instance, Apu talks about his autobiographical novel, in which there is going to be a lot of "fiction, imaginary characters, and a predominant love interest," Pulu cuts him short by wondering what Apu could really *know* about love, since "you have really had no experience of it."

Immediately, we are reminded of an earlier scene in which Apu had closed his window when he had found the neighboring girl staring at him from the window opposite. Previously, in the scene with the downstairs tenant, when the man had asked Apu whether he'd ever had a girlfriend who wrote to him, Apu had shyly shaken his head in the negative. The only women that Apu has known are his mother and sister; he does not know what love really means until Aparna unexpectedly enters his life. Here again, it is Pulu who first approaches Apu – on the day Aparna's original husband-to-be is discovered to be a demented half-wit – and asks him to marry her instead. It is Pulu, therefore, who provides Apu with the fulfillment of that part of his life, namely his emotional and sexual attachment to a woman.

It is Pulu, also, who is instrumental in leading the estranged and embittered Apu back to his son Kajal after Aparna's untimely death during childbirth. Pulu's common sense and insistence on responsibility is vitally needed to fracture Apu's overwhelming sense of hurt and stubborn egoism. "It is because Kajal exists that Aparna does not," he tells Pulu in their confrontation near the mine where Apu has taken a job. Apu wants to go abroad, but Pulu insists that he should take care of Kajal's future before settling his own: "And there is something called duty, or have you thrown that away as well, like your novel?" Pulu spurns Apu's pleas to play the surrogate father to Kajal, deliberately refusing in order to make the sensitive Apu feel guilty about his own selfish plans to get as far away from Kajal as he possibly can. He literally pushes Apu to go and visit his son, on whom Apu has yet to lay eyes. Wise as he is, Pulu knows that once Apu *sees* Kajal, the "father" who has been dead and buried for so long inside will be miraculously resurrected by the child's endearing presence and antics – a prophecy we later see come true.

Apu's sexual timidity becomes the first major characteristic that Ray cleverly inscribes through Apu's predominant *angika* or bodily movements of playing the flute. The first time we see this *abhinaya* is on the evening when Apu receives the good news that one of his stories is going to be published. However, before he can play something on his flute to express his joy, he suddenly sees a girl standing at a window in the house opposite, looking in. Apu cautiously slides backward, picks up his flute, and pushes his window shut with it. The girl has obviously heard him play the flute before. Instead of using the flute to attract her even more or strike up a friendship, however, Apu uses it as a tool to isolate himself from her. Both *angikas* clearly designate his shyness with women even though he holds the instrument through which romantic liaisons could be most successfully struck. In fact, Apu's character is given a mythopoeic significance by Aparna's mother at their first meeting because of his flute. Ray's mise-en-scène is brilliant, especially in portraying the subtle interplay of *angikas* and *vacikas* (utterances) that not only suggestively refer to Apu's identification with Lord Krishna, but further reaffirm his shyness and timidity with the opposite sex:

Pulu comes into the room with a child. He puts the child down and touches his aunt's feet. The room is crowded with young girls.

AUNT: *(blessing him)* There, there. How are you, my child?

(Apu comes in.)

PULU: *(to Apu)* My aunt.

(Apu touches her feet. Pulu's aunt stares at Apu, her eyes shining.)

PULU: Here I had such a good match for your daughter, and you fix Aparna's marriage somewhere else.

AUNT: Where have I seen this face?

PULU: You couldn't have seen it anywhere. This is his first visit.

AUNT: No, no. I know this face well. Oh yes! I know where I've seen it before, in the painting of Gods!

PULU: Lord Krishna incarnate. Complete with flute.

(Apu smiles, very embarrassed).[46]

When Apu enters the room, the only object he holds is his flute. We cut to Aparna's mother staring at Apu and his flute; behind her we see a row of girls doing the same. Now Ray cuts to a reverse shot, so that we see Apu, completely alone and embarrassed, in the frame. As bouts of shyness overwhelm his *angikas,* he becomes more appealing as the consummate object of desire for the predominantly feminine gaze, not only of Aparna's mother but also of the other women standing behind her. The Krishna pronouncement adds another layer to Apu; the flute immediately becomes the conspicuous *dhvani* that suggests the merging of Apu with that god. In the Krishna myth, the flute is his most potent weapon: While the women of Vrindavan labored at their chores, it was Krishna's flute that lured them to his presence and their ultimate seduction. Psychoanalyst Sudhir Kakar, in his section on the "Cult and Myths of Krishna," singles out the following qualities of this god:

In a country of many religious cults and a variety of gods, Krishna is unquestionably the most popular. . . . He is usually portrayed as a blue-complexioned child full of pranks and mischief, or as a youthful cowherd wearing a crown of peacock feathers whose beauty entrances all who see him or hear the irresistible call of his flute. . . . The later Krishna texts, *Vishnu Purana, Padma Purana,* and *Brahmavaivarta Purana,* are fascinated by and focus upon these aspects of the god: Krishna's freedom and spontaneity as the eternal child, the youth-Krishna's surpassing beauty and the seductive power of the haunting flute which breaks down human resistance to the appeal of the divine lover.[47]

Apu has Krishna's freedom and spontaneity as the eternal child. He also has his surpassing beauty and could have irresistibly conquered the maidens assembled in this room with his flute; but his timidity prevents him from capitalizing on his Krishna attributes. Ray alerts us to this by describing in the mise-en-scène the suggestive entrance of Pulu with a child. The child clearly suggests Apu himself, who, knowing no one in this household, follows Pulu close behind. The room is full of girls who are all attracted to Apu's strikingly good looks – a collective attraction conveyed most suggestively through Aparna's mother's *vacikas* and the *sātvika* (involuntary reaction) of her shining eyes, dazzled by Apu's close resemblance to a painting of Krishna she has seen somewhere. Wanting to free himself from all this attention, Apu hurriedly and shyly leaves the room. In fact, during the wedding preparations, we never see Apu sitting or talking with anyone in the house; rather, we always see him *away* from the house, wandering all by himself. Ray usually positions him near the river, reading a book or playing his flute softly to himself. Pulu's remark that Apu is a good match for Aparna is of course made in jest to his aunt, but its *vacika* significance is clearly revealed when Apu conclusively becomes the first choice to take the demented bridegroom's place. Nobody, we notice, offers any opposition to Apu.

After Apu leaves Aparna's mother, Ray cuts to a *shehnai* (classical pipe instrument) player. He then cuts to Aparna (our first glimpse of her) being prepared as a bride by the household women. From here Ray moves outdoors to a shot of the bridegroom's *palanquin* or covered litter approaching the bride's home, shouldered by a band that plays "for he's a jolly good fellow" – referring of course to Aparna's intended. As Ray's camera tracks the groom's progress at a lower level, it also focuses on Apu sleeping with his flute under a tree on an elevated embankment, visually instigating a link between the two men. We then cut to Aparna's father and the males getting ready at their home's entrance to welcome the bridegroom and his party. As the litter halts before the gate, Ray tracks in toward the man seated inside. To our horror we see him muttering incoherently and tearing to shreds all the floral arrangements around him. In a long-held shot we see Aparna's male family members, one by one, peering with horror at this mad groom, who is far from the jolly good fellow the music had wickedly but erroneously suggested. We cut to the bride's mother and the weeping Aparna in her room. The mother slams the door on Aparna's father, who in desperation turns to the calm Pulu for help. Once again Ray moves outdoors, cutting to a close-up of the sleeping Apu being awakened by Pulu. When Pulu discloses the sad details about the groom and requests Apu to take his place, Apu's reaction is predictable: His timidity and outrage make him shrink from Pulu and the elders who stand before him with folded arms. While they retreat (off-frame), Ray focuses on an agitated Apu pacing feverishly beside the tree. We now cut to a long shot of Aparna's house. Slowly Apu's arm enters the frame. In a series of shots we see him hesitantly approaching the house (and hear a child cry) – passing, as he does so, the *palanquin* bearing away the mad groom. In midshot Apu approaches Pulu and agrees to marry Aparna.

Flattered by Aparna's mother's comparison of him to Krishna, Apu patronizingly asserts his own godlikeness to Aparna, across her father's four-poster bed, the first moment they find themselves together after their nuptials: "Believe me, the marriage was forced upon me. I was strongly against it. But the way the request was made, I thought I was doing something noble." A god's duty is to save people in distress, and Apu feels he has saved Aparna and her family honor by agreeing to marry her. For Aparna's parents, his decision is welcomed in fact as "a blessing": One of the guests watching the wedding whispers to Aparna's beaming mother, "The curse has turned into a blessing for you. Your daughter hasn't worshiped Shiva in vain." The next time we see Apu playing the flute, it is solely for Aparna's benefit and delight. This occurs on the morning after a night of sexual and emotional plenitude. Now the window of his house is kept permanently open, and the flute's melody soars high above the noise and smoke of the shunting engines in the railway yard. Krishna has finally found his Radha, and he wants the whole world (including the neighboring girl) to know it.

In *Aparajito*, when Ray had shown Apu weeping over his mother's death, his camera had tracked *away* from the bereaved son, indicating not only Apu's orphaned state but also the opening up of opportunities for him in a wider, bigger world. In *Apur Sansar*, when Aparna's brother Murari conveys to Apu Aparna's death during childbirth, the camera tracks *in* on Apu's shocked face. At first, as Apu unlocks his room's door, he doesn't see Murari, but we do. We then cut to Murari from Apu's perspective, followed by a reverse shot of Apu from Murari. As Murari murmurs "the baby came too soon," Ray tracks into Apu as he turns briefly and then resoundingly strikes his brother-in-law across the face. This brutal *angika* (hand movement) *abhinaya* powerfully conveys to us Apu's total impotence in the face of such a calamity. His wife's untimely death seems completely to cripple him. A kind and well-meaning neighbor offers Apu the birth of his son Kajal as a compensation to balance Aparna's death ("Well it's a good thing the child was saved"), but Apu is unwilling to accept that. His later remark to Pulu, "It is because Kajal exists that Aparna does not," confirms both the agonizing loss of Aparna and the subsequent violence, perpetuated first on the hapless brother-in-law and next on Kajal, who is cruelly neglected by Apu for the first five years. The *rasa* of *karuna* as compassion is wonderfully supported here by the *rasa* of *rudra* or anger.

The poignancy at Aparna's demise is intensified by the scenes that immediately precede the revelation of her death to Apu. In these, the consistent *abhinaya* displayed by Apu is the reading again and again of Aparna's most recent *prempatra* or love letter to him. At first, we see him trying to read the letter at work behind the shelter of his typewriter. As the camera zooms in to enhance the moment's intimacy, the *vacika* of Aparna in voice-over spells out its utterly charming contents to us: Apu owes her eight letters, and she insists that he now come and fetch her. We cut to a clock that announces closing time. Now Ray situates us with Apu. On his way home in the tram, Apu takes out the letter again and reads the part where Aparna warns him not to open their bedroom window because she is very jealous of the girl next door watching him every morning and evening. Once again Ray zooms in on Apu, excluding all the other passengers breathing down his neck. As Apu grins, Ray cuts to a fat middle-aged man standing beside him and staring at him inquisitively. Cut to Apu in long shot on a bridge; he descends, then approaches the camera, continuing to read her letter as he walks home beside the railway tracks. Now we are privileged to hear the letter's conclusion, a plea that Apu should not laugh at her spelling mistakes but come and fetch her as she misses him terribly. Aparna's *vacika* (speech) and Apu's *angika* (bodily movements) are brilliantly juxtaposed through the simple vehicle of this letter to show the intensity of the marriage bond. Aparna misses Apu every moment in her wealthy parents' home, just as Apu seems to carry Aparna with him everywhere he goes. The fact that this bond is soon going to be ruptured, however, is first indicated by the three "nevers" intoned by Aparna in her letter: "I'll never speak to you – never, never, never, if you don't come soon." Apu laughs and picks up a child playing dangerously near the railway track; this will be the last caring act Apu will perform for some time.

The inclusion of the *child* in the mise-en-scène is quite suggestive of that earlier moment when Apu had resolved to marry Aparna. As he approached her house, we heard very distinctly the crying of a child on the sound track. That crying was later linked to the shot of a child learning how to walk toward its mother, which the crying Aparna had seen from Apu's room on her first entrance into Apu's shabby and poverty-ridden room, and which had made her stop weeping. Now, the crying of a child not only points to what could have happened to *this* child had it been hurt by a train but foreshadows that messenger of doom who awaits Apu on his doorstep with the news that his wife died because "the child came too soon." This kind of presentation manifests strongly the *rasa* of *karuna* as compassion, subordinated as it has been by the *rasa* of *sringara* or erotic love through this letter-reading sequence.

The final section of the film deals with Apu's confrontation with his son Kajal. The predominant setting is the maternal grandfather's house. When Kajal is introduced to the spectator, he is wearing a devil mask as a disguise; when this is removed, we are shown a remarkably sensitive yet rebellious face. Apu, on the other hand, has grown a beard in the period since Aparna's death. Kajal's devil mask and Apu's beard become very appropriately the two visible signifiers behind which both conceal their anger. These become the chief physical indicators from which the characters of Kajal and Apu have to emerge in order to finally accept themselves in their prospective roles as "son" and "father." Both have created damaging myths of each other for themselves, and these are expressed through the *vyabhicharibhavas* or accompanying emotions of mistrust and suspicion. For Kajal, Apu is the absent father who lives only in fairy tales and will never come to take him away from his strict grandfather. For Apu, Kajal is responsible for causing Aparna's death during childbirth and thus undeserving of a father's love and protection. The only reason Apu has come to fetch Kajal is to take him off his father-in-law's hands and leave the little boy with his own uncle in his village before going abroad. The *vyabhicharibhavas* of mistrust and suspicion must be expressed and expelled from the wounded psyches of father and son before the *santa rasa* of *peace* as an intensely felt state of mind can be attained. For the spectators, the positive emotion of *sama* (serenity/calmness) emanating from the reconciliation is thereby transformed into the *santa* or quietistic *rasa* itself.

Kajal is introduced to us as a rebellious young boy of four or five. In the very first incident we can see him participating in a cruel act of mischief: picking up a dead bird and dangling it over an old peasant woman, frightening her. When an old man who has witnessed this prank threatens to tell his grandfather, Kajal yells at him: "Go ahead. You tell him. I'll tell my father. Then he'll come and break your neck." This remark reveals very suggestively how much the little boy misses his father, whom he has never seen but about whom he has obviously heard a lot. Moreover, what he has heard about Apu, especially from his grandfather, has created in Kajal's mind the image of a father very much like himself: rebellious, always getting into trouble, someone whom these old people clearly *don't* seem to like. However, the fact that Apu is never there also indicates to Kajal that maybe his father doesn't like *him* either.

When Apu enters Kajal's room, he sees Kajal asleep on the same large four-poster bed across which he had dramatized to Kajal's mother, on their wedding night, his Krishna-like nobility in marrying her in spite of his orphaned existence in the big city. The *dhvanis* or suggestions of Kajal's orphanhood are movingly indicated here. Visually, a tiny boy curled up on such a massive bed without his parents' comforting presence intensifies Kajal's aloneness also. As Apu approaches the bed and stares at his son for the first time, a romantic song of a boatman is heard outside the window. This reminds Apu of that earlier scene when he had recited Tagore's poem about his "Fair One" in the boat and elicited a foolish grin from the boatman. The camera slowly tracks out as Apu goes and sits by the window. Ray cuts to a close-up of Apu as he rises and touches Kajal. When Apu utters his name, Kajal rolls off the bed and runs out of the room, out of the house, and stops at the gate. Apu runs after him.

When Apu informs him, "Kajal, I'm your father," the child retaliates by hurling a stone at him. This *abhinaya* conveys three possible *dhvanis* or suggestive meanings: First, Kajal wants to hurt Apu in the same way he had hurt that dead bird, that old woman, and that old passer-by. Second, he knows intuitively that his father is strong and wants to show him that, although a child, he is strong too. Third, the stone throwing is a test, and Kajal wants to see how Apu will respond to it. When the grandfather, who has observed this defiance, now rushes in to thrash Kajal with his cane, Apu intervenes bodily to protect his son. Kajal grasps that when threatened, he will now have his father to protect him. The camera pulls back as the grandfather leaves. We cut to a toy train whizzing toward Kajal, who is now back in his room.

Having reached a first plateau of reconciliation, Apu's winding up and sending this toy train toward Kajal is another friendly *abhinaya* on his part; but the train is hurled back at him in anger. For Kajal, the toy train suggests both a useless mechanical bribe of friendship and the strong possibility of his father once again leaving, going away on an actual train. Kajal needs something that intrinsically belongs to his father, not something that can be mechanically wound and unwound. Sensing this, Apu approaches his son, who is now pretending to sleep, and offers to tell him stories: "I know lots of stories. Will you be my friend, Kajal, and listen to them?" Kajal does not respond, but from his face we know that he is willing. Though he is not yet ready for tactile contact with Apu (he pushes Apu's hands away from his shoulders), Kajal does not reject Apu's role

Figure 5. Apu (Soumitra Chatterjee) and Kajal (Aloke Chakravarty) confidently confronting their future in Apur Sansar (The World of Apu, *1959). (Photo courtesy the Ray Archives, University of California at Santa Cruz)*

as storyteller. He wants his father's voice to enter his tiny frame. Here, the second plateau of their reconciliation is attained sensitively and movingly by Ray.

After these initial rejections, when Apu prepares to leave without Kajal, the young boy follows him, keeping all the while at a distance. When Apu turns and waits for his son to close the actual as well as the metaphorical gap between them, Ray, wonderfully, has them discuss the "father" in the "third person." Kajal has surmised that Apu really *is* his father; but he is still hurt by Apu's long neglect. If Apu has to earn acceptance as his father in the "first person," then he will have to ascend from the "third person." Kajal asks Apu, "Do you know my father?" When Apu says he does, the child asks, "Will you take me to him?" When Apu, with tears in his eyes, proclaims the definitive *yes* – "Yes, Yes, Kajal, I will, I will," the "son" rushes into his "father's" arms and is immediately hoisted up on his father's shoulders. As father and son, now completely reunited by that *yes*, prepare to leave, we who now have been witness to this can enjoy the *rasa* of *sama* as both Apu and Kajal confidently stride into the future, a dyad of faith and heroic performance [Fig. 5]. Peace and happiness now await them on this *pather panchali* (little road), leading them to their future.

Jalsaghar (1958): A Critical Evaluation Rendered through *Rasa*

J. L. Masson and M. V. Patwardhan define a *rasa*-induced experience as follows:

How does the tradition regard a viewing of *Sakuntala* from the point of view of *rasa*? The *vibhavas* [sources] belong to the characters represented on the stage. The *alambanavibhavas* [primary sources] will be Sakuntala and Dushanta. The *uddipanavibhavas* [settings] will be the physical beauty of both characters, the spring flowers, the bees, etc. . . . The *anubhavas* will also belong to the characters and are the physical indices of love like trembling, sweating, etc. . . . These are the essential elements of the preliminary stage. Now we come to the more problematic three: the *vyabhicharibhavas* [also called *sancaribhavas*], the *sthayibhavas*, and finally *rasa* itself. *Vyabhicharibhavas* are emotions that accompany the primary feelings of the character. They are liable to change and are not inherent to the character's personality. Examples are *harsha* [joy], *autsukya* [longing], etc. . . . all of which belong exclusively to the characters. Now the *sthayibhava* is a state of mind which because it is more deeply felt dominates all other emotions. It belongs to both the characters and the spectator. The difference is this: Once the character experiences this *sthayibhava* he has reached the height of emotion. But the spectator can go further and deeper. For when "love" is awakened in him it is not like the love that the original character felt. The spectators do not fall in love with Sakuntala. This *sthayibhava* is transformed into what is called *rasa* or an extraworldly state. This enables him to retain *aesthetic distance,* the name for which is *rasa*.[48]

A close examination of the opening scenes of Ray's 1958 film, *Jalsaghar* (*The Music Room*), displays a skillful working of the author's *prathibha* or imagination in establishing, consolidating, and setting the stage for the further promotion of the dominant *rasa* of *karuna* or sorrow. According to Bharata, the *karuna rasa* arises from the permanent emotion of sorrow. Its *vibhavas* (sources) are separation, downfall from a respectable position, loss of wealth, misfortune, destruction, death, and calamity. Its *vyabhicharibhavas* (accompanying emotions) are world-weariness, mental and physical exhaustion, lifelessness, paralysis, depression, insanity, and so on. We then reach the *sthayibhava* of *soka* (grief), which when transformed, gives us the *karuna rasa*.[49]

Jalsaghar opens with a close-up of the lifeless face of a man who has exiled himself from the rest of the world. The lips move and ask Ananta, the servant, to fetch him his hookah and his glass of sherbet. As the camera slowly pulls back, the *uddipanavibhava* or setting fixes Biswambhar Roy in his environment. It is one of abounding space in which time seems to be frozen. Biswambhar, an old *zamindar* – a landholder responsible for collecting and paying to the (British colonial) government the taxes on the land under his jurisdiction – is seated on the terrace of his vast *haveli* or mansion. Patches of broken concrete and cement are peeling from the walls all around him. As he walks up and down the terrace, Ray's camera focuses first on what he sees in the distance outside his *haveli*, then slowly pans over the interior of Biswambhar's mansion below. We see, from the *zamindar*'s point of view, a horse quietly gazing, an elephant playfully lounging, and the Padma River rippling and lapping at the borders of the mansion – all of these images juxtaposed beside the dark and shadowy enclosure in which furniture and objects are displayed like ghostly possessions covered by drapes and mosquito nets. Dust is everywhere. When the strains of the *shehnai* or classical pipe waft in, we are introduced to Mahim Ganguly, the new *zamindar*, a nouveau-riche moneylender who (as Ananta tells his master) is celebrating his son's sacred-thread ceremony. Biswambhar's dried-up face manages one further utterance before being plunged into its first flashback: "Ananta, what month is this?"

Like the opening of Kalidasa's *Sakuntala*, in which the deer's dance manifests the *rasa* of fear through the principle of *camatkara* or wonder, this opening scene is the elaboration of an emotion. We are totally hypnotized by the weariness and indolence this face signifies. Its sole vocalization – "What month is this?" – points to its complete isolation from the space and time around it. Since we don't know yet what painful particularities have led to this exhaustion, we are totally transported by the *rasa* of *karuna* or sorrow that emerges from the series of *dhvanis* suggested by this face. The eyes are blank. The mouth appears parched. There is no will to any movement except a slow walk that signifies the burden of certain painful memories being dragged a million times back and forth on this terrace. All these signifiers create an appalling beauty: The *zamindar*'s face dominates our entire field of vision and the film frame; it inspires around it a suggestion of interminable waiting. As the mouth slowly drinks the sherbet and puffs meditatively on the hookah, the servant awaits its next commands. The animals are also shown in a state of waiting for their master to come and pat them or ride them. The lapping river, the silent mansion, the covered furniture – everything seems caught in a mysterious state of stasis, which enters the spectator directly as the *karu-na rasa*. Having introduced the *zamindar*'s character in the very first scene as the film's sole *alambanavibhava* or primary source, Ray now plunges him into a lengthy flashback to establish certain characteristics of this man that are shown to remain constant during the rest of the film. This extended flashback is presented in the form of a recollection, deliberately chosen by the *zamindar* to suggest a comparison between his past and his present. The strains of the *shehnai* drifting in from Ganguly-*babu*'s son's thread ceremony dissolves into the *shehnai* played at the thread ceremony of Biswambhar's own son. In the flashback, the proud and haughty Biswambhar announces that he will celebrate the auspicious event by holding a *jalsa* or classical music and dance performance – even though his manager, Taraprasanna, informs him that the banks will not lend him any more money. To meet this expense, he orders his manager to pawn some of the family jewels. This consolidates the *vibhava* or source of the *zamindar*'s downfall, which lies principally in his obsessive love for classical music and the extravagance with which he consummates this passion.

For Biswambhar, the most important area in his mansion is the *jalsa-ghar* or music room. All of his illustrious ancestors from whom he has inherited this fatal love for music are assembled on the walls, their posed presences straight and erect within their picture frames. Ray now concentrates on a series of *abhinayas* that Biswambhar executes in the mise-en-scène as he deliberately stands before the room's wide and resplendent mirror. Biswambhar does this to personify the power of his *zamindar*-ness not only for the servants and manager who are present but also for Mahim, who has surreptitiously arrived to ask permission to lease some of Biswambhar's property. Biswambhar's posturings before the mirror (he is still attired in his riding costume) suggest to his audience that, in spite of his sagging bank balance, his *vacikas* and *angikas* still qualify him as *the zamindar* of the province. The mirror, then, becomes a substitute picture frame, validating Biswambhar's straight and erect position beside those of his ancestors looking down at him from their portraits on the walls.

His *zamindar*-ness is further confirmed in the flashback by the next costly *jalsa* he plots to give on Homage Day (when subjects of the *zamindar* are expected to call on him with thankful offerings for his patronage). This he does to humiliate his rival, Mahim Ganguly, who has organized a *jalsa* on the same day to inaugurate his newly constructed modern house in keeping with his own recently acquired status of *zamindar*. Biswambhar's Homage Day *jalsa* is to be funded, like his earlier one, by pawning family jewels from the already dwindling Roy estate. Mahim, appropriately humiliated, has to abandon his own *jalsa* and attend Biswambhar's. That same day, however, the boat carrying Biswambhar's wife and son (returning from his father-in-law's village) is caught in a storm. The news of their drowning leaves Biswambhar a broken man, and it is here that the first flashback ends.

Besides confirming the main character's dominant qualities, the flashback suggests a prolonged moment of reminiscence that is euphoric even when it revives an extremely painful past. This becomes apparent when we see a sudden change of color, voice, and language in the *vyabhicharibhavas* or accompanying emotions of Biswambhar as he comes out of his reverie. The flashback seems to revitalize him. Liberating him from his lifeless condition on the terrace, it propels him back into the land of the living. The loss of his wife and son is far outweighed by the delight he feels again at the humiliation suffered by Mahim on that accursed Homage Day. Since this extended flashback bears convincing testimony of the intensity of the *zamindar*'s memory, it also serves to anticipate future problems. We realize that Biswambhar could act in the same reckless manner if a similar opportunity arises in the future; and when it does arise, the spectator relishes the *rasa* of *karuna* or sorrow even when Biswambhar is shown losing every single *mohur* (gold coin equal to fifteen *rupees*) and is reduced to the level of a pauper. This is conveyed most notably by Ray's skillful presentation of Biswambhar's preparation for the third or last *jalsa*.

First, Ray shows the maniacal zeal with which the head servant obeys his master's extravagant orders in the organization of that fatal *jalsa*. Like a man possessed, Ananta unfurls the carpets directly into the camera, dusts the music room (opened for the first time four years after the family tragedy), polishes the brass lamps, pours imported brandy into the glasses, and fixes the candles inside the chandeliers. All of this activity arouses in us a feeling of *utsaha* or dynamic energy. Ananta's frenzied movements are counterpointed by Biswambhar's gradual emergence from his grieving passive state into the world of the living. As he waits for Ananta to unlock the *jalsaghar*, Ray cuts to a close-up of Biswambhar's fingers nervously tapping the knob of his cane. As he enters his favorite room, he is greeted by a spectacle of dust, cobwebs, spiders, and bats. From a top shot we see the *zamindar* stagger inside. The room is now in a state of abject decay, and Ray's mise-en-scène powerfully extends that rot to Biswambhar as well. The once bright chandelier is swathed in spider webs; Biswambhar slowly raises his cane to feel the forgotten tinkle of glass. As Ray's camera, from Biswambhar's perspective, pans 360° around the room, one by one familiar objects come to view: the ancestral portraits on the wall; the pillows and cushions scattered over the rug; the bottles, glasses, and a hookah – all left exactly as they were during the Homage Day *jalsa,* when the room had been filled with *raga* (a traditional form in Hindu music), and he had rushed from it to confront the swollen body of his drowned son carried by a fisherman.

Memory forces him to collapse on the rug. Then we see him rise and stagger toward that same mirror where he had once displayed his *zamindari abhinayas.* Ray shoots this moment from the perspective of the manager, who has breathlessly arrived in the room. As Taraprasanna watches his master slowly wipe away the thick coat of dust from the glass, he is horrified to hear that once-familiar voice asking him in that same arrogant tone how much money that celebrated dancer hired by Mahim Ganguly would need to be persuaded to dance instead for Biswambhar Roy. In spite of this *vacika* and recklessness displayed by both master and servant, we look forward, once again, to Mahim's humiliation. We know we are also going to witness the sad spectacle of a foolish man going to his ruin, and yet we are fascinated by this sudden Dionysian plunge into the inevitable abyss that awaits Biswambhar. We thus await with *vismaya* or astonishment the unfolding of Biswambhar's last *jalsa.*

Ray's mise-en-scène in the previous *jalsas* had articulated very accurately the *abhinayas* of the musicians and the spectators as they responded to each other during the musical performance. Whereas Biswambhar was shown completely enthralled by the music, Mahim's foolish antics playing the role of music connoisseur were humorously parodied. Through the sustaining metaphor of *music,* however, Ray reaffirms the crucial historical fact that feudal *zamindars* like Biswambhar Roy were indeed great patrons of Indian classical music. (Biswambhar's joyful immersion in all his *jalsas* validates his presence in that room above everyone else, even when we know that his main intention is to humiliate Mahim.) India's classical musicians, we are made to realize, owe a great deal to these aristocrats who had an authentic passion and deep understanding of their art, whereas the nouveau-riche like Mahim Ganguly, who succeeded the old *zamindars,* only *pretended* to take over this patronage. They had neither the temperament nor the ancestry to appreciate classical music, which was and continues to be one of India's finest art forms. What is also suggested by the film is the inevitable collapse of that feudal order with its dying tradition of pomp and pageantry to which this doomed *zamindar* still clings.

In the final *jalsa* this is indicated through the *abhinayas* or gestures performed almost unconsciously by Biswambhar. We see him puffing at the hookah, fingering the bangle of garlanded flowers round his wrists, caressing the small bag in which his entire family fortune has been collected, meditatively sipping imported brandy from the glass that his eager servant keeps refilling – all transpiring in an autonomous space that still retains a very suggestive cultural history. This carefully created ambience of the *jalsaghar* commemorates and continues that noble tradition of all those other *jalsas* that had been celebrated in this very same room by so many of Biswambhar's "noble ancestors." More important, however, it is in the final *jalsa* that Biswambhar scores his greatest victory over Mahim Ganguly through an *abhinaya* for the spectator's aesthetic satisfaction: As his cane comes down on his rival's wrist – restraining Mahim from throwing his lucre at the feet of the dancing artiste (*baiji*) – Biswambhar, with great pomp, flings instead the small bag containing all the gold *mohurs* of his depleted treasury. He will not allow a fake patron like Mahim to reward the exquisite *nritya* or dance of this great danseuse; dance of such exalted order needs rewards that come only from a genuine source. The dignity with which Biswambhar achieves such an *abhinaya* makes us relish all the more the *karuna rasa* arising from such a superbly etched cinematic moment. Although Biswambhar will experience the *sthayibhava* of *soka* or grief as a result of this excessive gesture, for the spectator this mental state has been effectively transformed into the *karuna rasa* to be enjoyed and savored from an aesthetic distance.

In a play (or film) constructed in accordance with the Sanskrit aesthetic principles of *rasa*, the dominant emotion exists because of a set of sustained and intelligently maintained contrasts with other emotions. As A. K. Ramanujan and Edwin Gerow point out: "It is rather the constant interplay of various transitory emotional states with or against the dominant emotional tone that both establishes the tone and maintains it."[50] As they further maintain:

The dominant emotion of a play [or a film conceived on similar classical Sanskrit aesthetic lines] does not exclude other emotions. . . . In fact the greatest achievement of the dramatic poet consists in his use of other, potentially dominant emotions as subordinate motifs in his statement of the primary emotion. . . . In *Sakuntala*, the dominant emotion is love. But the fifth and sixth acts are devoted to expressing the *rasa* of pity, first of the shunned Sakuntala, then of the king despondent at what he has done.[51]

In *Jalsaghar*, the dominant emotion is *karuna* or sorrow; but Ray uses the *rasa* of *bhayanaka* or fear as a continuous subordinate motif to strengthen the dominant emotion with compassion in order to "qualify it, bring it to life and mediate its intensity."[52]

Ray introduces the subordinate *bhayanaka rasa* primarily through the River Padma, which is inextricably linked with the *zamindar*'s tragic condition. The Padma makes its initial presence felt when Taraprasanna, the manager, warns his master that he should do something about the river's gradual erosion of his mansion. At this point Biswambhar laughs it off. The portentousness of the manager's warning dawns on Biswambhar only when his wife and son become the river's drowning victims on that fateful Homage Day. Ray reaffirms the erosion motif when he shows Biswambhar retreating into his own solipsistic world the day after this tragedy occurs. His self-imposed exile takes on *bhayanaka* or fearful tones, thereby maintaining and qualifying the dominant *rasa* of *karuna* or sorrow. Biswambhar refuses to come down to the ground floor of his mansion. Lapsing into a stony silence he chooses to shut himself off from the world, turning his back on reality. Ray's camera constantly encircles him as he mopes and drinks in his room upstairs, surrounded by his family photographs and the familiar objects that used to be handled by his wife and son. When Ray shows him strolling on his terrace, he draws our attention to the *zamindar*'s eyes staring vacantly into space; but his gaze is conspicuously averted from the Padma, over whose waters Ray's camera often lingers as the river naggingly laps the shores of Biswambhar's estate and his memories. He orders his music room to be locked and his ancestral furniture to be covered under white ghostlike shrouds. In these scenes, the *zamindar* seems to age before Ray's camera, becoming a faded presence in that silent oppressive mansion.

It should also be pointed out that Ray presents the *bhayanaka rasa* of fear arising historically out of the dichotomy that is cinematically established by the presentation of two Indias: the feudal India of the past and the industrial India of the present [Fig. 6]. Time and again Ray skillfully juxtaposes these two visions. In one scene, as an *ustaad* (master musician) plays a soothing *taan* on the lutelike *sarod* for a sad Biswambhar, the insistent hum of Mahim Ganguly's electric generator pierces the air and enters the *zamindar*'s room. It becomes progressively louder and annoying, destroying the aesthetic and emotional architecture of that wonderful musical moment, which has to be abruptly abandoned. On several occasions we see electricity intruding on Biswambhar's vision, as he is forced to watch from his isolated and empty mansion the twinkling lights in Ma-

Figure 6. Biswambhar Roy's (Chhabi Biswas) feudal India confronted by Mahim Ganguly's (Gangapada Basu) industrial one in Jalsaghar (The Music Room, *1958). (Photo by Nemai Ghosh; gift of Ben Nyce)*

him's recently constructed modern villa. The flickering candles inside his ancient glass lamps cannot compete with them.

This subordinate *rasa* of *bhayanaka* is further reaffirmed by Ray's iconic use of Biswambhar's horse Toofan and his elephant Moti. The names themselves are quite significant: *Toofan* literally means "storm," and *moti* "wealth." Since they can no longer figure in the *zamindar*'s present destitute condition, both animals function as empty symbols of a glorious past that has ceased to have any value or meaning for the grieving man. The *rasa* of fear is constantly manifested because Biswambhar refuses to accept or rectify his current displaced position. In another scene, Ray frames him watching Toofan and Moti grazing in the distance. As he is about to break into a smile over these two animals, vestiges of his feudal past, Mahim's noisy construction truck enters the film frame, swirls both animals in an obliteration of dust, and roars out of frame, destroying the old *zamindar*'s brief moment of nostalgia. In another scene, when Biswambhar sends his manager to distribute invitations for his final *jalsa*, he insists that Taraprasanna go mounted on the elephant. The very sight of an elephant trundling down a modern Indian road full of cars and trucks transforms the beast into an absurd symbol of the past. Moreover, this elephant, whose name betokens wealth, belongs to a pauper: After this final *jalsa* there will be nothing left in the *zamindar*'s treasury but penury and bankruptcy. He will have to give up all his claims to his house, his elephant, his horse, his servants, everything. Toofan, meanwhile, will become the appropriate instrument of his master's impending death: After the ruinous *jalsa*, as a drunken Biswambhar, attired in full *zamindar* regalia, whips and beats his horse for a last reckless ride on the banks of the River Padma, he is thrown to his death by the terrified animal before the fearful eyes of Ananta and Taraprasanna. When Ananta, his servant, sees blood oozing from his dead master's nostrils he cannot believe it. "Blood? Blood?" he cries to himself in astonishment. How could such an immortal being die so mortally, the desperate victim of his favorite horse?

When Ananta rises from his dead master's side and observes Biswambhar's *zamindari* turban soiled by the sands and wind of the riverbank, he is dumbfounded. Ananta's awe for Biswambhar, fueled by his own subservient status and an adoration bordering on madness, is conclusively transformed at this instant to *karuna* or pity. By concentrating on this transformation Ray enables the spectator to maintain that aesthetic distance whence to enjoy the combination of the fear and sorrow *rasas* created by the mise-en-scène and the responses of Ananta. It is the subordinate *rasa* of fear, however, that gives the dominant *rasa* of sorrow just the right amount of ironic edge – especially at the film's end, where the demise of not only this unfortunate *zamindar* but also the entire tradition of the *zamindari*, of the feudal system itself, is powerfully enunciated. A master humbled before his servant, both by an animal and by nature, remorselessly personifies the extinction of that feudal order.

Concluding Remarks

Lest I be accused of valorizing the Indianness of these early Ray films, especially ones on which his international reputation was established, the need to examine them under Indian concepts of criticism arose precisely because of the reception these films received when they were first released in India. Since Ray's films never fitted the contemporary molds of Indian cinema, they were often categorized as "art" films – an absurd and meaningless label. Two reasons were advocated for this: Since Ray never made mythological, melodramatic, romantic, satirical (etc.) Indian films, his films were not popular to Indians; and since his films were very popular in the West, it was claimed that the craft in his films utilized Western norms of expression rather than Indian forms that Western audiences and critics could well understand and appreciate.

Let me cite two responses from Western critics to validate these claims. In his paper "*Rasa* as a Category of Literary Criticism" for the 1972 International Conference on Sanskrit Drama, held in Honolulu, Edwin Gerow offers these remarks on Satyajit Ray:

Ray, whose films don't seem to respond to any Indian need at all, is terribly well received in the West because his films conform recognizably to our own [i.e., Western] notion of a direct personal statement of the human condition.[53]

A little later he makes the more damaging claim that Ray's films "are difficult to account for in [Indian] classical terms" and are "therefore, in a technical sense" tasteless "except to those Indians who have imbibed something of a western taste in these matters."[54] Robin Wood's attempt in *The Apu Trilogy* is once again to forward the claim that Western audiences find Ray's films very accessible because "Ray appears to have learnt his art mainly from the western cinema."[55] He goes on to enumerate Jean Renoir, Vittorio De Sica, John Ford, Frank Capra, Ingmar Bergman, and Alfred Hitchcock as directors either who have directly influenced Ray or on whom Ray has showered a lot of admiration in his numerous interviews. Ray's particular remark in an interview that he had Mozart in mind when he made *Charulata* gladdens Wood, who then proceeds to universalize it by noting that

the reference to Mozart is an important clue to the nature of Ray's art. It points up his affinities with Renoir. . . . This *emotional complexity*, the *delicate balancing of responses*, what one might call the Mozartian aspect of Ray's art, which links him with Renoir, *is already characteristic* in *Pather Panchali*.[56]

My attempt in this chapter has been to show precisely how Ray's films are *not* difficult to account for in Indian classical terms and are highly sophisticated in a technical sense *especially* to those Indians who have imbibed a lot of *Indian* taste in these matters! True, Ray *has* learned a lot from Western cinema but not to the *exclusion* of Indian arts or aesthetics. His "emotional complexity" and "delicate balancing of responses" that Wood singles out as being from Mozart and Renoir are also inspired by intricate Indian theories of *rasa*. And why *only* Mozart and Renoir? What about Bibhuti Bhusan Banerjee's cinematic eye in the Apu novels and Ravi

Shankar's haunting Indian classical music compositions in the trilogy? *Rasa* informs their art too.

By emphasizing Ray's intricate use of *rasa* and reasserting the Indian-ness of Ray's cinema, I have tried to free his work, especially these early films, from rigid and often misleading and one-sided contextualizations, to give them an Indian dignity they richly deserve.

2

From Gazes to Threat: The Odyssean *Yatra* (Journey) of the Ray Woman

To my wife,
Pravina,
who emblematizes superbly
all of these ennobling
qualities of the Ray woman

The "Roles" of the Indian Woman as Determined by Hindu Society: A Historical Background

In Satyajit Ray's cinema of the 1960s and 1970s, the predominant concern is the degraded status of the Indian woman in Indian society. As a synopsis of the "Report of the National Committee on the Status of Women in India" (1971–4) makes clear:

Any assessment of the status of [Indian] women has to start from the social framework. Social structures, cultural norms, and value systems influence social expectations regarding the behaviour of both men and women, and determine a woman's role and position in society.[1]

Indian psychoanalyst Sudhir Kakar categorizes the dominant realities of an Indian woman's life by condensing them into the following three stages: "First she is daughter to her parents. Second she is wife to her husband (and daughter-in-law to his parents). Third she is a mother to her sons (and daughters)."[2] This indicates that an Indian woman can never be independent. Historically, this was not always the case, as historian A. R. Gupta informs us in his thought-provoking study of *Women in Hindu Society*. Gupta points out that:

the status of women in India in the pre-Vedic and Vedic periods was equal to that of men in religious and social duties. But in the later period, a steady deterioration took place, when persons like *Manu*, the great Hindu law-giver, made the following observations:

It is the nature of woman to seduce man in this world, and hence the wise are never unguarded in the company of the females.

In the course of time, a formidable list of vices came to be attributed to the woman, who was later on debarred from the performance of sacremental rites and

75

even the study of sacred texts. Thus the woman was deprived of her social and educational rites and her role came to be restricted to the domestic spheres which ultimately led to her economic slavery to man. . . .[3]

– and thus to the establishment of the definition of the ideal Hindu woman. The two emblematized women who were chosen to personify the ideal Hindu woman were Sita, from the influential epic *Ramayana,* and the legendary Savitri. In both cases what a Hindu woman was expected to do and not to do was subject to the dictates and demands of her chosen husband. In Hinduism this is called the principle of *pativrata (pati* = husband, *vrata* = devotion), which a Hindu woman is expected to exercise. In his exploration of Indian sexuality, *Intimate Relations,* Kakar defines *pativrata* in the following vein:

> Above all, in the ideals of the traditional culture, the "good" woman is a *pativrata,* subordinating her life to the husband's welfare and needs in a way demanded of no other woman in any other part of the world with which I am familiar. . . . We can understand the underlying male concerns when in the *Mahabharata,* the goddess Uma, laying down the guidelines of right conduct for women, describes a *pativrata* as one "who does not cast her eyes upon the Moon or Sun (both male in Hindu cosmology) or a tree that has a masculine name." The goddess, however, goes further. . . .
> The husband is the god which women have. The husband is their friend. The husband is their high refuge. Women have no refuge that can compare with their husband, and no god that can compare with him. . . . If the husband that is poor or diseased or distressed were to command the wife to accomplish anything that is improper or unrighteous or that may lead to destruction of life itself, the wife should without any hesitation accomplish it.[4]

When Sita is kidnapped by the demon Ravana and manages with her *pativrata* to put off her abductor's lustful salvos and sexual overtures, her efforts are not appreciated by her husband, Rama. When Rama wins her back after a long and arduous struggle with Ravana, Sita is forced publicly to prove her state of purity to satisfy not only her husband in the role of "wife" but also his subjects in the role of "queen." As A. R. Gupta comments:

> When despite her innocence, her husband Rama forsook her in the interest of public confidence, Sita as the perfect wife went through the fire ordeal to prove that she had remained unsullied by Ravana's temptation. Another step further, [Rama is not convinced because his subjects still seem to gossip about his wife's chastity] she leaves home without a murmur when her lord Rama decrees it so.[5]

In no way is Sita allowed (even from her powerful position as the king's wife) to plead her case or display an active resistance to the inhuman treatment meted out to her by her husband and his subjects. What is demanded, instead, are "the comparatively negative virtues of passivity and fortitude"⁶ which she is forced to embrace for the sake of *pativrata*.

When we turn to the Savitri story, what is emphasized is Savitri's Sisyphean struggle as a "wife" to win back her dead "husband" from Yama, the Lord of Death. However, certain details from the Savitri text clearly show how the *pati* (husband) is subtly and slyly valorized even when the narrative is centered around the *patni*'s (wife's) struggle to raise him like Lazarus from the dead. For instance, after they are married, Savitri is told that according to her husband's horoscope he is destined to die in a year's period. Observe Savitri's response:

The die is already cast. It is only once that one can say "I give away." Whether he has a short or long life, I have selected my husband once and for all and I will not select a second one.⁷

These words not only thrill the masculine Hindu ear and heart but even succeed in winning her dead husband back from Yama. In fact, granting her husband a second life becomes Savitri's lifelong goal and passion. So monumentally *worthy* was her husband (his name was Satyavan, which roughly translates as "the truthful one") that his wife was prepared to duel with death himself to grant him life all over again. We can see that even in such a sanctified position, Savitri's status is still subservient to that of her husband.

Prof. Gupta further defines Indian womanhood in relation to three important ideals: the sacramental, the sociological, and the individualistic or hedonistic. In his definition:

The sacramental ideal is overwhelmingly influenced by the dictates of religion.
    The sociological ideal is governed by the motives in the interest of society.
    The individualistic level has always been looked at mainly from the point of view of the happiness of the individual concerned.⁸

Our study of Ray's exploration of Indian womanhood in his films of the 1960–70s shall observe the operation of all three of these ideals. The sacramental and the sociological ideals cruelly trap and imprison the Ray woman, who has to undertake a long and painful *yatra* (journey) to break out of the Sita/Savitri mold, and to fight for what is her right as a woman. This emancipation is achieved through three crucial stages cited by Gupta:

(i)   the fight for woman's rights
(ii) the moral emancipation of the woman
(iii) the liberation in which the very fundamentals of the equation of the male–female relationship are questioned.⁹

These stages are precisely what Ray succeeds in establishing in his women-centered films. By implementing them Ray exposes a host of prejudices and customs governing many of the "roles" an Indian woman is expected to perform in her quotidian existence. Her instinctive fight, therefore, is to reassert her position as "woman" *over* and *above* all "roles." Ray becomes the perfect spokesperson on behalf of all the Ratans, Charulatas, Bimalas, Aratis, Sutapas, Aditis, and Karunas (etc.) of India.

Ray's analysis of the Indian woman's struggle also arises out of the historical situations in which they find themselves. Their struggle necessitates a variety of determined responses carved out of the historical changes taking place in Indian society. In the words of sociologists Rhoda Lois Blumberg and Leela Dwarki, this brings the Indian women "into contact with beliefs and standards different from those they have known."[10] If Ray is instrumental in showing us these changes, he prefaces this important step by first projecting and examining that other crippling Indian principle of "adjustment" that every Indian woman is expected to make as part of her *dharma* or duty to society. Blumberg and Dwarki delineate this principle – along the very same lines pursued by Ray's filmic inquiry when he shows his heroines acting and reacting to this specter of adjustment – as follows:

"Adjustment," the woman's duty, is used very broadly to refer to any situation in which [an Indian] woman is placed in a new, different or disagreeable position. Thus, if the parents refuse to allow her to work, she adjusts; if she goes to live with orthodox in-laws, she adjusts to their ways; in doing so, the woman adopts rationalizations which help to accept her fate. Adjustment takes the form of a highly developed sensitivity to the needs and wishes of others. The most artful women become masterful at manipulation, learning to wait for the proper time, circumstances and issues on which they can express their own viewpoints.[11]

In his *At the Edge of Psychology*, political scientist Ashis Nandy particularizes the important role played by Bengal and its artists, intellectuals, and social reformers in dramatizing the herculean struggles of the Indian woman. Nandy points out that when we look

at the styles of creative self-expression during the last two hundred years, a period characterized by a fast tempo of social change and the breakdown of many aspects of older life style, one cannot but marvel at the crucial role that woman as a symbol and womanliness as an aspect of Indian identity have played. This linkage is clearer in some parts of the country than in others, because some communities, such as in Bengal, have a greater tendency than others to dramatize the psychological problems of society at large. . . .[12]

Woman Redefined in the Tagore Triad: "The Postmaster," *Charulata,* and *Ghare-Baire*

Satyajit Ray and Rabindranath Tagore are two of the prominent Bengali artists and intellectuals who have been seriously concerned with the constricted roles that Indian women have had to play in Indian society in general and in Bengal in particular. Both have depicted with extraordinary clarity and empathy women's isolated and self-denying status in a male-dominated system. Ashis Nandy, while including Ray in this Bengali pantheon, strangely leaves out Tagore when he says:

At least from Rammohan Roy to Ishwar Chandra Vidyasaghar in the area of social reform, from Bankim Chandra Chatterjee through Sarat Chandra Chatterjee to Satyajit Ray in literature and art, from Vivekananda to Aurobindo in religion, womanhood as a symbol and womanliness as a subject of study have been the centerpieces of creative consciousness in different sectors of Bengali life. . . . Some like Rammohan Roy and Ishwar Chandra Vidyasaghar tried to redraw the traditional definition of woman and identity, trying to introduce into it new elements drawn from reinterpreted tradition. . . . Some with mass appeal like Sarat Chandra Chatterji . . . among writers and Vidyasaghar and Gandhi among reformers, tried to legitimize woman's wifely role in particular and public role in general by stressing in them aspects of her motherliness.[13]

But Tagore must be included, especially when three of Ray's woman-centered films are adapted from his writings. Tagore, in his novella *Nash-tanir (The Broken Nest,* 1901), novel *Ghare-Baire (Home and the World,* 1919), and short story "The Postmaster" (1891), and Ray in his adaptations *Charulata* (1964), "The Postmaster" (in the tripartite *Teen Kanya [Three Daughters],* 1961), and *Ghare-Baire* (1985), deepen this Bengali exploration of the Indian woman by showing very explicitly how she resolves to redefine herself by devising, in the words of Nandy,

means of de-emphasising some aspects of her role in her family and society and emphasizing others so that she may widen her identity without breaking totally from its cultural definition or becoming disjunctive with its psychological distinctiveness.[14]

The ensuing sections examine these three Tagore-adaptation films, in which Ray depicts the Indian woman's willful and radical participation in a revolution to gain her emancipation. In this Tagore triad, Ray focuses on her attempt to force the Indian man to acknowledge her equality; to provide her with the necessary opportunities to *be* a woman; and to view her femininity as an essential part of her personal identity.

The Indictment of Patriarchy in "The Postmaster" (1961)

The urbanite postmaster who takes up his duties in a small Indian village in Ray's short film sketch is portrayed as a confirmed representative of the insensitive, middle-class Bengali *bhadralok,* the cultivated man of education.

The postmaster Nandalal, cut off from all his friends, family members, and his city of Calcutta, is presented by Ray as an orphan in this remote village. He doesn't like his surroundings, and among the villagers he appears ill at ease. Ratan is the illiterate, twelve-year-old, actual orphan who functions as his housekeeper. The postmaster, exiled from the love of his mother and sister and bored by his rural surroundings, decides in his spare time to teach Ratan the Bengali alphabet. This is the first pivotal scene, in Ray's film, through which the Bengal patriarchal culture is clearly indicted: In spite of the sophisticated, literary education it imparts to its young men, it blinds them to the needs and feelings of others, in this case, the little girl Ratan.

Ray's indictment of the postmaster begins in the scene where Nandalal resolves to teach Ratan how to read and write. The scene opens with Nandalal lying on his bed, his face toward the camera, gazing at a postcard in an open book. Behind him in the frame, the mise-en-scène very accurately defines his lonely existence: There is a large photograph of his mother and sister on the wall. Hanging nearby from a peg is an enormous umbrella that he carries with him everywhere. The sheltered son and brother is not only suggested by the conspicuous family portrait but reaffirmed by that massive umbrella, which protects him from the inclement weather, stray animals, and the village madman he daily encounters.

However, the one who really cares for him and protects him, little Ratan, he clearly ignores. Ray shows Ratan entering the frame wearing freshly washed clothes. She positions herself in such a way that he can notice her appearance, carefully prepared for him, yet he does not: He is too engrossed in the postcard he has received from home. When he excitedly tells her that it is from his "mother," we see Ratan quickly run to the family photograph and correctly point out the mother's figure to him. When she hesitatingly asks who the *other* woman in the photo is, and is told that it is his "sister," she looks a little unhappy and asks him, "Can your sister read and write?" At this juncture, he turns his back on her and replies, "Yes. And she can sing too. She's not like you." Undeterred, Ratan answers, "I can sing too"; but when she starts to sing, nervously clutching at her clothes, the camera slowly pulls back, cutting off Ratan to show only Nandalal in the frame, on the point of going to sleep. Hurt by this rudeness, Ratan, offscreen, breaks off in the middle of her song. Nandalal gets up and laughs. As the camera now tracks toward him, taking in Ratan again, we can see him saying, "Your song was very good. I must teach you how to read and write. Then you'll be like my sister." He tells her to take some money from his coat pocket to buy some chalk pieces and a slate. "If you study hard I'll give you more," he assures her, as Ratan shyly takes the money and runs excitedly out of the frame. Still, Ray holds onto the shot until Ratan predictably enters and stands before him once again. "Oh," he finally notices, "you have washed your clothes."

Throughout this scene, Ray makes us see that it is Ratan who is making all the efforts to get herself noticed. She wants desperately to win his approval so as to become, in some way, a part of his family, the one he adores. Ray indicates this through the carefully articulated movements of both characters. Ratan initiates this process by pointing out the mother's photograph, but Nandalal offers no signs of approval. Instead, he hurts the little girl by sarcastically emphasizing his sister's superiority over her. Not content with that, he further humiliates her by thoughtlessly remarking about his sister's singing talents. When the camera literally cuts her off and concentrates only on his dozing presence, we are made to feel not only his callousness but also the little girl's isolation. She grasps that she cannot compete with his sister; she has far too many handicaps. As a result, she chokes on her song, leaving it unfinished. When Ray's camera tracks in and brings both together in the frame, Nandalal pronounces his resolve to educate her – not because we see him in any way moved by her inarticulate song, but because he *wants* to have the patriarchal privilege of educating her so that she can become literate like his own sister in Calcutta. It is a condescending gesture and not a philanthrophic one. He wants to play the proverbial *bhadralok* Henry Higgins. However, the rewards he wants to bestow on her efforts are not, as Ray immediately shows, the fruits to be gained from the educational process itself; rather, they will take the form of bribes he promises to give her *if he* feels satisfied with her progress. The emphasis, we are repeatedly reminded by Ray, is always his, never hers. Moreover, she has to make another effort to display her well-groomed appearance before him. He never tries to confirm his awareness of her. It is always she who has to construct an elaborate mise-en-scène for him to finally acknowledge her presence.

One significant difference between Tagore's story and Ray's short film must be noted. Tagore ends on a melodramatic note: By overstating Ratan's second orphaning (once the postmaster makes her know he intends to go back to Calcutta), he reduces it to bathos. Ray, on the other hand, avoids falling into this trap. His ending is cast more in the stoic and de-sentimentalized mold of the contemporary artist. In Tagore's story:

The postmaster said: "You need not be anxious about my going away, Ratan. I shall tell my successor to look after you." These words were kindly meant, no doubt: but inscrutable are the ways of a woman's heart. Ratan had borne many a scolding from her master without complaint but these kind words she could not bear. She burst out weeping, and said: "No, no, you need not tell anybody anything about me. I don't want to stay on here." The postmaster was dumb-founded. He had never seen Ratan like this before. The new incumbent duly ar-rived, and the postmaster having given over charge, prepared to depart. Just be-fore starting he called Ratan and said: "Here is something for you. I hope it will keep you for some little time." He brought out from his pocket the whole of his month's salary, retaining only a trifle for his traveling expenses. Then Ratan fell at his feet and cried: "Oh, Dada, I pray, you don't give me anything, don't in any way trouble about me," and then she ran away out of sight."[15]

In Ray's film, Ratan, orphaned and ill-treated at a very early age, espe-cially by Nandalal's predecessor (Ray's addition to the text), is already a little adult when we first meet her. That is why her conduct at the film's end is not that of the whimpering child begging for security and comfort as in the Tagore original. Both Tagore and Ray have conditioned us to an-ticipate that events are not going to work out for Ratan as she had imag-ined them; but whereas Tagore's drama sentimentalizes the denouement by an excess of emotion, thereby distancing us from the little girl and rob-bing Ratan of all the dignity she had displayed, Ray *maintains* Ratan's dignity by making her deliberately *ignore* the postmaster when the time comes for them to part. Her hurt is very intense but she does *not* run away from it. She remains conspicuously within the postmaster's gaze without betraying any sign of her injured feelings. When she steps out of his gaze, however, we see her weeping quietly as she draws water from the well. The moment her master calls her, she wipes away all traces of her tears. In the film's final scene, she walks past him carrying the water bucket, and haughtily ignores the money that he clumsily wants to offer her.

One can clearly see the ideological differences between Tagore's and Ray's portrayals. Ray's 1961 Ratan is *not* Tagore's 1891 Victorian waif abandoned in a cruel and merciless world. Ray's Ratan is a contemporary child of suffering and endurance. She will somehow survive and subdue her misery as effectively as she earlier subdued and controlled the terrible village madman (another Ray invention) who always frightened her mas-ter and made him rush indoors.

It is Nandalal who *is* the real orphan in the film. He is the one who constantly keeps "missing his mother and sister." When Ratan plays both these roles during his illness, he fails to acknowledge or recognize them. If he had any backbone, he wouldn't have gone running back to them in Calcutta, since he had already found both in little Ratan. At the end of the film the grown patriarch returns to Calcutta, but he will have no tales of conquest to relate to his friends. A twelve-year-old girl who will end-lessly draw water from the well for his successor has, in the final analysis, triumphed.

The Indian Woman in the Doll's House – Charulata *(1964)*

In her introduction to Tagore's novella *Nashtanir (The Broken Nest,* 1901), on which Ray's *Charulata* is based, Indian critic Mary M. Lago defines for the non-Bengali reader the important meanings implied in the three principal characters' names:

Charu's full name is Charulata. The Bengali word *caru* means "beautiful" and *lata* is a "forest creeper," a "clinging vine." . . . The husband's name is Bhupati. The word *bhupati* means "sustainer of the world." Amal is the name of the lover. The word *amal* means "stainless," "pure."[16]

Whereas both masculine names are given connotations of importance, in-dependence, and patriarchal privilege, the feminine name is not allowed any autonomy. In keeping with the codes of Hindu patriarchy, the Indian woman is expected to be beautiful and accomplished because of her *cling-ing* to the world of man: usually the husband, or other men like her hus-band's cousin, Amal. Man, on the other hand, is supposed to adorn her beauty and *sustain* her in her travails. In return, she has to feed the vanity of the male ego in order to keep it *stainless* and *pure*. In the course of the film, Ray forces us to witness the cruel victimization of a beautiful, independent-minded, intelligent woman, destroyed by the Hindu extend-ed family of nineteenth-century India [Fig. 7].

In the film's first seven minutes, Ray brilliantly sets up a visual version of the Hindu "doll's house," in which we see how a beautiful and lonely woman is bound by her tradition to the confines of her house, her all im-portant "nest." Whereas the space of the Hindu house should normally assume intimacy, warmth, security, and safety for the Indian woman, Ray subverts this idea by showing us how this "nest" is, in reality, a *prison*. In a series of slow-moving images we see Charu wandering aimlessly from one room to another, humming a melancholy tune, with the camera mimicking Charu's boredom, both through the image and the movement. Ray shows her passing her fingers listlessly over a row of books she must have read a million times. She picks one out and playfully makes up snatches of tunes with the author's name (Bankim) to amuse herself. The sound of a monkey man's drumming outside diverts her attention. We now see her hurrying to her bedroom where, a little excited, she removes a lorgnette from a drawer. At this point, the imitative camera accelerates: Her image and her movement quicken, and Ray focuses conspicuously on the swinging lorgnette, seen in a wonderful tracking movement through the balcony railing along which she is hurrying. These eyeglasses now become the instruments through which she chooses to alleviate her ennui: From the window shutters of her husband's study, we see her focusing her lorgnette on the monkey man (a common sight in Indian cities) performing with his monkey in the world outside.

Ray shows his heroine obeying her age's code of Hindu femininity by observing the world as she is expected to – from a *distance*, discreetly, through a pair of glasses that articulate and *reaffirm* that distance! She can only watch; she cannot participate. The house, therefore, becomes the only world in which she is allowed the freedom to "wander" – one of the favorite words of another trapped woman, Judy in Hitchcock's *Vertigo*. We see Charu tied to this house and its rituals just as the dancing monkey outside is tied and performs to the commands of his beggar-master. She is about to close the shutters when she spies a fat, oily, Bengali waddling across the street with an umbrella and a pot of sweetmeats. She rushes to the drawing room and follows his comical Pickwickian gait through its windows. Boredom sets in once again as he turns the corner and is gone. She is forced to close the shutters, shutting out the world once more.

In this opening tableau, the spectator is invited to construct the history of this lonely woman's bored existence. The carefully selected images, the particularity of her gestures, the objects she touches and handles, the juxtaposition of the signifiers that designate her isolation and boredom in this house – all become invested with social meaning. Ray's indictment of the marriage is made clear in the closing stages of this tableau, when he makes Bhupati intrude into his wife's space and become the particular object of her consuming gaze.

Silence weighs heavily on this opulent house of brocade wallpaper, embroidered rugs, chiming clocks, and floral motifs splashed so resplendently on the doors and walls. Undecided in her movements once again, after she has closed the window shutters, we see Charu approach the piano, lift the lid, and casually try out a tune. The piano is slightly out of tune and

Figure 7. Charulata (Madhabi Mukherjee) in Bhupati's (Sailen Mukherjee) and Amal's (Soumitra Chatterjee) "doll's house" in Charulata (1964). (Photo by Nemai Ghosh; gift of Ben Nyce)

will not yield any music to distract her; but at this moment, she hears the sounds of footsteps padding across the corridor. It is Bhupati, in his shirt-sleeves, going absentmindedly toward his bedroom. We see Charulata come out of the drawing room and stand in midshot by the door, lorgnette in hand, waiting for her husband to return. He does so, his nose buried in a book. Stopping to turn a page right beside Charu (a pause, wonderfully attained in the mise-en-scène), he fails to notice her presence. We are made to see his gradually receding figure from her point of view, and just before Bhupati exits from her gaze, we see her playfully bring her lorgnette up to her eyes. As though seen through its lenses, Bhupati's image in the shot that follows is suddenly magnified and brought very close to her. As he disappears down the staircase to his printing press, we see Charu slowly lower the lorgnette with an air of intense loneliness and resignation that registers very poignantly the yawning gulf between them – an alienation affirmed by the camera abruptly zooming out from Charu as she lowers the lorgnette.

Up until this zoom-out, Ray's camera has given us the vision of Charu and of her world. When he zooms out from her, he does not distance her from us; rather, he imposes another vision in which Charu's vision is transformed and reflected. The use of the zoom doubles our perception of her, not only as a bored, unloved wife but as a woman on the verge of *losing* her identity as a wife. It enables her, in Deleuzian terms, to enter "into a 'free indirect' relationship with the poetic vision of the director who affirms himself in her, through her, whilst at the same time distinguishing himself from her."[17] Animated by his heroine's individualistic element, Ray presents the neurosis of her character on the sociological level (governed by the motives of her Hindu societal world) while reflecting it in a pure form of poetic consciousness via the zoom, which takes us beyond Charu's subjective vision. It reflects not only the *content* of Charu's precarious emotional state, but also the *form* of Ray's aesthetic consciousness.

Here the opening tableau ends. No words have been said, but Ray's evocative and suggestive mise-en-scène enables us very accurately to construct the painful history of Charu's marriage in the India of 1879. This tableau inscribes an active desire on Charu's part to become the object of her husband's gaze. Though this may be a narcissistic desire, it is shown to be a necessity that will prevent her from feeling neglected.

As the typical nineteenth-century aristocratic Bengali housewife, Charu is forced to function within the traditional boundaries that her position as a Hindu wife in the patriarchal, extended-family structure allows. She is expected to sew (which we see her doing right at the beginning of the film, embroidering a "B" on her husband's handerkerchief), supervise all domestic chores, serve meals to her husband, and cultivate her idle moments in the practice of "feminine" pastimes like playing cards, embroidery, reading, playing the piano, and decorating herself for her spouse. Writing, of course, is a male prerogative, and both Bhupati (a journalist) and Amal (a poet) feel slightly threatened when Charu's writing gets published for the first time in an important Bengali journal.

It is very daring, then, on Charu's part to signal her emancipation from such a routine by boldly expressing her attraction toward her husband's younger cousin, Amal. Ray makes this explicit in the scene between Charu and Amal in the garden, overflowing with the writing and recitation of poetry, bright sunshine, and deep lurking passions. In this mise-en-scène Amal is on the ground, writing and reading, and Charu is positioned on a swing, observing him. This sunlit garden becomes a very important space where we are shown directly for the first time Charu's conscious definition of her hidden desires for Amal, which she articulates not only to us but also to herself. Ray, however, has implied the ultimate direction of these desires all along: the embroidered exercise book that she had stitched exclusively for Amal and in which he is now writing his poems solely for her; the brand-new slippers she has hidden in her cupboard and hopes to surprise him with soon; her insistence that he eat only the betel leaf that she prepares; her mending of all his torn clothes. All of these small events occur so innocuously in the film that Amal, the spectator, and even Charu seem to miss their real intent until her gaze at Amal churns them up.

Amal's passion for reading, writing, piano playing, and argument reflect all those pursuits Charu has secretly wanted to share with a man. Now he makes her participate in them and, in Sudhir Kakar's words, "reflects back with favor and with a confirming glow . . . all her acts of relationship."[18] Thus, her gaze confers on Amal "an incorporation of the Idealized Other in whom [Charu] seeks to merge, hoping therein to find a way to build cohesiveness and strength into her own self."[19]

Since Charu's desire for Amal was still unconscious when she performed her little acts of kindness for him, she thought she did all these tasks out of a protective sense, almost like a mother for the orphaned Amal. (Bhupati and Charu are the only family Amal has.) Even for Amal it is a part of the Hindu familial tradition to be fussed over and spoiled, almost like a second husband. Lago offers us an interesting insight here:

Amal, who is Bhupati's country cousin and a member of the household while he attends college in Calcutta, is regarded as a young son of the family. As such he may come and go freely in the woman's quarters where he is likely to be thoroughly spoiled by doting female relatives. Sisters-in-law or cousins of his age group are approved companions.[20]

The mock flirting and teasing that thus ensued between Charu and Amal was innocent, predictable, and totally acceptable within the universe of the extended family. Even for the spectator all these actions by Charu were seen as extensions of the same kinds of "games" she had to constantly invent for herself to relieve her from her housebound ennui. However, the moment she leaves her "indoors" space – the rigidly ordered parameters of her Victorian household or, in Eliotian terms, the perfectly enunciated objective correlative of a strict and conventional Hinduism – she is liberated. The garden with its bright "outdoors," the tantalizing swing, the lush garden vegetation, and the exciting splash of spilled sunlight on the grass – all strengthen her continuous and persistent gaze on the handsome Amal, who is sprawled on the mat spread out on the ground, literally at her feet.

By shooting the entire scene from Charu's subjective point of view, Ray conveys accurately and subtly the changes of desire occurring within her at this memorable moment. We see only what Charu's gaze selects. Every time Charu's feet hit the ground while she is swinging, the exuberance of the editing literally *and* psychologically elevates her desires to ascending levels of bliss. The dizzying "outdoor" vision of the garden, trees, and sky reflects the blur of her own passions precariously at tilt with her hitherto normal and placid "indoors" world. After she stops swinging, a cool and collected Charu trains her lorgnette brazenly on Amal. As his magnified face appears in close-up prominently before her, we realize that she has confronted herself openly and freely with her forbidden desires. Since she has willingly revealed this secret to us, Ray, by making us then share her gaze, alerts us to the way she will henceforth act.

In depicting his heroine in this way, Ray is doing something very bold. Normally, when a Hindu woman is confronted with a forbidden desire, she satisfies it only in a fantasy. Sudhir Kakar gives us some very interesting examples from his study *The Inner World:*

There exist, of course, elaborate codes and rituals of social behaviour and discretion between the male and female members of an extended family, such as the injunction that the elder brother never directly address his younger brother's wife. . . . Like most taboos, these are broken in fantasy. In a Bengali folk song, for example, a woman expresses her desire for amorous relations with the elder brother of her husband, regretting that he is not the younger brother so that her desire may be gratified.[21]

In Charu's case, this idyllic garden is not a creation of her fantasy. It offers her the alternative between a loveless domestic marriage and a fulfilling, though forbidden, romantic entanglement. She opts for the latter and does not shirk from her lover's bold profile in close-up. In fact it is the men, both Amal and Bhupati, who are shown losing control of their space and their male dominating positions when Charu goes a step further and dares to make her emotional demands *known* to them.

Amal slinks away from the household like a thief literally in the night. He leaves behind an impersonal letter explaining his abrupt departure. For a man who "admires the spirit of Byron" and writes prose poems and essays on "romantic passion" and "commitment" in the Byronic vein, Amal fails miserably when Charu wants to confront him. Bhupati acts in a similar cowardly manner when faced suddenly by Charu's confessed passion for Amal: Shocked, he rushes out of the house instead of having the courage to stand his ground and face her. The onus, in fact, falls on Charu to effect the final reconciliation with her husband when he returns.

Charu's first step is to tear up Amal's letter to Bhupati (in which no mention is made of her), suggesting that from now on Amal will cease to have any power over her. She goes to the mirror, takes a pinch of *sindhur* (red powder), and applies it to where her hair is parted – a sign representing a Hindu wife's legitimate married status. When Bhupati knocks and hesitates to enter his own threshold, it is Charu who extends her hands and asks him to "come in." The shocked husband has for the moment *lost his voice* and cannot utter a word. He extends his hand, and she hers, but just before they meet Ray freezes the frame. A number of still shots follow the freeze:

1. a frozen Charu with a tilted head;
2. Bhupati's grief-stricken face;
3. a servant holding a lamp;
4. a medium shot of husband and wife with their extended hands in the doorway; then,
5. a slow pull-out, the camera still focusing on Charu and Bhupati trying to reach out to each other, half an inch between them.

The half-inch gap between their outstretched hands, on which the film ends, *becomes* intuitively the silence that will always remain between the two; yet it claims for Charu her final ethical victory, for it finally awakens Bhupati to a recognition of the crucial reality around him that he had abandoned and neglected in his overriding passion for journalism and politics. It makes him confront his situation and his marriage. If, on one level, it acts as a defense for Charu against any neglect, its also gains from her husband his recognition of her not only as his wife but also as a vital, intelligent, and emotionally whole woman who needs to be loved and understood. Ray's ending is different from Tagore's pessimistic conclusion, wherein Charu and Bhupati are unable to reconcile. At the end of the novella, Bhupati reluctantly agrees to take Charu with him to another city, but she refuses – and this refusal seals the marriage's doom. In Ray's film, however, it is the wife who finally shows the husband the way by which their broken "nest" can be made whole again. The gap through which Charu achieves such a reconciliation is all the more noteworthy since it shows her finding a viable place for herself in the male-dominated culture of nineteenth-century India as a *woman*, irrespective of the different *roles* she is asked to play in it.

The Indian Woman: Neither at Home nor in the World:
Ghare-Baire *(1985)*

Set against the stormy period of the Swadeshi or Freedom Movement in
India (1903–8), Ray's film *Ghare-Baire* (*The Home and the World*) presents the central female character of Bimala as a woman confronted by
the seduction of two distinct worlds that her husband Nikhil and her lover
Sandip want to impose upon her. When we first meet Bimala she has been
happily married to Nikhil for nine years. Nikhil is a sensitive and highly
educated Bengali *zamindar.* Wishing to emancipate his wife from the strict
isolation of his aristocratic Hindu family (where a wife was supposed to
live in obedient seclusion from all males except her husband), Nikhil
wants Bimala to have an English education. Next, he wants his wife to
utilize this knowledge in order to *find who she really is* so that she can
blossom in the wide world outside, under his proud scrutiny and that of
his other male friends, like Sandip. He endorses this venture as the expression of what true love should really mean between him and Bimala
[Fig. 8]. If she is "his" in the "home," he wants her to be "his" in the
"world" too after she has experienced it.

History provides Ray's heroine with another emancipatory alternative
through the Swadeshi Movement, which succeeded in penetrating even into the *zenana,* the women's private and secluded chambers of nineteenth-
century Bengal. In 1907, Lord Curzon, the British Governor General of
India, decided to split up Bengal and divide its population of Hindus and
Muslims. Capitalizing on the racial hatred that had already existed between the two, Curzon's aim was to keep them in a continuous state of
tension and enmity in order to exercise British hegemony over Bengal. In
protest to this policy, Indians launched the Swadeshi Movement, demanding a ban on all *videshi* (imported) goods and a promotion of *swadeshi*
(Indian) goods. In spite of its nationalistic intentions, however, the movement ironically helped the British to exercise its unjust policy of divide and
rule: Since imported goods were cheaper and of better quality, the poor
Muslim traders of Bengal, who benefited from selling these in the market-
place, were the ones hardest hit by Swadeshi. Terrorized by Swadeshi leaders and upstarts into selling Indian goods, their already precarious finan-
cial condition was crippled to such an extent that the Muslims launched
their own campaign of violence against the Hindus. This suited the British
perfectly.

In the film, Bimala feels the effects of Swadeshi not as an idea but as
a passion, and it is at this critical moment that Sandip makes his entrance

Figure 8. Nikhil (Victor Banerjee) introduces the Westernized kiss to his Bengali wife Bimala (Swatilekha Chatterjee) in Ghare-Baire *(The Home and the World, 1984). (Photo by Nemai Ghosh; gift of Ben Nyce)*

into Bimala's life. Captivated by his Swadeshi rhetoric, she falls a willing victim to his clever flattery, which extols her in his eyes as the "Shakti [supreme strength] of the Motherland" and the "Queen Bee" of the Swadeshi cause. She is made to feel, through Sandip's constant instigations, that this new cause needs her beauty, her passion, and her sacrifice; and when this direction is skillfully altered to satiate his sexual longings for her, Bimala finds herself captivated by a man *other* than her own husband.

Bimala's unique position in Ray's text lies in her honesty to record in her diary, like a Bengali Lady Genji, the intimate details of her psychological struggle between her eroding loyalty toward her husband and her increasing fascination with his best friend. Both Nikhil and Sandip are viewed through her confused consciousness. From Bimala's point of view, Nikhil appears as an Apollonian figure who is noble but in many ways unapproachable, whereas Sandip emerges as the Dionysian one who, in spite of being potentially threatening, satisfies a lot of her repressed and unspoken desires. Ray puts Bimala in the same position as Tennyson had placed Guinevere in *The Idylls of the King*. Nikhil is the Arthur figure, the noble *zamindar* who, by his lofty ideals, sets up difficult standards of morality in devotion, behavior, and motivations. Sandip is the Lancelot figure bringing temptation, heat, and color into Bimala's life, making her illicit eros glitter in the dark.

Nikhil creates a tiny Camelot for Bimala and himself. Like Arthur, Nikhil displays unstained virtues. He does not drink and is not given to dissipation. He brings the English governess, Miss Gilby, to educate Bimala and introduce her to the modern age, where the English language with its manners and customs reigns. He adorns Bimala with the masquerades of perfumes and exotic garments. Whatever she asks for, he gives. He remains consecrated for her at all times, like a prince, so full of perfection and personification of the thoroughly good man that he gradually loses the mystery and challenge of personality that sustain and nurture a marriage. Bimala, initially attracted and comforted by his fairy-tale kingdom, soon begins to tire of it. The excitement of manliness that is absent from this Camelot is provided by Sandip, who comes to Bimala's neighborhood with his followers to preach Swadeshi. Bimala, with the other women, sits behind a screen to hear what he has to say. Into this collective feminine gaze Sandip makes a grand entrance, seated in a big chair hoisted on the shoulders of ten or twelve youths. When he begins to speak, Ray shows Bimala impatiently pushing away the screen from her face. From this moment Sandip becomes the consuming object of her fixed gaze. Not only does his voice and presence free her from her hidden space in Camelot, it also brings her into the "world" of other men, just as Nikhil had wished.

To a large extent Ray's film is a faithful adaptation of Tagore's novel. It sensitively portrays a wife's confused passion, a husband's misguided nobility, and a lover's shrewd exploitation of these qualities to suit his own Machiavellian ends. Both husband and wife suffer, but since the lover conveniently exits and the husband pays the price by getting killed, it is the wife who is ultimately victimized.

In Tagore's novel, there are three distinct points of view – Bimala's, Nikhil's, and Sandip's. In the film, however, it is Bimala who significantly becomes the focus. We see her seduced by two different worlds in which her liberation is promised but never delivered. Each world and the culture it embodies becomes in the film a strategic "mirror" in which both men try to impose their own version of the Hindu woman they want Bimala to be. Their ownership of Bimala is determined by the measure of success that each achieves. The mirroring device become the film's central motif, and Ray uses it masterfully to chronicle the painful odyssey of a woman whose image is never fated to be her own.

The first "mirror" in the film in which Bimala is made to function is
the Anglophile world of the English governess, Miss Gilby. Nikhil hires
her to teach his wife the English language, Highland songs, piano playing, and proper British etiquette as observed in social rituals, like pour-
ing tea for invited guests. Miss Gilby teaches Bimala a particular English
song:

> Tell me the tales that to me were so dear
> Long long ago, long long ago.
> Sing me the songs that I wanted to hear
> Long long ago, long ago.

When Ray frames Miss Gilby singing this song, it very poignantly
evokes her own isolated condition, expressing her longing for the green
shores of England. When Ray then cuts to Bimala singing this song alone
in the frame, it designates Bimala's forced emancipation from her Indian
moorings and enunciates her progress in obtaining some kind of mastery
over another culture's language and customs. However, when Ray focuses in the next shot on both women singing the song in unison within
the same frame, we see the divided selves of each confronting the other.
Although they belong to separate cultures, the women share a common
identity: Both are controlled by Nikhil, one playing for this *zamindar* the
role of "teacher," the other the role of "student." Later, after Bimala has
been smitten by her first glimpse of Sandip and is preparing herself in her
bedroom to invite him for tea the next day, we see her singing the same
song she has been taught. As she sings it, she picks up from the mantel-
piece Sandip's portrait (which Nikhil has given her, by way of introduction), and directly addresses it with a very suggestive verse from the song,
one we have not heard before:

> Now that you're come
> All my grief is removed.
> Let me forget that
> So long you have wooed.

Ray very shrewdly alerts us to the new direction that Bimala's eros is going to take. Nikhil is present in the room and watching her; and through
this song, Bimala is already indicating to him that she is unwilling to be
the recipient of his suffocating kind of love and that she would like to
be wooed by another man. Ray strengthens this resolve through carefully
planted Hindu signifiers. When Nikhil, irritated by this English song, asks
Bimala to sing a native Bengali song, Bimala switches to a *bhajan* (devo-

tional song) by mystic-poet Mira Bai, in which that famed married Rajput princess openly confesses her love for Krishna and asks this love god to come quickly and consummate her passion. By fusing the Sandip/Krishna icons, Bimala's yearning to explore eros with another man is enunciated very strongly. Earlier Bimala had introduced this idea daringly to Nikhil (and us) by declaring that she "envied Draupadi with her five husbands." (Draupadi was the joint wife of the five Pandava brothers in the Indian epic *The Mahabharata*, and she was loved and enjoyed by each without conflicts or jealousy.) If Nikhil's enterprise insists on her Westernization, then Bimala also expects him to accept her as a contemporary Draupadi figure when she claims his best friend's attentions.

Although Nikhil wants to free Bimala in the style, as he tells his widowed sister-in-law, of the "great women who were never in *purdah*" (i.e., kept systematically "curtained off" or segregated from men), he adds that "man must have his fancies too." Ray establishes his intent when he shows Nikhil watching the spectacle of Bimala preparing herself for him before her bedroom mirror. He has forced a narcissism on her, and we see Bimala constantly making and unmaking herself as the sexual object for her lord and master. When Sandip meets Bimala for the first time at tea the next day, he imposes another kind of narcissism on her by granting her the twin titles of Mother Goddess and Queen Bee. Her "feminine intuition," about which Nikhil regularly teases her, is quick to acknowledge Sandip's dual personification of her femininity: as the powerful "mother" who can preserve and nurture *and* as the sexual "queen" who can attract and entice. In the emancipatory mirror offered by Nikhil, we are made to witness a woman who is reduced to a decorative object. All that Bimala can do in this assumed state is to manifest herself as a presence demanded by her husband. When we see Sandip granting Bimala the privilege of infatuation, we see how Bimala is provided with an opportunity to express herself for the first time as an attractive object for a man *her* desire has chosen. Even in Sandip's emancipatory mirror, however, she is reduced to functioning as a sexual prisoner: He woos her endlessly with his public oratory of the Swadeshi cause only because he wants her to surrender herself sexually to him. Thus, Ray positions his heroine between the mirrors of one man's ineffectual enlightenment and another man's sybaritic sexual politics.

The mise-en-scène during the tea sequence establishes Bimala's growing attraction toward Sandip, who is gradually shown as becoming the sexual object of her gaze. Ray registers this evocatively by a careful arrangement of tracking shots and slow zooms that first draw Bimala's eros to the surface and then target it on the man as a sexual object. Ray places Nikhil and Bimala on the sofa together; Sandip sits opposite them on a chair. Abruptly, we see Sandip getting up to sing a stirring patriotic song, the song aimed right at Bimala. As he sings, the camera is focused directly on Sandip from behind Nikhil's head. It slowly tracks sideways until it comes to rest behind Bimala's head. Then, from her perspective, Ray slowly and very unobtrusively zooms in on Sandip's passionate singing face. A reverse-angle zoom follows, this time from Sandip to Bimala's face, completely enthralled by his song. As the zooms accelerate they are intercut with medium shots of all three, in which Nikhil is often seen removing his glasses and wiping them. Such an action brilliantly registers the gradual *loss* of the wife from the husband's gaze, whereas the repeated zooms seem to bring Bimala and Sandip closer together in an implied space from which Nikhil has been clearly evicted.

In another scene between Sandip and Bimala, Ray registers their growing awareness of each other through the important signifier of a particular brand of British cigarette that Sandip is shown smoking: "Pompadour," whose name on the packet is represented by a flirtatious lady in a large flouncing dress. For all his Swadeshi politics (in which the banning of all English goods was the most distinctive principle), Sandip cannot bear to smoke an Indian brand. Although Bimala has been told by Nikhil that "our Sandip has had many affairs of the heart with women, not all of them *swadeshi*," she coquettishly picks up the "Pompadour" packet, stares at the lady on it, and in a sly whisper murmurs half to herself and half to Sandip: "I know you won the hearts of many . . . ," leaving the sentence deliberately unfinished. With this wonderfully staged moment Ray displays Bimala's desire to prove to Sandip that *swadeshi* women like herself can be as attractive and as seductive as that British lady with the flouncing dress on the cigarette packet. Moreover, the fact that Bimala is dressed in a very bold red *sari* only for his benefit emphasizes this sexual claim as well: A red *sari* being exactly what a traditional Bengali woman wears on the day of her marriage, she is actually hinting to Sandip that she is preparing herself for her seduction by him. The next time they meet, Sandip confirms this expectation by telling Bimala that the thrill of politics is far inferior to the thrill a man like him feels when faced with the challenge of "winning the heart of a woman" like her.

Another revealing scene between the two occurs when Bimala says she is prepared to offer Sandip any amount of money for the Swadeshi cause should he need it. What is interesting here is Ray's cunning reversal of the gender roles of a normally active Sandip and a quietly passive Bimala. It is Bimala who is now constantly shown circling the stationary Sandip in the diegesis. She seems to be completely absorbed by his presence, and we can sense from her predatory movements her desire to elicit from him a strong affirmative response in which politics and sexuality are powerfully commingled. The normally ebullient Sandip is now frozen in a stunned posture as Bimala continues to run circles round him, physically and mentally. When he initially fails to respond to this new version of Bimala, she resignedly moves to go, prompting him at last to act in the way she has wanted all along: He runs, blocks her exit, and finally grasps her hands. She does not resist because she wants him to control this relationship from now on. She has literally put herself into his hands. The dominant positions in Sandip's patriarchal mirror have changed, and Ray allows his heroine a brief victory before the storm breaks and Bimala is confronted by Sandip's true designs of sexual exploitation.

When a repentant Bimala weeps uncontrollably before her bedroom mirror, Nikhil takes her into his arms but refuses to block her tear-stained image reflected in the mirror. He wants that image to show Bimala her fall from grace, not only in his eyes but in her own. It is only then that he can offer her the privilege of his forgiveness. Ray articulates this privileged male position most remarkably when in the film's final scene he reduces Bimala to the position of widow through three apocalyptic dissolves. His filmic presentation powerfully inscribes how Hinduism finally *fixes* Bimala and strips her of her femininity and womanhood. From the rich wife of a *zamindar*, bedecked with luxurious hair, expensive clothes, and jewelry, the Hindu forces of her age reduce her in these three cruel dissolves to a weeping widow with shaven hair, a plain *sari*, and an unadorned self. Such an ending is more shattering than Tagore's: In the novel, Nikhil's funeral pyre had significantly provided Bimala with a cathartic purification in her widowhood. Through this purification, the writer had redeemed Bimala, whose eros had plunged her into the forbidden fires of desire for another man and had finally made her attain a defiant stoical stance in which she feared neither herself nor anyone else. Ray's final image of Bimala is just the opposite: a Bimala completely emptied of her essential female self before the all-pervasive and judgmental forces of Hinduism. Ray makes her the inevitable victim of a history that finally forces her to occupy a position neither at home nor in the world of her time.

The Ray Woman – Under the Male Hindu Gaze

Ray's concern with the Indian woman, her assumptions of roles and problems of "identity," and her struggles in Indian society continue from *Devi*

(*The Goddess*, 1960), through *Kanchanjungha* in 1962, *Mahanagar* (*The Big City*, 1963), *Kapurush-o-Mahapurush* (*The Coward and the Holy Man*, 1965), *Nayak* (*The Hero*, 1966), *Aranyer Din Ratri* (*Days and Nights in the Forest*, 1970), *Pratidwandi* (*The Adversary*, 1970), *Ashani Sanket* (*Distant Thunder*, 1973), to *Shatranj-ke-Khilari* (*The Chess Players*, 1977).

In *Mahanagar*, the moment Arati gets a job and proves herself to be good in it, she becomes the central troubled object of her household's gaze. Her job is an outdoors one, selling sewing machines, and through work she discovers a whole new world. She begins to enjoy her job, the company of her sister-saleswomen, and her professional visits, which often take her into the houses of the affluent Bengali upper class. Edith, an Anglo–Indian girl with whom she strikes up a close friendship, presents her with her first lipstick and a pair of stylish sunglasses. Even the boss, Mr. Mukherjee – the only other male in the office beside the clerk – takes a liking to Arati and expresses his admiration for her sales efforts. On the days she works late, he even drops her home in his car. However, while success characterizes her in her professional space, her hitherto warm-and-cozy domestic space at home undergoes a dramatic change. By stepping beyond her family's rigid, middle-class, Bengali threshold, Arati seems to whip up a turmoil within her own family *angaan* (courtyard). Her father-in-law refuses to speak to her. Her mother-in-law does the same, while secretly envying Arati's liberated position. Her little son sulks. The one most affected is her accountant husband, Subrata, who had forced her, in the first place, to take up the job when his bank salary fell short of the family's increasing needs [Fig. 9]. He views Arati's transformation of personality with grave anxiety and concern. Ray's camera makes the spectator identify with these predominantly male gazes objectifying Arati on the screen. To her silently pained husband (the film's most central gaze), she appears suddenly confident and radiant. Her vocabulary, to his alarm, changes its gender: She no longer discusses domestic feminine issues with him but traditionally masculine issues like "sales," "salaries," and "commissions." She mentions Mr. Mukherjee's name more often than her son's. By emphasizing these details, Ray calls attention to Subrata's troubled male gaze as he observes Arati's rapid metamorphoses.

Arati's new presence as the salaried woman makes her a secondary wife, a secondary mother, and a secondary daughter-in-law. She disrupts and displaces the traditional position of the Hindu woman from within the periphery of the family. Sylvia Harvey, in her essay "Woman's Place: The Absent Family of Film Noir," provides a still of Joan Crawford as the title character in the 1945 film *Mildred Pierce*, under which she remarks:

The astounding Mildred Pierce ... woman of the world, woman of business, and only secondarily a mother, is a good example of this disruption and displacement of the values of family life. The image of Mildred, in a masculine style of dress, holding her account books and looking *away* from her lover, typifies this kind of displacement.[22]

In Ray's film, the image of Arati is built exactly in the opposite vein: She becomes more feminine in her role as the attractive saleswoman of sewing machines because the sale of her product depends largely on her attractively presented personality. What Arati does share with Mildred Pierce can be accurately defined through Pam Cook's observation that like Mildred, Arati "invades the territory of men: that of property and investment."[23] Arati's striking physical appearance and constant talk of money not only disturbs her predominantly male household but further threatens it by her attempts to take over the place of her husband (and his retired father) as *head* of the family. In this respect, Arati is a forerunner of Sutapa (more on whom later), that confident and glamorous young woman in Ray's 1970 film *Pratidwandi* who decides to run the household when her two brothers are found wanting.

The one object that Ray features as culturally threatening Subrata's myopic gaze in *Mahanagar* is the lipstick Edith has given Arati. Ray shows Arati applying her lipstick only in her professional role as a saleswoman, since it adds to her inherent traditional Indian beauty just the right touch of Westernization so necessary in her job of selling sewing machines to the wealthy, Westernized, bourgeois Bengali housewife. When Subrata discovers the lipstick in Arati's purse, however, he is shocked: From his strict and narrow-minded Hindu point of view, the lipstick is a threat, signifying his wife's liberation from her traditional role as the Hindu wife. When Subrata confronts Arati with the offending cylinder, she promptly throws it away, but she reminds Subrata that "I don't care what others may think or say. I don't want *you* to misunderstand me." She wants her husband to have faith in her new liberated self, to *refocus* his gaze on her so that he can accept her as a joint breadwinner of this house. She wants, in this new version of herself, to be seen as someone who participates in the outside world and has therefore to make radical adjustments, even improvements, over her traditional makeup and roles of the accepted Hindu wife, mother, and daughter-in-law at home.

In the last reel of *Mahanagar*, we see Arati standing not *behind* Subrata but *with* him. Sending in her resignation after a heated dispute with her boss over the unfair dismissal of her coworker-friend Edith, Arati descends

Figure 9. Arati (Madhabi Mukherjee) detaching herself from her husband Subrata's (Anil Chatterjee) patriarchal gaze and contemplating stepping out into the world outside her domestic space in Mahanagar (The Big City, 1963). *(Photo by Nemai Ghosh; gift of Ben Nyce)*

the staircase where the now-unemployed Subrata waits. Subrata has lost his job because there was a run on his bank; Arati, on the other hand, loses hers because of her principles. Although this might have made her stand *before* her man in that last reel, she doesn't. Linking her hand with his, Ray has Arati and Subrata set out *together* to find their future in the *mahanagar*, or big city, of Calcutta.

Having earlier cited Arati's resemblance to Mildred Pierce, it is interesting to note the radical difference in Arati's position at the film's end compared to Mildred's. Mildred reunites with Bert, her estranged husband, and the two of them walk into the proverbial dawn, penniless but happy. However, because Mildred had neglected her family for the sake of her business, and because that had proved very costly for her – losing her jobless husband (who had walked away) and her jealous daughter, Veda (who had killed Mildred's second husband), it is highly unlikely that Mildred is going to step out of the patriarchal family again at the end of the film.

Mildred is given a second chance to become wife and mother. In Ray's film, Arati is determined to find another job. In addition to confidence she has acquired worth. Subrata is proud of her; so (one hopes) will be her household. Indeed, *Mahanagar* has found a *maha* (great) heroine.

In his 1970 *Pratidwandi (The Adversary*, also known as *Siddhartha and the City*), Ray intensifies his exploration by showing how a woman, once having become the object of the male gaze, is quite capable of presenting herself in a calculated way for the male look. The woman in question here is Sutapa, Siddhartha's younger sister. Ambitious and good-looking, she knows she is a definite social success. Instead of submerging her sexuality under her modesty as the Hindu code of femininity demands, she is shown flaunting it in a calculated fashion, defying the suffocating conventions of the rigid, middle-class Bengali family. She delights in telling Siddhartha how she is using her presence to manipulate her boss's male gaze in order to gain his attention, admiration, gifts, and steady promotions in her secretarial career. After all, she is her family's *only* reliable and consistent breadwinner now: Her father is dead; Siddhartha is trying and repeatedly failing to get a job; and the only other brother, Tunnu, is studying and participating in dangerous acts of political terrorism. Siddhartha responds to her by taking up the conventional position of the outraged Hindu brother determined to beat the living daylights out of her scoundrel boss. When he makes this resolve known to her, Sutapa merely laughs: She knows the social codes that have allowed Siddhartha to reach such a predictable conclusion.

Sutapa's laugh very cleverly delineates the site of the Hindu family melodrama within which Ray places this transaction between a failed brother and a successful sister. Siddhartha is critical of Sutapa's petit-bourgeois aspirations. He is down on his luck, unemployed, his masculinity tarnished. Sutapa's defiance clearly reveals her rejection of the patriarchal order. Her laugh rejects Siddhartha's criticism, expels her paternal uncle from her dead father's place in the home, silences her whining mother (who wants to know what Sutapa does after her office hours and why she comes home so late), and establishes herself as the father/provider. She certainly has all the qualities (lacking in the men) to run the household – strength, attractiveness, industry, ambition – but her resolve predictably leads to a deterioration of order in her family.

Siddhartha and the elders are agonized to learn that Sutapa is taking dancing lessons after work. This immediately equates her (as we shall see in greater detail a little later) with the Westernized woman living her life in the fast lane. Another discovery is even more threatening: Sutapa has spent several evenings with her boss decorating his newly purchased summer home. In fact, she is not ashamed to display all his gifts to them. Has she become his mistress? The final blow is delivered by the boss's hysterical wife, who makes a sudden appearance at the family's house and dramatically portrays Sutapa as a home wrecker.

What is interesting is that Sutapa continues to rule the house in spite of all these threats. Moreover, when she insists that her relationship with her boss is platonic and that his wife suffers from hysterical breakdowns, Siddhartha reluctantly backs her up – though he's not happy at all with her dancing lessons. When Sutapa drags Siddhartha to the terrace and displays her techniques of the dance, we are watching her demonstrate the representation of her body through the language of masquerade, with its deliberate hyperbolization of femininity. Her exhibitionism fixes Sutapa for Siddhartha and for the Indian spectator as the femme fatale: the woman who thrives by creating scandal, going out of her way to upset the word and the Law of the dominant, male Hindu world. As she whirls gracefully before him, Ray amplifies Siddhartha's troubled gaze by translating her therein from this solitary terrace dancer to another imaginary setting of a cocktail party, where she is shown dancing indiscriminately and intimately with many men. "How you've changed," he opines after emerging from this reverie. "So has everyone," she calmly retorts. For him, Sutapa has already become the fallen woman. For Sutapa, though, the masquerade she adopts is crucial: It enables her to reappropriate her subjectivity by dictating to her jaundiced brother that this is the only way she is ever going to fulfill all her desires, because no one else in the family can help her realize them.[24]

Sutapa's dance clearly encourages her brother's misperception of her as the femme fatale via his fantasy. Since Siddhartha himself has been reduced to a victim by virtue of his jobless state and economic dependence on Sutapa, his fantasy reduces her to a victim too. Once this is achieved, Siddhartha identifies with Sutapa. Thus, her dance and his concurrent fantasy dramatize for brother and sister the loss of their close relationship and respect for each other. As she dancingly moves *toward* Siddhartha on the deserted terrace, she seems to articulate an intense enjoyment in her own body; she appears to be telling Siddhartha that it is the dance that has really made her discover her own body. As she moves *away* from him, however, she seems to map out an escape from her stifling life in her crowded home where she has become the sullen object of scrutiny and surveillance. When Siddhartha fixes her dance in his fantasy, the distance has been irrevocably lengthened, and Sutapa has become only a lost object in the arms of so many strangers with whom she is seen dancing.

Women as Possessors of the Gaze

When Ray's men become the objects of their women's gaze (as we have seen earlier in this chapter's discussions of *Charulata* and *Ghare-Baire* (*The Home and the World*), the women do *not* lose their feminine characteristics. In fact, through this gaze reversal, they reveal a greater honesty in coming to terms not only with the men who are the determined objects of their gaze but, more important, with their own selves. Ray's 1966 film *Nayak* testifies to this position of women.

In *Nayak* (*The Hero*), it is the film idol Arindam Mukherjee who finds himself confiding his misgivings regarding his own career and his character – under the gaze of the "formidable young woman," Aditi Sengupta – in the dining car of a Delhi-bound train. She edits a modern women's magazine called *Adhunika*, she tells him in their initial meeting. Although she is not interested in him or his films, he would make quick-selling copy, she bluntly explains; hence, she would like to interview him. Still, in the course of this arrangement she makes no attempt to humiliate or even condescend to him. She not only maintains her traditional feminine characteristics in her role as interrogator and possessor of the gaze but also succeeds in allowing the authentic "man" in Arindam to emerge from behind his assumed persona of the "hero." Her initial antagonism toward his professional presence quickly gives way to a genuine empathy and concern as she helps him understand the difficult terrain of success and fame in which he confesses to be trapped.

When they first meet, Aditi is standing in front of the seated Arindam, looking down at him. She asks him for his autograph and, as he obliges her with a flourish in typical film-hero style, she undermines his vanity by adding that the autograph is not for her but "for a cousin of mine." Arindam stops writing and looks up, amused. When he starts to write again, his pen won't work; he has to dip it in a glass of water to let it function again. Attracted by her forthright approach, he ventures an exploratory remark:

ARINDAM: I take it you don't like our [Bengali] films.
ADITI: Too remote from reality.
ARINDAM: Quite right – educated ladies shouldn't burst into songs at the slightest provocation.
ADITI: And heroes shouldn't be so Godlike.[25]

Instead of taking offense, Arindam seems to admire Aditi's resolve to fracture the image of the hero that has always trapped him. Aditi first asks him, in the course of her interview, if "in the midst of having so much, don't you feel there's something missing in your life? Some emptiness somewhere?" Arindam proceeds to defend his life-style, reminding her that an alternative one would have only "hurt my box office." However, as Aditi makes him the object of her gaze and forces him to confront this unsettling question that he has been avoiding, he feels infinitely relieved. He reciprocates this concern in his last meeting with her by repeating her very own words to her:

ADITI: How are you?
ARINDAM: You know everything. You tell me.
ADITI: Fine.
ARINDAM: Not quite.
ADITI: Why not?
ARINDAM: There's something missing . . . Some emptiness somewhere.

Before he meets Aditi, we see Arindam looking at the world through his dark glasses. Ray makes effective use of the glasses in *Nayak,* as he did the lipstick in *Mahanagar.* Arindam needs these glasses because they provide him with detachment from a world that looks at him always as a hero and never as a human being; but the moment he becomes the object of Adati's gaze, we see him *abandon* his dark glasses before her open-eyed scrutiny. Moreover, he doesn't mind her regarding him through *her* glasses during the interview. Once the process of this examination is over, Aditi is shown tearing up all the interview notes. When Arindam asks her if she is going "to write from memory," Aditi gives him a long, transparent look before replying that she'll "keep it in [her] memory."

In *Charulata,* the heroine's lorgnette brought into close-up first her husband and then her lover; but both men were so absorbed in their own male-dominated worlds of journalism and poetry that they failed to acknowledge Charu's gaze (via her glasses), which objectified them without neurosis, hysteria, or anxiety. When she replaced the husband with the lover in her glasses, no negative connotations were imposed on her by Ray: His investigative gaze, along with our's, accepted Charu's transference of passion from husband to lover. Her glasses, therefore, became the predominant signifiers of her hidden desires. In *Nayak,* when we first glimpse Aditi with her cotravelers Ajoy and Shefali, Ray's script describes her as follows: "the young girl opposite them [is] about 25 years old and has a serious intelligent look about her." Her glasses signify that serious intelligent look, but still Aditi is presented as a journalist, asking subscriptions from Ajoy for her magazine. The notorious Arindam Mukherjee, who is subsequently glimpsed traveling in the same train, is then proposed as making interesting material for her feminist magazine. Still, she refuses to see herself as a journalist. Observe the following exchange when Aditi comes into the dining car and has her second encounter with Arindam.

ARINDAM: Another cousin?
ADITI: Do you mind if I bother you again ... I just wanted to ask you some questions.
ARINDAM: My God! You're not a journalist, are you?
ADITI: No, I edit a woman's magazine.

By scrutinizing Arindam through her glasses, Aditi makes it clear to him that she's not interested in him as a mere item of gossip for her readers. She knows his personal and popular history and feels "what they have been writing about you is not very interesting." She wants to edit these out and reach his psyche. She wants to resurrect the real Arindam, make him reveal his hidden desires, beliefs, and fears. Moreover, once Arindam becomes objectified for her as a lonely vulnerable person, Aditi stops being even an editor of a woman's magazine: The earnest, formidable woman in glasses becomes a confidant to whom he can reveal himself honestly – hence the abandonment of his dark glasses. Now when they talk, he is no longer a film star hiding behind glasses and she is no longer an editor scrutinizing him as a journalist's subject through her glasses. This interview, therefore, cannot be published: Their identities during the process have undergone a radical change. What we have witnessed is, in the memorable words of Robert Bresson's country priest (in *Journal d'un curé de campagne*), "a soul for soul" transaction between two immensely attractive personalities. Ray has even had us mildly entertaining the traditional love-story ending with the hero walking away hand-in-hand with this attractive woman. What could be more romantic than such a pair coming together at the end, even if our film star happened to be traveling in a first-class, air-conditioned compartment and our woman editor in an ordinary third-class, chair coach?

Nothing of the sort ever happens, however: The gulf between the first-class traveler and the third-class one is rigorously maintained throughout the film. The interview takes place in a neutral spatial area: the dining car. There, amusingly, it is the attractive pair of Arindam and Aditi who are repeatedly shown coming under the collective gaze of all the other diners inside the train and the spectators on the railway platforms, who crowd round their dining-car window whenever the train makes its scheduled stops. Just before they part for good, they have the following exchange:

ARINDAM: I don't suppose we'll meet again . . . And you're not likely to come into our line.
ADITI: No. You live in a different world. We're out in the streets, in trams, and buses . . .
ARINDAM: If three of my films flop in a row, I might go back into that world.
ADITI: Don't say that. I'm sure you'll stay right where you are, for a long time yet. Your box office will stay good.

It is morning when the above conversation takes place in the dining car. Breakfast time is *not* the traditional romantic hour for farewells, and the dining car, again, is *not* the traditional romantic spot (although Hitchcock marvelously turned it into one in his memorable *North by Northwest*). Both time and space, therefore, have been brilliantly used by Ray to defeat all romantic expectations of their coming together. The above conversation further intensifies the gulf that already exists between their different worlds – she "out in the streets," free, independent, anonymous, and vital; he, a prisoner of his own fame, unable to move freely like her "in trams and buses" because of his overexposed visibility, but still vital as long as his image means something in the box office.

Ray makes them part with mutual respect but without any display of emotion. Aditi *namastes* (i.e., bows slightly with palms together), tears up the interview notes, and leaves. We see the train approach Delhi station and slow down at the platform. Arindam stands at the door. He is immediately spotted by his fans, who surround him as the train grinds to a halt. From the third-class compartment, Aditi descends. Arindam alights also and is immediately garlanded. He salutes his fans with a profuse greeting of the *namaste*. As he does so, Aditi passes him by, chatting animatedly with her uncle who has come to receive her. Arindam turns to catch a final response from her. He fails. He turns round, smiles, and begins to move with the crowd. Surrounded by an adoring multitude (his "public"), the one honest recognition that Arindam needs, even here on a territory in which he is so completely at ease, *is* from Aditi; but she is so engrossed in conversation that she walks by without even acknowledging his final glance. Arindam has ironically become for her (in keeping with her last words to him) a "memory." When the camera moves in for the final close-up of our hero, we notice that he has put *on* his dark glasses again. The mythical persona of the *nayak* is once again assumed.

Two Ray Women – in Masquerade

In *Mahanagar*, there is a puzzling moment where Ray overarticulates Arati's liberated presence. This occurs in the scene when we surprisingly see the actress Madhabi Mukherjee dressed in a peculiarly transparent blouse through which her white bra can clearly be seen when she goes out on one of her sales calls. Within the mise-en-scène, this seems not in keeping with Arati's character as it has been developed by Ray. Not only would her family at home not allow such a brazen sartorial display, but even her own Bengali boss would be scandalized if any one of his Indian saleswomen dared to dress in so obvious a revealing outfit. Neither has Arati been shown as being tempted to change her image so dramatically under the Westernized tutelage of her Anglo–Indian friend Edith. Nonetheless, Madhabi Mukherjee as Arati is allowed this supreme moment of erotic meaning in the complete *absence* of her husband, her boss, or any other *male* character within the narrative space itself.

When the spectator sees Arati dressed in this unique and daring masquerade, it articulates her representation as a conventional Bengali housewife who has liberated herself from her stifling family's gaze by such an act of narcissistic display. Arati is revealing to the spectator a forbidden aspect of her femininity that the rigid codes of her patriarchal family had forced her to conceal from herself and the world. By reestablishing her image for the spectator through the assumption of such a masquerade, Ray succeeds, it seems to me, in effecting the defamiliarization of the icon of the traditional Bengali housewife. This strengthens his attempts to disarticulate the Hindu male's traditional viewing of the Bengali woman. The time has come for women like Arati to subvert the Hindu male codes by which Hindu women are forced to be seen. Such a masquerade is quite successful, then, in fracturing the network of Hindu male hegemony.

Such, however, is not the case with Ray's use of Sharmila Tagore in his films. When Ray first used her in *Apur Sansar* (*The World of Apu*) and *Devi* (*The Goddess*), Sharmila was not a full-fledged actress. There was something wonderfully innocent and vulnerable about Sharmila as Aparna in the former film and as Doya in the latter. Her intuitive interpretation of these women and her appealing simplicity made these two characters very moving and credible. Sharmila herself acknowledged this in an interview given to a local film magazine of Bombay – *after*, we must note, she had become a very big star in the commercial Hindi film world. She stated categorically:

The pictures I make, I realize, won't stay. They will be dead. Nobody will remember them in fifty years. Perhaps only *Apur Sansar* and *Devi* will stay. . . .
Devi was what a genius got out of me, not something I did myself. He saw my
face, my eyes. He said to himself: she will be my mouthpiece, my canvas. I had
no eye in me then. You can see now, how little of "self" we artists really have
in our work? In the process of becoming a star, there is a little alienation.[26]

Ray has never been able to repeat this Sharmila "magic" in his later films
with her. In them she comes through as a seasoned professional. Even
though her acting is very sincere and competent, there is a noticeable tension in her image. Sharmila seems to be *aware* of how Ray is using her,
and of the kind of fascination he has for the Bengali woman she as the
character is supposed to represent and connote; but this awareness seems
to make her extremely self-conscious before Ray's camera. It seems as if
she is playing the scenes for Ray himself, appealing to his creativity to get
something original out of her. Such an understanding, however, results
in a distancing from the character she is supposed to be playing. This
prompts Ray to use Sharmila in films where her status as La Tagore "on
display" can function meaningfully within the film's narrative context.

   The moment Sharmila, as Aditi, appears in *Nayak,* Ray focuses our
attention on the fountain pen clipped in a very casual way to the upper-
right-hand part of her blouse; but her blouse is cut low, and the pen heaves
a bit too suggestively. We have seen Sharmila playing this version of the
liberated Indian woman in countless Hindi films; Ray's version, in Aditi,
seems not to improve it but merely repeats it. As Aparna in *Aranyer Din
Ratri* (*Days and Nights in the Forest*), Sharmila's elaborately made-up face
lit by Ashim's cigarette lighter; an excessively mannered walk in a provocatively draped *sari* or tight pants; a carefully arranged hairdo; dimpled
smiles, pouts, silences, and gently whispered remarks – again and again
these are offered as token "displays" gleaned from her unfortunate immersion in Bombay's Hollywood. In *Seemabaddha* (*Company Limited*),
her glamorous appearance as Sudharshana clashes very unconvincingly
with her narrative presence – the shy, small-town woman from the rural
and conservative town of Patna coming to visit her more glamorous and
attractive sister, Dolan, who is married to a rich executive in the bustling
metropolis of Calcutta. Moreover, Sudharshana is supposed to be in love
with a fiery revolutionary back home. Surely, such a character could not
fit in so easily and comfortably as she is shown doing in the film when her
brother-in-law takes her through a whirlwind of upper-class activity: cocktail parties, the race course, golf-club lunches, and so on. Again we have

a Sharmila on "display," going through all her commercially imbibed gestures for Ray and us. She tries very hard but is unable either to overcome or to eliminate the masquerade altogether.

The Victimized Woman Who Dares to Humble the Father

Richard Lannoy offers us the following narrative of an Indian woman psychologist, as quoted by Margaret Cormack in her study *The Hindu Woman:*

In our country the father is still not a family friend, but a dictator . . . culturally we expect the father to be a sort of authority, and every member of the family must try to keep him happy. The family is ready to accept this type of dictatorship. . . . We still feel that we are not able to speak frankly or discuss all our desires with our fathers. Whenever children want to ask something they speak with their mothers. This is because of fear of the dictatorship, and not fear of the father as a person.[27]

What Ray specifically emphasizes in his indictment of Indian patriarchy is the authoritarian and powerful role of the father, under whose hegemony the Indian woman, in all her different roles of daughter, daughter-in-law, mother and wife, is expected to function as an obedient slave. Ray portrays her in these roles both as "victim" in his 1960 film *Devi (The Goddess)* and as a "rebel" in his 1962 film *Kanchanjungha.*

Although the drama of Ray's *Devi* is supposed to take place in the India of the 1830s, the film's referential target is modern India. The ubiquity of superstition that Ray strongly indicts clearly points to a crucial blindness that continues to be at the core of contemporary Hinduism. Ray's depiction of a young woman's unfortunate apotheosis into an assumed goddess figure and her ultimate death reveals a dual masculine myopia: in those like the father figure of the *zamindar* Kalikinkar Roy, who endorses such a metamorphosis, and the husband figure of Umaprasad, who in spite of being liberal and rational finds himself powerless to intervene and save his wife Doya from her unfortunate fate.

The film is very daring in its Freudian explication of both men wanting to possess Doya as the mother. The old *zamindar* has a dream in which he is convinced that the goddess Durga tells him that she has descended into his house in the human form of Doya, his daughter-in-law. Doya replaces the image of the goddess in the old man's dream, and from then on, he derives pleasure in seeing her (incarnated or otherwise) as the mother figure. What is most impressive about Ray's presentation is the idea that even when the oppressed Indian woman is granted such an apotheosis, ultimately she becomes a devastated victim.

The paternalistic *zamindar* is alienated from all the members of his extended family but one: Doya, the outsider, who is constantly shown mothering him. The same tender look enters his eyes when he observes her performing the family *puja* (prayer ritual) to the Divine Mother as when, being a dutiful daughter-in-law, she massages his feet every evening.

The scene begins with Kalikinkar relaxing on a tiger-skin chair. In mid-shot Doya enters his room with a glass of milk. He coaxingly addresses her as "little mother." The little boy Khoka, who is very fond of Doya, is shown leaving the room in anger in the background when he sees his favorite aunt entering his grandfather's chamber. When the camera pulls back we see Doya pressing the old man's feet; as it slowly zooms in, we see Kalikinkar making fun of Doya's "Christian husband," not as a father but as a rival. Strengthening the old man's attraction to Doya is the overtly sexual way in which Ray positions him in the mise-en-scène: sitting with his legs willingly spread before the kneeling young woman. Ray's editing also fixes the old man's gazes covetously devouring Doya as she shyly comes into the room, delicately places the milk, monosyllabically responds to his flirtations, and dutifully rubs his feet. Geeta Kapur's remarks from her excellent essay "Mythic Material in Indian Cinema," especially on the above-mentioned scene, accurately set the stage for Doya's impending victimization:

[T]he core of this film is revealed when an unintended eroticism unwinds in the heart of the old aristocrat and destroys the old order. As Kalikinkar Roy watches his beautiful, young daughter-in-law perform the ritual *puja* before the goddess, and as he receives her devoted attentions, we see a visible conflation of motives: the deification of a desired object. The dream that is forming in the old man is still, in terms of the plot, to be revealed: in terms of the image it is already established in the body and performance and cinematographic capture of Kalikinkar.[28]

To fix Doya as goddess is easy for this *zamindar* since he has the power, the class, the sex, and the age in which a prevalent Hindu society makes its people support superstition blindly. Ray inscribes this notion quite clearly through the credits, where the smiling face (actually a white mask of the Divine Mother) receives in successive dissolves its fetished embellishments of ornaments and decorations. The film portrays these commodities of ritual and *mantra* as indices of an aristocratic excess by which an innocent woman can be trapped and doomed. The film traces Doya's ordeal as she is slowly stripped of her essential femininity, successively made to relinquish all her human roles, and forced to put on the *mask* of a goddess. When she finally abandons this mask, she has to don another mask of madness before the furies finally claim her. In the film's final shot, we see her fading into the flowers where death awaits her, her face smeared with ash and holy powders, her hair in disarray [Fig. 10]: a sorrowful and frightened spectacle of sacrifice and guilt, all from the impotent point of view of her husband, who has been unable to save her from the demented Brahminic power of his father.

In a crucial scene, the old man's drunken elder son, Tarapada, explains to his wife that the reason he has accepted Doya's deification is because "All belongs to father here: this house, this property, this money, everything." From this scene Ray cuts to a comic play being watched by Umaprasad (the younger son) in Calcutta. In the scene being presented, there is a father who is being constantly insulted by his sons because they are not his legitimate progeny. In juxtaposing the two scenes, Ray is indicting Kalikinkar: By robbing Doya of her legitimate role as his son's wife and his daughter-in-law, he has transformed her illegitimately to a *devi* or goddess. In the scene when Doya was massaging his feet, he had called her "little mother," adding that "to call your name is to become pure." But his love for her *is* impure, and the only way he can symbolically possess her is by deifying her.

During the credit sequence, Ray focuses on a ritualistic sacrifice where a goat is being offered by Kalikinkar Roy to the goddess Durga. In his study of Hinduism, Nirad Chaudhuri offers a historical explanation of this act of worship, which, from a Hindu point of view, is a "contract of mutual help":

For example, goats, sheep and buffaloes are sacrificed to the Goddess Durga at her annual worship and the goat is told: "The goddess will be pleased to receive your flesh mixed with blood." When the head has been cut off, it is taken to the image of the goddess with some blood, and the goddess is apostrophized: "Thou who art fond of sacrificial meat, O great goddess! accept the blood of the beast with its flesh." . . . Since the goddess has been given her due, the worshipper (actually the priest on his behalf) feels entitled to utter this prayer: "Om! Give me long life, give me fame, O goddess! give me good fortune, give me sons, give me wealth, give me all things desirable." She is also asked to give immunity from blindness, leprosy, poverty, diseases, great bereavements, loss of friends and relatives and all distressing situations.

Then comes the thanksgiving:

Figure 10. Doya (Sharmila Tagore) fading into the flowers: a sorrowful and fright-ened spectacle of sacrifice and guilt in Devi (The Goddess, *1960). (Photo by Ne-mai Ghosh; gift of Ben Nyce)*

I am blessed that I have done my duty, my life has attained to its fulfillment be-cause you, Great Goddess! have come to my dwelling.[29]

Ray's film emphatically negates Kalikinkar's contract with the goddess. As her worshiper, the old *zamindar* gives the goddess her due and she in re-turn gives him two sons: the elder, who mimics him and obeys him out of fear and also because he wants a larger share of the old man's inheritance, and the younger, who is determined to upset his father's Hindu Brahminic essence with a Westernized rational one. Regarding good fortune, the old man has none. Instead of granting him immunity from blindness, the god-dess blinds him in his desire for his younger daughter-in-law. By deifying her, he drives her to suicide, thus depriving his younger son of a wife and a happy married life. He also causes bereavement in the older son's fam-ily when Doya's goddess powers fail to cure Khoka, and the old man makes the little boy die on her lap. In the end, the goddess leaves the *za-mindar* in a distressing situation with his younger son, who, having just witnessed Doya's suicide, rushes in and accuses his father of killing both his wife and Khoka. The wealthy *zamindar* who gave the goddess a goat at the film's beginning is left, at the end, empty-handed and a murderer, with no grandson or daughter-in-law.

What intensifies the tragedy in the film is Doya's own trapped femininity, which forces her to confront herself as a split subjectivity: dying and being born everyday, now as a woman/mother, now as a domestic/Divine Mother goddess. Ray's depiction of her as a confused presence is memorably achieved through the objective correlative of the skeletal papier-mâché image of the Durga goddess Doya sees *half-immersed* in the water when she and her husband go out secretly to the riverside one moonlit night, while making plans for their imminent escape to Calcutta. After seeing that image, however, Doya refuses to flee and expresses doubts about the kind of normal life she is expected to embrace once she starts her life with him in Calcutta. Like that strange half-human, half-divine image of Durga, one part of her wants to run away and start a new life in the city but another part of her wants to remain behind and be worshiped as the incarnation of the goddess. It is this latter part that finally drags her to her death by drowning. So insistent is she in her arguments that her husband finally relents, and both return to play out the father's doomed Brahminical game of apotheosis.

Further proof of Doya's victimization is offered imagistically by Ray capitalizing on actress Sharmila Tagore's diminutive presence, expressing her helplessness through her smallness. In Geeta Kapur's observation:

How little she is derives from the young small body of the actress, and in the way she is held and cherished and also spoken of by the husband, whose entire agony about her absurd transformation is expressed in one sentence to his mentor in Calcutta: she is only seventeen.[30]

When Umaprasad returns home, he is not allowed to see Doya. Religion stands like a wall between the horrified husband and his wife sitting on her shrine like a goddess. Here her smallness becomes all the more ironic when we compare her to the large clay icon of the goddess at the film's beginning. Whereas the clay goddess inspired awe and reverence, Doya's manufactured goddess presence evokes only our fear and pity. Geeta Kapur registers this irony:

In fact her littleness seems to become an insistent motif especially after she has been deified: seated in the shrine you see her from near enough but you also see her as the camera saw the clay icon at the start, tilted, about to fall back. You see the signs of a trance showing on her weary face (a trance evoked as much by the claustrophobia of priests, chanting, incense and beseeching pilgrims as by her own half-doubt about her status) but when she actually swoons and falls sideways like a doll, the camera has withdrawn and you see her in long shot, bereft, broken.[31]

Ray keeps the fear and pity overwhelmingly in check by constantly emphasizing Doya's divided feminine sensibility. As she kisses her husband in the privacy of her room, she is humanized by his closeness and bodily contact. However, when he asks for "proof" sanctioning her divine metamorphosis, she is too perplexed to react: She needs to escape with him, out of this room, out of this mansion, into nature, where she hopes to breathe again. Eagerly she responds to the song of a passing boatman, which drowns out the agonizing peal of bells she has been exposed to while seated all day on the shrine; but the half-immersed Durga skeleton she sees cuts the ground from her feet. Stopping among the giant weeds by the riverbank, she whispers to her tall, so out-of-reach husband, "I'm afraid, I'm afraid, I'm afraid, maybe I am really a goddess."

Indoors or outdoors, Doya appears to be trapped. There are, however, significant moments in the film when her desire is allowed representation by Ray. She empathizes, for instance, with the household parrot whose "wings have been clipped." Her toes curl up and shrink under her *sari* in confusion and shame when her father-in-law bends down to touch her feet with his head. There is one memorable scene when we see Doya leaving the prayer room with all her goddess decorations still on her body. Ray shows her crossing the corridor where one of the servants is playing with her little nephew, Khoka. The servant suddenly stops and looks at her, not knowing how he is expected to react to this vision: Is she *still* the goddess *avatar* (incarnate) or has she reverted to her normal mistress self? As he stands stupefied, Doya, aware of his confusion, quickly enters her own bedroom. The camera tracks with her into the room's enveloping darkness. There is a long pause before we see a reflection of light playing on a wooden panel that we can now discern in that darkness. As we approach that light source, we are now able to see Doya quite clearly. She is shown opening the drawers of a desk and taking out a packet of love letters written by her husband. She looks at them very longingly and then raises her eyes dreamily to some distant offscreen space. That look indicates clearly how such innocent pleasures are completely denied her in this decorated version of herself as goddess, ironically displayed before the camera's persistent gaze. She has been reduced to a visible spectacle and has become the unfortunate receptacle of other peoples' desires, which her goddess powers are supposed to fulfill. Her own desires, however, can be expressed only secretly, in darkness – but to whom can she express them? There is

neither god nor man willing to accept them now. The only person with
whom she can behave normally is her little nephew, Khoka; but here
again, her manufactured goddess presence intervenes and deprives her of
Khoka's innocent affection.

Ray makes this estrangement poignantly clear in a scene that begins
with a top shot over Doya resting on her bed. We cut to an open door
through which we see, from Doya's prone position on the bed, Khoka
playing with a ball. In the next shot we see the ball rolling into Doya's
room. Normally, Khoka would have rushed into his favorite aunt's room
to collect the ball. Now, we see that he does not. As Ray holds on to that
shot, there is a long pause. Suddenly Khoka rushes in, grabs the ball, and
runs out. There is no acknowledgment of Doya by the child: This is not
his aunt who used to give him sweets and tell him stories of "witches who
like to munch the bones of children"; this is a strange woman who sits
on a tall platform as many many people bow to her. She is said to be a
goddess, but who knows, she could be a witch. So when he falls critically ill, and when her assumed goddess powers fail to save him from his
death, we see Doya inexorably drifting into a madness brought on by her
mourning and her melancholia over that innocent child's death. Instead
of deflecting her hatred toward the family and the father who has trapped
her in this deadly divine state, she turns her anger upon herself by finally
committing suicide.

In *Kanchanjungha* (Ray's first original screenplay), which he made in
1962, Ray defines even more clearly the entrapment of the contemporary
Bengali women under the constant surveillance and domination of the
powerful Hindu father. This film, however, also presents the end of the
father's oppressive hegemony. Supported by many of the family members'
collective moral force, the youngest daughter, Monisha, arises as her father's first formidable rebel.

Indranath Choudhury, recipient of a British title and chairman of five
companies is the all-powerful father in the film. (In Hindu mythology, Indra is the King of Gods.) He is as solidly set in his ideology as the Hima-
layan mountain range in this health resort of Darjeeling, where he has
come with his family for a holiday. He has ruled over his family with an
iron hand and has driven each family member into some kind of a humiliating submission. However, this last afternoon is not going to be an ordinary one for him: In the next hundred minutes of the film, while Indranath
hopes to catch a clear view of the majestic Kanchanjungha peak, obscured
as it usually is by fog and mist, the women in his family will assert them-

selves and topple his unchallenged reign of tyranny. The major victors in this scenario are going to be Labanya, the eldest woman and his once obedient and passive wife, and Monisha, his most sensitive and gifted youngest daughter.

Ray shows Indranath as a typical upper-class Bengali Anglophile, who even in an independent India continues to place himself on par with the English. He dislikes Indians who are critical of the British Raj and goes out of his way in his obsequious "good mornings and good afternoons," which he flings with carefully rehearsed clipped accents to every English tourist who passes him by on his daily walks at this tiny hill station. His memories are always of a preindependent India under the British, and he determines every individual's worth by his proximity to an acquired British colonial culture. Thus, he approves of Monisha's "match" with Pranab Banerjee, a smooth-talking, well-established, ambitious young engineer, recently returned from a long stint in England. Pranab has fallen in love "at first glance" with Monisha at Darjeeling and is, with the old man's conniving, on the point of proposing to her.

Success and wealth have made Pranab excessively glib and assertive. He thinks he can woo Monisha by laying at her feet clichés like how lonely and empty his life has been without a soul mate in spite of all his materialistic luxuries, and so on. Monisha, who is a bright student of Bengali and English literature, is alert not only to Pranab's verbal triteness but also to the bribes that Pranab cleverly attaches to them every time he flings a new proposal at her. She refuses to respond to him because, in Pranab, she very clearly sees a reflected version of her own father. Thus, even in scenes when the father is not visually present, we see his absent presence mirrored. Ray makes Monisha triumph ultimately through a deliberate stance of silence, which he has her adopt repeatedly to erode Pranab's incessant and excessive garrulity. This lack of a traditional feminine response makes Pranab's assertive masculinity all the more desperate, since Monisha denies him access to both a shy "yes" or a hesitant "no" to his marriage proposal. Either would have satisfied his chauvinistic demands, but Monisha chooses to register her denial through an assertion of stoical silence, and she appears visibly delighted every time a loud peal of the neighboring temple bells, aiding her silence, successively drown out Pranab's empty rhetoric of useless words. In the end Pranab is forced to admit defeat, which Ray makes him acknowledge by having him give an entire Cadbury's (British) chocolate bar (another "bribe" with which he had hoped to sweeten Monisha) to the tattered Nepali beggar boy following them.

What might have become of Monisha as Pranab's wife is commented on very clearly when Ray trains his cinematic gaze on the unhappy marriage of her elder sister, Anima. Anima, we gradually learn, was pushed into a marriage with Shankar by her domineering father to confirm and further his own family name in upper-class Bengali circles. The only positive fruit of this loveless transaction is their six-year-old daughter, Tuklu. Within this marital imbalance Ray reveals Anima's crucial discovery that her secret love affair of many years' standing had been known to her husband all along, and it was because of this that his "protest" had taken the conspicuous forms of drinking and gambling. Ray makes us see how Shankar has tried, through such behavior, to punish her emasculation of him as the replaced husband-lover. Still, the man truly responsible for the forces of cruelty practiced by each spouse on the other is Indranath – the family's remorseless fountainhead.

Shankar's protest doesn't stem only from his unhappy arranged marriage: Since his marriage makes him part of Indranath's extended family, he has to now accept Indranath as the symbolic ideal father and obey all his injunctions. This leads to a desire on Shankar's part to break free. As historian Richard Lannoy puts it:

[T]he word used in connection with the joint [extended] family in all ancient lawbooks of the Hindus is not "jointness" but *unseparatedness.* . . . The result . . . can often be a state of suppressed hostility, overt quarrels, and restlessness.[32]

Shankar is not alone in displaying all three of the above-mentioned symptoms of rebelliousness; so too does Anil, Indranath's son, a marginal character in the film. Ray portrays him as a playboy chasing every pretty girl who crosses his path in Darjeeling. This is, one assumes, a persona Anil puts on deliberately to defy and anger his properly behaved and Anglo-etiquetted father – his way of trying to subvert Indranath's Law by making his strict and unapproachable father somehow responsible for the son's rude and wayward behavior.

Since the mother is the one who feels this kind of victimization most acutely for her children, especially her daughters, the revolt against Indranath must include Labanya. As Anima and Shankar's daughter Tuklu rides past her in a crucial scene, Ray fixes Labanya's gaze, first on her granddaughter, then panning from her to a barren tree from her customary position on a roadside bench. Labanya knows what has happened to Anima, and she knows how the same thing could happen not only to Monisha but *also* to *Tuklu* when she grows up if the Law of the Father is allowed to determine her future!

Ray's bonding between the grandmother and Tuklu (who also stands in here for the absent Monisha) is crucial here because it enables him to defeat the patriarchal practice of separating the daughter from the mother. Ray shows Labanya speaking for the granddaughter from a feminist position as (grand)mother. By focusing on Tuklu as she rides around her estranged parents and a silently grieving grandmother, Ray articulates in the conditional tense the hypothesized ambivalence that daughters bear toward their mothers in most patriarchal cultures. If Indranath in the future has his way regarding Tuklu's marriage (as the film shows him doing when he executes the Law of the Father with Monisha's marriage), then Tuklu, as a grown young woman, would be angry with Anima and Labanya, her mother and grandmother, because, in Ann Kaplan's words,

first, they did not give her the independence she needed, or the wherewithal to discover her identity; second, because they failed to protect her adequately against a [known] patriarchal culture by which she could be psychologically, culturally, and (sometimes) physically harmed[33]

– as were they. The denuded qualities of that tree become a metonymic extension of the impending fates of Monisha and Tuklu if Labanya, as the eldest matriarch of the family, chooses not to intervene. After years of suffering, Labanya suddenly realizes that her own condition is very similar to the bareness she sees in this tree. She has been deprived of kindness and love that, again in metonymic terms, suggest the appropriate foliage under which a happy family and marriage are expected to shelter the Indian woman – foliage missing permanently from her life and temporarily from that tree, as it stands before her in its winter condition.

Suddenly a new resolve takes hold of her: She will advise her youngest daughter, Monisha, not to be bullied by her father's proposal but to go ahead and marry the man of her *own* choice when the right moment arrives. She knows that her elder daughter Anima will fully endorse this; so will her husband, Shankar. Her resolve is articulated through a romantic song that we see and hear Labanya singing – a song she "hasn't sung for years," as she tells her brother, Jagadish. He doesn't have to ask her why: He has silently empathized with her victimization. Now, as she confides her new resolve to him, he asks her to sing this song again, and as it fills the sound track, it seems to lift the very mists from her accustomed humble presence. Proudly she rises, and still singing gets up to fight for her younger daughter's and granddaughter's emancipation.

Hinduism's patriarchal structure was so designed to erase the mutual, intergenerational bonds among women. Ray's unique stance in *Kanchan-*

Jungha resurrects these bonds between daughters and mothers (Anima or Monisha and Labanya) and between granddaughters and grandmothers (Tuklu and Labanya). Unaffected by the dominant gaze of Indranath/the Father, Ray's film sets in motion a mutual gaze that the women of the family circulate among themselves to fortify their combined presence and then defeat the partriarchal gaze, which can no longer reduce them to submission. Ray's film boldly and movingly enunciates a return of matriarchy that not only prevents the impending victimization of the "innocents" – Monisha and Tuklu – but allows a mother–daughter–granddaughter bonding before which the dreaded father is not only overwhelmingly humbled but decisively replaced.

The Articulation of the Ray Woman – From a Space She Can Call Her Own

Confronted by Hinduism's patriarchal construct, the Indian woman, in the words of Sudhir Kakar,

> turns her aggression against herself and transforms such a cultural devaluation into feelings of worthlessness and inferiority. . . . The internalization of [this] low esteem also presupposes that Indian girls and women have no sphere of their own, no independent livelihood and activity, no area of family and community responsibility and dominance, no living space apart from that of men, within which to create and manifest those aspects of feminine identity that derive from intimacy and collaboration with other women.[34]

Ray rectifies feminine identity by articulating a female bonding that enables the women to succeed not only in regaining their worth in their own eyes but also in freeing themselves from the overwhelming patriarchal structures in which they have to function on a daily basis.

In *Mahanagar*, Ray conspicuously shows all of Mr. Mukherjee's saleswomen bonding into a very intimate work group when they relax between sales calls in the "rest area" of the office, which they seem to have taken over as their own private space. It is here that they chat, tell each other intimate details of their lives, and plan out future strategies relating to the world of "males" in general, both in their domestic as well as their professional spheres. The intimate bond on which Ray concentrates is the one that Arati shares with the Anglo–Indian Edith, her friend, coworker, and the group's most outspoken candidate. Arati is attracted to Edith's honest and open manner of talking about herself and her family. Her Western upbringing has created in Edith a no-nonsense approach and a fierce spirit of independence. She is brutally honest with this group of conventional and passive Hindu women who, with the possible exception of Arati, admire her from a distance. When Arati extends her hand of friendship, Edith grabs it and becomes her mentor.

Hence, when Arati becomes aware of her Bengali boss's racist behavior toward Edith, which culminates in Edith being fired, she rises to a spirited defense of her wronged friend, barging into Mukherjee's office and flinging down her own letter of resignation, as a protest, on his table. Her actions reflect a oneness with Edith, necessitated by their oppressed positions in Indian society. This is affirmed by Ray's carefully constructed mise-en-scène: All intimate confidences between these two women are exchanged, we note, within the office's protected sanctum of the "ladies' restroom" and, most revealingly, before the mirror above the washbasin. When we see Arati receiving her first paycheck, for example, Ray endorses her narcissism by having her rush straight into the restroom, where the first person to whom she shows her hard-earned money is her own virtual image in the mirror. She is proud of herself, and this gesture adds to her self-esteem. She compliments herself, knowing that very few or none will be forthcoming at home.

At this moment, Arati's actual image (before the mirror) and her virtual image (in the mirror) conjoin and peak: Her virtual image as the successful professional woman becomes actual via the mirror. In Deleuzean terms, when this exchange takes place, Arati's actual image becomes "visible and limpid." She is proud of its visibility and limpidity, and Ray's presentation clearly shows her acknowledging this to herself. When Arati's actual image becomes virtual in its turn, however, what Ray makes us see in that mirror are Arati's "opaque and shadowy" features that help her to sustain her autonomy as a woman and fight the patriarchal order.[35] It is precisely these attributes, facilitated by the exchange, that reaffirms Arati's narcissism and clearly upsets her family and her boss, who do *not* want Arati's domestic Hindu image to undergo any radical metamorphosis. Her narcissism is not merely self-oriented or of a passive kind, however; it extends itself to purposeful action as well.

It is once again in this restroom, before this mirror, that Arati encounters the weeping Edith after she has been fired. Edith's first reaction to Arati is, "Oh Arati, what will I tell my boyfriend? He'll kill me." It is not her widowed mother (with whom Edith lives) about whom she is worried, but her boyfriend: He will be scandalized by the shattering of her virtual image as the successful saleswoman and antiestablishment activist; he will reject her, she feels, in her actual image as the unemployed and disgraced "fired" employee. For Edith, the "exchange" augments her victimization and clearly reveals to us the masculine myopia of her own Anglo–Indian community as well.

Arati, on the other hand, doesn't even think of her own family when she charges into the office of her Bengali boss and demands an immediate "apology" from him for his disgraceful behavior with Edith. Subrata, Arati's husband, has recently lost his job at the bank, and the whole family is being supported by her. Despite these pressing circumstances, Arati lays her own job on the line, and when her arrogant boss hints to her that he will brook no further intimidation from *any* of his saleswomen, Arati promptly resigns before he can have the satisfaction of firing her too. She remains faithful to her feminine bond with Edith, over and above her own familial bonding – a bold and an unusual step for a Hindu woman to take, both outside and inside the traditional Hindu patriarchal courtyard.

In Ray's 1984 *Ghare-Baire* (*The Home and the World*), Bimala's widowed sister-in-law similarly acts as a contrapuntal mirror image of bonding for Bimala (until the film's final scene, when Bimala herself has to embrace widowhood). Widowed at a very early age by a dissipated husband, the sister-in-law, Gopa, has been forced by the strict codes of Hinduism to forgo all claims to feminine embellishments like jewelry, colored clothes, and perfume. Ostracized from any real mirror – a Hindu widow is forbidden even to *look* at, let alone scrutinize, her own image in the glass, lest old passions of vanity and pride be stirred up – the elder woman makes repeated attempts to reflect her former actual self in the younger's virtual one – an "exchange" in which she could actualize the joys of her own eros vicariously through Bimala. In return she tries to share her few happy memories with this younger "self," offering her all kinds of salacious gossip, sexual tips, and intimate woman-to-woman chatter; but Bimala, completely engrossed in satisfying, through her own "exchange," her husband's virtual image of her, indifferently rejects this bonding, replacing it cruelly by her own rituals of constant narcissism before her own bedroom mirror.

The only "mirror" left for the unfortunate widow is her own memory. In one moving scene, Ray slowly zooms in on her actualized widowed presence. Ray shows her clutching Bimala's bedpost quite suggestively, reminiscing about the limited joys of her own unfulfilled eros, while Bimala fusses with her own virtual presence before the mirror in the background as she awaits the evening's lovemaking with her spouse. What Ray does in this memorable scene is point to the denouement, which is reached through what Gilles Deleuze refers to as "the principle of indiscernibility." At the end of the film, when Bimala is prematurely widowed, she too is reduced to the same actual image of the woman as widow – the bonding that she resisted is thrust upon her. The two women's prewidowhood virtual images also get locked in a similar resemblance, thereby completing the bonding framework to which Bimala and her sister-in-law will, through the passage of time, ultimately resign themselves.

In *Ashani Sanket* (*Distant Thunder*), Ray's 1973 film, the bonding that occurs between Ananga (the wife of Gangacharan, the Brahmin priest) and the jolly Chutki, a local peasant woman, is clearly an attempt by the women to assert their superiority over the men with whom they share their lives. Ananga is the typical submissive Brahmin wife, feeding her husband's arrogance and appetite as a dutiful Hindu wife is expected to do. She cooks his meals, washes his clothes, prepares the coals for his hookah, rubs his feet, satiates his libido, and never questions any of his actions, whims, or demands. Still, without her presence, as Ray pointedly shows us, Gangacharan could never survive: Ananga is the only person to whom he can turn during the famine, when the whole village isolates him. At the end of the film, when she opens the gates of her house to welcome the neighboring Brahmin's family, she chooses this precise moment to convey to her husband that she is expecting their first child. This gesture, heroic in itself, speaks of her conviction, not only as to enduring the famine but also to facing the future confidently in spite of there being so many mouths to feed. This optimism is also reflected in Chutki: In the midst of the famine, when she gives herself sexually to Jadu, the hideously scarred kiln worker, for a bagful of rice, one thinks Ray is out to portray her as an exploited woman of her time. However, when we see her attempting to build some sort of redeeming relationship with that frightened and angry young man, whose burned face has made him a social pariah and an Untouchable in the eyes of the other villagers, we see her displaying the same kind of courage and confidence that Ananga shows with her husband. Chutki's intuitive acceptance of her deformed lover as a whole human being who needs human love, care, and compassion is similar to Ananga's acceptance of another starving and homeless family in addition to her own child and husband. Both women will sustain their men and their families in the best of times and in the worst of times.

Ashani Sanket opens with a close-up of sunlight reflected on the surface of a smooth sheet of water. As the camera directs our gaze to the water's limpid surface, we become aware of a human hand slowly rising from below, then quickly breaking through the surface. Focusing on the hand as it now plays sensuously with the water, Ray slowly pulls the camera

Figure 11. The actual and virtual presences of Ananga (Babita) via her hand playing sensuously with the water in Ashani Sanket *(Distant Thunder, 1973). (Photo by Nemai Ghosh; gift of Ben Nyce)*

back to reveal Ananga, whose hand it is. The two actions of her hand that we have just witnessed – playing with and breaking through the water – imply the actual and virtual presences of Ananga [Fig. 11]. She can sustain and delight, and she can break through and survive. The same qualities are extended also to Chutki.

Once again Ray makes luminous Deleuze's principle of indiscernibility. Using Deleuze's terms, Ananga shines with the "visible and limpid" light of wisdom in face of the impending darkness of the oncoming famine; but Chutki's actions, while making her withdraw into an "opaque" life with her hideously scarred lover and be pushed into performing "obscure" tasks, "become more like faith as in an Augustianian 'illumination.'"[36] Both women confront their environment with what Deleuze defines as "the internal disposition of a seed" that promises for each in life or in death a singular victory.[37]

The Ray Woman's Politics of Silence

When the Indian woman is victimized by male cowardice and treachery, she feels ultimately consigned to a domain of silence. Here, she is forced to employ silence as a desperate strategy to defeat a garrulous and selfish Indian phallocentric domination. Ray's heroine, Karuna, in the 1965 film sketch "Kapurush" ("The Coward," part of the diptych *Kapurush-o-Mahapurush* [*The Coward and the Holy Man*]), speaks to us from the center of a silence into which she has been consigned by a male conspiracy. The silence that she emblematizes can accurately be categorized by what the French writer and filmmaker Marguerite Duras defined in an interview in *Signs* (1975), where she talked of the darkness and silence that have enveloped women living in a male-dominated culture for centuries: "Behind men, there is distortion of reality, there are lies. . . . The silence in women is such that anything that falls into it has an enormous reverberation."[38] Ray presents Karuna's victimization at the hands of her lover, Amitabha, in a flashback insert. Amitabha had loved Karuna once very much but, bowing to family pressures, he had callously abandoned her and conveniently disappeared from her life. Now Amitabha, as a successful screenwriter stranded one evening in a small tea-plantation town in Assam (where he has gone to collect material for a new script), is befriended by Bimal Gupta, a local tea-estate owner, and invited to spend the night in his home. There, Amitabha is shocked to confront Karuna as his host's wife. (Her name is significant: As we saw in Chapter 1, *karuna* is one of the nine *rasas* in classical Indian aesthetics and denotes *sorrow* or *compassion*.) As Amitabha learns more about Bimal, he realizes that this marriage is not a happy one for Karuna. Irresistibly attracted to her all over again, Ray's camera fixes him, tossing and turning in his bed later that night, unable to sleep (the aforementioned flashback occurs here), so Karuna gives him a bottle of sleeping pills. The next day, the three go on a picnic. When Bimal falls asleep, Amitabha scrawls a hasty note to Karuna: "I will wait for you at the railway station. If you still love me, come. I won't let you down this time." In the evening, as the hour of his departure nears, he waits impatiently for her. When Karuna does turn up, he feels relieved, but his triumph is short-lived: She has come only to retrieve the bottle of sleeping pills she had lent him the previous night.

Karuna's strength is expressed conspicuously through Ray's visual style and the dominance he bestows on her over the two men by his artful arrangement of the three characters in his mise-en-scène. Our first view of Karuna occurs when Bimal ushers Amitabha into the living room of his opulent bungalow. Karuna is positioned very close to the camera, facing us; her back is to the two men shown diminutively in the back of the frame. The agony on her face is clearly displayed for us: Both of these men (placed strategically by Ray before the entranceway) have caused her pain. As she turns around, the grief on her face is quickly replaced by a mask of cool indifference. Amitabha senses this, and we can see the cowardice in him making him retreat as Karuna slowly advances across the room and pretends to be introduced to him by her blustering husband.

In another scene, as the two ex-lovers find themselves alone in a mise-en-scène from which the husband is momentarily absent, Ray positions Karuna in the center of the frame under an archlike awning, standing on the threshold between the hall and the dining room; Amitabha is positioned further right in the foreground, closer to the camera. Nothing is said. Karuna, dressed in a striped *sari*, looks over her shoulder penetratingly at Amitabha. Amitabha, dressed in a striped shirt, cannot return her gaze. He bows his head and looks down *away* from her to the left-hand side of the frame.

Her silent gaze is made quite eloquent here by her strategic positioning in the mise-en-scène: The arch above her head suggests a wedding stage. The threshold points to the kind of marriage into which Amitabha's cowardly action has pushed her. The striped *sari* enunciates her joyless and caged condition. The surrounding emptiness metonymically reminds him of her empty day-to-day existence. All of these are collected in Karuna's gaze and flung back at her cowardly lover, who acknowledges his defeat before her by bowing his head. No words are needed to articulate her domination.

In the scenes featuring the three of them together, eating at the dining table or relaxing in the living room, Ray has Bimal occupy the center of the frame, with Karuna and Amitabha on either side of him. At the dining table, all three characters are dressed in stripes: Bimal's shirt and Karuna's *sari* have large black and white stripes; Amitabha's shirt has gray ones. Bimal is facing us. Unaware of the tension between the two, he entertains Amitabha lavishly, not only with a generous spread of food and drink but also with long, tiresome monologues in which only he himself figures prominently. The same performance is repeated later in the living room. This time, Ray has Bimal in the center, with his back to us, but that does not stop him from talking endlessly about himself. He thinks he's truly at the center, the life and soul of the party, but in reality he is not: He is merely an obstacle. We are more interested in Karuna and Amitabha, who, while offering Bimal the customary polite verbal responses, seem to converse tacitly and tensely through him [Fig. 12]. In the latter scene, Ray cunningly places a telephone near Amitabha, but there is little or no communication here: Each individual, trapped in his or her own cell, is just playing the role of host, hostess, or guest. Bimal's words are like the empty ticking of the clock: They help to pass the time; nothing more. The di-

Figure 12. The dialectic between Karuna's (Madhabi Mukherjee) and Amitabha's (Soumitra Chatterjee) silence and Bimal's (Haradhan Banerjee) garrulity in Kapurush-o-Mahapurush (The Coward and the Holy Man, 1965). *(Photo by Nemai Ghosh; gift of Ben Nyce)*

alectic between words and wordlessness – between man, who uses words, and woman, who protects herself from them with an armor of silence – is now set into motion and brilliantly explored by Ray.

Although Karuna plays the perfect hostess to her ex-lover, and makes no effort to hide her marital unhappiness from him, she does not encourage Amitabha, in any way, to repeat the past. Through Karuna's determined adoption of silence, Ray shows how a feminine crisis can be movingly expressed without verbalization – which, given the phallocentric Indian culture, would permit (as Kaplan puts it) only "male articulation, functioning, and understandings."[39] Both Amitabha and Bimal are obsessed with words. Amitabha is a scriptwriter, and it is his profession to seduce the audience with words. One is reminded of Eve Kendall's evaluation of advertising executive Roger Thornhill's verbal facilities in Hitchcock's *North by Northwest:*

EVE: You're very clever with words. You can probably make them do
anything for you . . . sell people things they don't need . . . make women
who don't know you fall in love with you?

Bimal is a typical, garrulous, Bengali *boxwallah* (Indian peddler of British
goods), obsessed with his own sweet smell of success. He loves to talk endlessly about himself, and his self-obsession excludes his wife Karuna, who
is ignored not only verbally but also visually. Amitabha's presence is thus
crucial for Bimal, who can finally talk about his success to another successful man, who he feels will acknowledge it. All his remarks are therefore addressed to Amitabha; at no point is any reference made to Karuna.
A happily married man would include his spouse, even when speaking of
himself; thus Bimal's talking *only* of himself, and only to another man, indicates a need to break the stifling boredom he feels is characteristic of his
marriage. (Further indications as to the failure of love between Bimal and
Karuna are two notable absences: the absence of family and the absence
of children. Amitabha becomes another painful reminder of the failure of
romance, especially for Karuna, as is clear in the scene in which, left alone
with him, she stares at Amitabha silently from the threshold.)

In the presence of such male talkers, Karuna says very little; but when
she does verbalize, a phrase or two is enough to undermine the privileged
male source and speaker. For instance, Amitabha asks her for "two sleeping pills," but she gives him the entire bottle. When he jokingly asks her
what would happen if he chose to take "more than two," she mockingly
affirms for him that "you won't." The implication, here, is that he is too
much of a coward to commit suicide out of guilt for trapping her in this
loveless marriage.

In the end, when Karuna comes to the station and silently asks for her
bottle of sleeping pills, it suddenly dawns on Amitabha that she *could*, one
day, take an overdose and kill herself! Her silent request is no gimmick;
it completely disorients Amitabha, who, visibly stricken, dumbly gives her
the bottle. Karuna's silence is shown triumphing over the oppression of
Amitabha's language and rekindled passion, so patriarchally exposed in
his arrogantly written message, "If *you* still love *me*, come. *I* won't let *you*
down, this time" (emphasis added). His words have failed to overpower
her into submission. When Karuna now resists his discourse at the railway station, Amitabha is shown becoming disconcerted and uncertain.
There is fear etched on his face as we see the train taking him away.

During the earlier picnic scene, Ray shows Karuna adopting the same
determined silence and deliberately avoiding the gazes of both husband
and ex-lover. She refuses to look at them; in fact, she masks her gaze by

wearing a pair of dark glasses. She sits alone on the rocks with her back usually toward them. She refuses even to take part in the men's conversation. Ray here creates a boundary between his heroine and the two men, his camera clearly emphasizing the separation between Karuna's inner world and the two men's outer one. Moreover, we see her in the picnic scene wearing the same striped *sari*, whose vertical lines suggestively codify her as a woman trapped in her femininity by the cruel patronage of a lover in her past and a husband in the present. Silence, then seems to be her only voice, her only defense against domination.

The Ray Woman as Hedonist

Aware of the kind of silence just described, the Ray men often feel the women exercising a palpable threat. Sudhir Kakar pinpoints this threat accurately:

Underlying the conscious ideal of womanly purity, innocence, and fidelity . . . is a secret conviction among many Hindu men that the feminine principle is really the opposite – treacherous, lustful, and rampant with an insatiable, contaminating sexuality.[40]

This fear is generated especially by the woman who refuses to be selfless, acts on her own initiative, and is determined to reject all the submissive roles patriarchy has reserved for her. This makes us arrive at the hedonistic or individual level on which the Ray women are now shown to be functioning. Ray endorses their threatening capacity in very interesting ways, especially through his portrayal of the tribal women – Duli and her sisters in his 1970 film *Aranyer Din Ratri (Days and Nights in the Forest)* and the two upper-class Bengali women, Aparna and her widowed sister-in-law Jaya, in the same film.

Although Duli and her tribal feminine group in *Aranyer Din Ratri* are considered, in the local caretaker's words, to be "dirty women," all the men – the locals as well as our educated Calcutta group of Ashim, Sanjoy, Hari, and Shekar – *fear* them. They are very uncomfortable when these dusky, scantily clad, overtly sensual tribal amazons deliberately articulate their power over them by boldly drinking the country hooch with them at the predominantly male local bar. When Shekar invites them to the bungalow to perform slavish domestic chores, the men, though enjoying this opportunity of sustained voyeurism, still feel uneasy as these half-naked women, conscious of the men's unease, dust, clean, and work the primitive overhead fan with arrogantly inviting motions and gestures.

Duli, the tribal group's acknowledged leader, is the source of these primitive women's power. Her threat to the men is expressed visually, both in the iconic way in which Ray presents her and through his visual style. Duli's iconography, as it were, is explicitly sexual: Her dark skin glows with sexual hunger. She wears no blouse, and her white *sari* is draped quite provocatively around her long-limbed body. She is tall and moves playfully as an uninhibited child of nature. When she walks, men stop and stare. When she talks, she stares brazenly at the men. When she sweeps the men's rooms she immediately becomes the compositional focus for all male eyes. As she moves from foreground to background, she directs and controls the lounging men's gazes. She has no desire to pull any shades over her self-induced exhibitionism. Shekar appropriately calls her "Miss India," but when she threatens to come close and drink with him in the local male-oriented bar, he panics and runs away.

The "memory game" that the men play with Aparna and Jaya later in the film conveys very clearly the threat that the *sophisticated* Tripathi women can unleash on the Indian male as opposed to those of which *primitive* women like Duli are capable. The game is one of the film's most important satellite events. The series of names of famous people that each participant selects to baffle and test the retentive memory of his or her opponent has two implications: First, it enunciates the degree to which each man or woman is determined to win, lose, or surrender. Second, the names chosen become, without the characters realizing it, important indices of their own secret yearnings and threats. In staging this game as a crucial battle between the sexes, then, Ray points very suggestively to the forging of subsequent relationships in which pairs of these men and women will find themselves playing out more disturbing and painful erotic games.

Ashim, the men's champion, immediately finds his authority threatened by Aparna's "phenomenal memory" (which, as Jaya constantly reiterates to the male players, "has never lost, not even once"). Aparna is always inclined toward famous people known for their aggressive personalities, such as Cleopatra and Bobby Kennedy. (When Aparna says, "Kennedy," a furious Ashim demands, "Which Kennedy?" Aparna coyly responds, "Why, Bobby of course!") Ashim contemptuously retaliates with names of famous individuals such as Shakespeare and Mumtaz Mahal: He wants to prove to Aparna that his ideal woman is not one who, like Cleopatra, created infidelities but rather one who had one of the wonders of the world, the Taj Mahal, consecrated to her as a divine monument of love. For Aparna, however, the threat that Cleopatra posed to Caesar and Antony, who were willing to set the world on fire for her, seems much more fulfilling than mere monuments of love being dedicated by a powerful king like Shah Jehan to his queen. As the contest narrows between the two, we see that Ashim is struggling with his powers of memory, which seem to be flagging with every successive round, whereas Aparna seems to grow more confident and combative. When she does concede defeat to Ashim, she does so deliberately so that he is not humiliated in public. When, later in the film, Ashim privately confesses his attraction toward her, he admits to being glad that she deliberately let him win the name game and not lose face before his male friends, whose acknowledged leader he is.

Although Aparna poses a serious threat to Ashim in the game, she is also portrayed by Ray as a very nurturing woman. When we first see her, she is not eager to meet with the city men in her pastoral retreat. She is aloof and lost in her own thoughts. Ray shows her occupying a separate place in the mise-en-scène. We see her visually passive and static. Ashim is instantly attracted to her, and when Aparna, on her father's instructions, is asked to show him her own private room in the guesthouse, Ashim is delighted by her choice of literature and music he finds there. Gradually she reveals to him her isolation and aloofness from the world. It comes from her internalized mourning for the poignant double loss she has suffered – her brother's (Jaya's deceased husband) death by suicide and her mother's in a fire.

It is when she makes these known to Ashim that she articulates her very first threat: "You haven't really suffered, have you?" she asks him point-blank. Aparna then sets out to puncture Ashim's thoughtlessness and arrogance, reminding him how his actions of moving into the bungalow without prior notification nearly cost the poor local caretaker his job. To reaffirm his selfishness, she takes him to that poor man's quarters, behind the bungalow, and forces Ashim to observe the filth and squalor of the surroundings, in the midst of which lies the caretaker's sick wife and wailing hungry children.

However, she also chooses to integrate Ashim from his alienated position. This is done imagistically by Ray when he links her to the wide open spaces of nature as opposed to the caretaker's space, which was narrow, dark, and full of threatening overtones. Her measured walk, gloomy face, and overall controlled presence is temporarily abandoned when Aparna suddenly spies a beautiful deer in the foliage. She is shown responding to it like a child, clapping her hands, jumping up and down, her face and voice erupting in a memorable visual and aural affirmation of "look, look, a deer!"

The same joyousness occurs twice more, though these instances are articulated as the second and third threats to Ashim. The second happens when her father's car, with her and Jaya in it, accidentally intrudes into the masculine space of our urbanized males trying to bathe with cold water, outdoors near the bungalow, dressed in their underwear. Hari quickly dives for cover behind the well, but poor Ashim soaping his half-naked torso is caught in the full laughing stares of the two women in the car. The third intrusion also occurs accidentally, when the headlights of Aparna's car, returning late in the night from a nearby outing, pin a drunken Ashim doing "a tribal twist" on the highway.

The memory game concludes the threats, but as the two reevaluate the game after Aparna pretends to lose to Ashim, we see Ashim accepting his redemption from her. He realizes his lack in her presence, and after she has confirmed these lacks, he wants to be made whole by her. His position is very similar to that of Arindam in *Nayak*, and both men are grateful, as Ray shows us, to these quiet formidable young women in putting them back on their feet again.

Meanwhile, the first two to be (quickly) eliminated from the memory game were the two ignorant male characters – Hari, the cricketer (who can think only of cricketers' names), and Shekar, the hanger-on. Quick-tempered, rash, and still licking his wounds after having been rejected by Atasi, his sophisticated Calcutta girlfriend, Hari has declared war on the female sex. Constantly tongue-tied and clumsy before Aparna and Jaya, he finally gets back at women by having a quick sexual encounter in the forest with the only female who seems to suit his outcast position – the tribal woman, Duli. Even here, however, his suggestion to Duli that she would look much better if she wore a wig (as had Atasi) indicates how threatened he feels by Duli's raw and primitive tribal appearance. Shekar, on the other hand, comes through as an asexual character not really interested in women. The only names he can come up with are those of crooked politicians like Atulaya Ghosh, racehorses on which he regularly loses a lot of money, and Helen of Troy, since Duli (his "Miss India") reminds him of her.

Sanjoy, the trade-union leader of the group, comes up with the appropriately referential names of Mao Tse-Tung and Karl Marx, whereas the likable Jaya (who is the first person to be declared "out" in the game) chortles with delight at remembering the missed name of Shakespeare, whose omission gets Sanjoy "out." This ostentatious young widow's tabs on Sanjoy's progress in the game (at one moment she even tries to prompt him) alerts him to her consuming interest in him. Sanjoy reciprocates by insisting that he go indoors and get her some pillows. After he collects his pillows from his room, we see the normally shy Sanjoy suddenly stop before a mirror and straighten out a fallen lock of hair. He knows he has become the object of this sensual "Cleopatra's" gaze, and, like a transformed "Antony" he hurries toward his queen to make her comfortable. However, when she later confronts him at her cottage, attired in full bridal array, her blatant sexual overtures (stemming from her premature widowhood and deprived eros) completely shatter poor Sanjoy. The outdoors game between him and Jaya is revealed to be not that innocent after all. Her preparation for this decisive indoors moment and his trembling rejection of her shows the extent to which both are victims of their stifling, upper- and middle-class, Hindu moralities, in which contaminated games of passion are not expected to be expressed or played out.

With extraordinary directness, Ray portrays Jaya's unrepressed sexual desires and Sanjoy's repressive response that destroys them. Ray inscribes Jaya's dominating presence potently through the sharply lighted signifiers of her heavily made-up face; the bridal jewelry with which she is adorned; her palpitating and heated presence in a deliberately darkened room; and a yearning that arches between a playful need for tactile consummation and a desperate one. Sanjoy freezes. He is petrified when Jaya takes his shaking hand and forcibly places it on her heaving chest. The ugly residue of cream that films over his cup of coffee becomes, as Ray's camera slowly pans over it, the metonymic extension of that false, carefree, cheerful persona behind which the grieving widow concealed her eros. She is, in metaphorical terms, willing to play Cleopatra; but he is not willing to play Antony.

In his 1977 film *Shatranj-ke-Khilari (The Chess Players)*, Ray goes a step further to valorize the Indian woman's threat, which becomes the only means by which the *nawab* (aristocrat) Mirza's wife, Khurshid, can entice her chess-obsessed husband into her *zenana*, or boudoir. In one poignant scene, we see Khurshid feigning a severe migraine attack in her bedroom to gain the attention of her husband, who is outside playing chess with his perpetual opponent and fellow *nawab*, Mir. Mirza reluctantly leaves to attend to his *begum* (wife; literally, a Muslim woman of rank), warning his opponent not to change the position of the pawns in his temporary absence. Once inside the bedroom, Mirza's wife attempts, but fails, to seduce him. Her sexual aggressiveness shocks her husband to such an extent that he fails to reciprocate and is unable to perform the act of coitus. In a stunning reversal of sexual *positions,* Ray shows Khurshid forc-

ing her husband to lie down with her above him. We see her taking the
"masculine" initiative of unbuttoning his clothes while he lies prone and
dazed. Unable to elicit any sexual response, Khurshid releases him, sits
on the bed, and looks away. The stupid ivory pieces on the chessboard
have absorbed all her husband's vital sexual juices, and she will have to
work extra hard to revive them in him. The only way she'll be able to do
this is by using her body as the appropriate site of sexual pleasure. Ray
makes her determination all the more sensuously Scheherazadean when
she calls for her servant Hiria and demands that the old woman come and
tell her a story. When she insists, "I want to stay awake all night," she
makes it clear to her departing husband that she will try again to ignite
his dormant sexual fires.

Later, a parallel scenario is marvelously manifested by Ray, this time
to enunciate Mir's cuckolding at the hands of his wife, Nafeesa. She has
gone some steps further than Khurshid and, in Mir's absence, has acquired
his nephew Aquil as her lover. What Charulata hoped to do with Amal,
but could not, is done by Nafeesa. Thus, we can see how far the Ray
woman has come in her determination to free herself. On one occasion,
when Mir actually surprises the pair in his bedroom, Nafeesa coolly informs her husband that Aquil is a refugee who does not want to enlist in
the king's army and, since he had rushed into her room a few minutes ago,
she was hiding him from the soldiers who were looking for him outside
– a story that this chess-obsessed *nawab* accepts unquestioningly. We see,
very clearly, how the threats of both wives are legitimized by Ray in the
film: In the first case, Khurshid is forced to feign a migraine to win her
husband's sexual favors. In the second, Nafeesa is forced to cheat because
her husband has no sexual favors left to offer her. Moreover, since both
stratagems have led to masculine impotence, the men, Ray seems to be
saying, are no longer entitled to enjoy their patriarchal roles as *nawabs*
(lords) of their *jagirs* (lands) *or* of their *begums* (wives)! Finally, if a lover
like Aquil can enter his uncle's wife's bedroom and conquer her, why can't
the British enter and conquer this kingdom, given the impotence of the
city's elite male aristocracy?

Concluding Remarks: In Praise of Satyajit Ray's Feminist Stance

Western feminists, like critic Toril Moi, despise the effort made by men to
speak out in women's defense: "Since this is precisely what the ventrilo-
quism of patriarchy has always done: Men have constantly spoken for
women, or in the name of women."[41] But India needs artists like Ray,

since the country still exercises in the man–woman contract what French feminist Hélène Cixous defines as "[t]he insistence on the proper, or a proper return, [which] leads to the masculine obsession with classification, systematization and hierarchization."[42] I have tried to show in this chapter how Ray's feminist stance has placed him against what Cixous calls "the pervasive [Indian] masculine urge to judge, diagnose, digest, name." Since in her view this realm is built on the male fear of castration, Cixous concludes that it is expected that "[e]verything return to the masculine. . . . If a man spends and is spent, [for example,] it's on condition that his power returns."[43] Ray, however, will *not allow* that return. He wants the Indian women to fracture this unjust economy because it clearly functions only for men's advantage, allowing women to be deprived and stripped of their identity. The traditional Indian woman's "ideal self" being expected to "give" in the spirit of self-sacrifice (see the opening section), Moi writes:

in the Realm of the Proper, the gift is perceived (ironically) as establishing an inequality – difference – threatening in that it seems to open up an imbalance of power. Thus, the act of giving [as seen from the male point-of-view) becomes a subtle means of aggression, of exposing the other to the threat of one's own superiority.[44]

But as I have shown, in Ray's films the women *do give* in the true spirit of the *Gita,* that is, without a thought for the fruits or returns. The Ray woman, therefore, endorses Cixous's claim that their giving *is* from spontaneous generosity.

In the final analysis, it is fit to say that Satyajit Ray rescues his women by making them live in a state of authenticity, or what the existentialists called "good faith," in spite of being denied the right to their own subjectivity and responsibility for their actions. Simone de Beauvoir's celebrated utterance – "One is not born a woman; one becomes one" – accurately applies to the Indian woman. Still, there are those like Satyajit Ray, who give their women voices of their own in an effort to make them distinct, unique, and triumphant in this all-encompassing process of *becoming.* Ray's giving, too, is from spontaneous generosity, and not a subtle means of aggression.

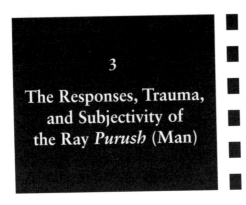

3

The Responses, Trauma, and Subjectivity of the Ray *Purush* (Man)

*To
Kironmoy Rahajee,
Gautam Kundu,
Narasingha "Ram" Sil, and
Suranjan Ganguly,
who have transcended all
traumas and define their
subjectivity authentically,
with grace, wisdom,
and dignity*

The Philosophical Determinant of Suffering and the Responses of the Ray *Purush:* Siddhartha's Response in *Pratidwandi* (1970)

Nirad Chaudhuri introduces us to three kinds of suffering in Hindu philosophy: "that which proceeds from the 'self'; that which comes from external sources, things or other living creatures; and that which is inflicted by supernatural agencies and acts of God."[1] We are concerned primarily with suffering of the first kind proceeding from the emotions of the self, which in Chaudhuri's definition include "lust, anger, greed, delusion, fear, envy, or sadness," and the suffering that results from "external courses which is of two kinds: that due to other living creatures or to inanimate things." The result of this suffering leads to a conspicuous "collapse of courage and vitality" of the protagonist "placed [very distinctly] in the secular order" of the Indian landscape in which he is shown as living and functioning.[2] Once this nadir is reached, in Hindu philosophical terms, he embraces what Chaudhuri defines as

the characteristic Hindu concept of *Tamas,* as the lowest of the *gunas* or attributes. The word *tamas* literally means darkness, but in Hindu thought and feeling it stands really for a very comprehensive term for all kinds of squalor – material, biological, intellectual, moral, and spiritual. Suffering in *tamas* was the Hindu hubris.[3]

One of the most conspicuous forms that *tamas*ic suffering takes is "frustration," which most of the Ray male protagonists exhibit, vocalize, or perpetuate in varying degrees depending on each one's hubris. Chaudhuri defines this frustration as *acedia* (spiritual torpor and apathy; ennui). He offers us two interesting variations: first, "acedia mingled with a more positive feeling – irritation and bad temper, which makes it a dangerously

134

active form of ennui." The modern Hindus, continues Chaudhuri, have made an addition to "this paralysis of the will . . . and supplemented the inertia with a continuous but *inactive* bad temper and a corrosive sense of grievance."[4]

In Ray's films, the Hindu home plays a major role in contributing to the male's acedic position. Chaudhuri characterizes the claustrophobic atmosphere of "a Hindu home as one of heavy and listless dullness, which drives the inmates out into the streets at all times of the day."[5] Ray's 1970 *Pratidwandi* (*The Adversary;* also known as *Siddhartha and the City*) clearly indicates the revelation of Siddhartha's male lack as a symptom of the larger Hindu acedic form of both active and inactive *tamasic* suffering of frustration. Siddhartha's acedia is revealed, in Kaja Silverman's words, as "a psychic wound that renders him incapable of functioning smoothly" outside in the city as well as indoors at home.[6]

Siddhartha's trauma and dislocation is visually conveyed through the opening scene, in which his father's untimely death is graphically portrayed – shot completely in negative. As Siddhartha stands brooding before his father's funeral pyre, the camera zooms in on him, and his image slowly becomes positive. The formal insistence on the negative inscribes the stress point in Siddhartha's present condition: His father's death forces him to abandon his botanical studies and take up immediate employment. Dislodged from his own position in the family as the eldest son, he has now to replace the dead father and look for a job in a city that becomes, with every step and turn, a powerful adversary. Returning home at the end of every frustrating day offers no solace either, since home reveals its own rivalry. Mercilessly caught between the city and home, Siddhartha's lack becomes a convincing exhibit offered by Ray as a contemporary display of male Hindu castration.

The two interview scenes in the film function as (borrowing Silverman's categories here) important suppliers of paternal representations and orchestrate for Siddhartha the projection so necessary to break through his privatized sense of male trauma, thereby leading to his gradual recovery of his sense of personal potency.[7]

In the first interview scene, Ray portrays Siddhartha as a humanist who stands up for his own principles. His assessment of the moon landing as being a less important historical event than the Vietnam War, and his admiration for primitive Vietnamese resistance over the capitalistic technology of moon buggies and astronauts brands him instantaneously as a "communist" in the eyes of the (paternal) interview board. This kind of radical thinking will persist in keeping him unemployed. He knows that, but he finds himself unable to change because of his prevalent "inertia," "continuous but inactive bad temper," and "corrosive sense of grievance" (Chaudhuri's words again) against the city and his home. At home he sees ambition nudging his attractive sister Sutapa to higher professional levels and a committed revolutionary zeal transforming his younger brother, Tunu, into a terrorist. Choked by Tunu's stinging criticism related to his own stasis – "you're still rotting away in the same spot, not doing anything" – Siddhartha plunges into the city, only to be met with the same circulation of disillusionment. Immersion in the air-conditioned comfort of a movie theater (ironically called The Lighthouse) is rudely shattered by the explosion of a bomb. An evening out with Adinath, a close college friend, gradually turns disastrous: Siddhartha is appalled to see Adinath stealing money from a Red Cross donation can. When Adinath offers him the triple delights of a Chinese meal, a glass of whiskey, and a Florence Nightingale daytime nurse moonlighting as a nighttime whore, Siddhartha refuses and walks out on him. His disgust, however, is cruelly undermined by Adinath's cynicism – "You, brother, are a thinker. Me, I'm a doer" – thereby implying that if Siddhartha has to make something of himself in this city, he will have to change.

In Chaudhurian terms, his acedia "will *have* to be mingled with a more active feeling of irritation and bad temper . . . a dangerously active form of ennui," and Ray presents us precisely with these symptoms in the film's second interview sequence. In fact Siddhartha is made to see his *former* state of inertia in all its passivity during this explosive event. Appalled by his submissiveness, he erupts like a volcano.

Seventy-one young men – all job aspirants – conglomerate under three ceiling fans. The applicants are shown sweating profusely from both heat and nervousness. Only one fan works; its irritating gnawing sound adds to the tension. As Ray's camera tracks past these traumatized males, it picks out one candidate who doesn't seem to fit in. Whereas most of the men, including Siddhartha, are dressed casually in bush shirt and trousers, this one is decked out in proper interview attire (suit, tie) and carries his papers confidently and officially. While the others slump, look out of the corridor balcony, clutch at handkerchiefs, and whisper (some indulge in wishful thinking: Maybe this suited candidate has a stammer?), he walks about calmly, his coat slung over his shoulder.

Siddhartha's acedia, which has borne all of these images and sounds with an inactive bad temper and corrosive sense of grievance, plunges into action when one of the candidates faints. Siddhartha leads a group into the main interview room to ask for more chairs. Not only is his request denied, but his name and number are quickly taken in case he causes further intrusions.

As he awaits his turn outside, Ray positions Siddhartha between two signs in English behind him on the corridor wall: "Strikers" and "Nonstrikers." Now occurs a powerful subjective shot that epitomizes what the ancient Hindu moralists, in Nirad Chaudhuri's scathing phrases, had discovered:

a mental state which was paralysed rather than irritated. They called it *Klaivya*, which meant impotence in the physiological sense . . . and was afterwards employed to cover all forms of mental inertia. This paralysis of will is universal among modern Hindus. . . .[8]

As Siddhartha looks down the corridor, he sees all the applicants, except for the suited candidate, as skeletons. The skeletal metamorphosis powerfully inscribes the physical and mental paralysis infecting all the waiting jobseekers – and provides Siddhartha with a reflection of his own Hindu *klaivya*. When the interviewing committee callously calls for a lengthy lunch break, Siddhartha's acedia undergoes a dangerous transformation. Full of irritation, bad temper, and positive feelings of protest, he storms into the committee room and proceeds to wreck all the phallic signifiers: He overturns the desk and throws a chair at the officials, says "I want an answer" (in English), refuses to be "treated like an animal," and smashes a desk lamp. He storms of the room, out of the corridor, into the snarling city outside, and keeps on going. When we next catch up with him, Siddhartha is on a train. He has taken a job as a small-town pharmaceutical salesman and is leaving the city for the country. His loss of belief in the family is ultimately compensated by his loss of big-city life, in which the adequacy of his maleness was always found wanting.

Throughout the film we see Siddhartha, defeated by his entrapment in the city and in his house, constantly escaping into his inner space. Ray visualizes this space as a deliberately created imaginary site into which Siddhartha can withdraw in order to strengthen and reaffirm his desire to abandon the familiar, which revolves around his home and the urban world of Calcutta. Ray intimately renders his antagonist's predicament by shooting over Siddhartha's shoulders as he urgently pounds the pavements of his city looking for a job. The hand-held camerawork not only immerses Siddhartha in crowded, overwhelming Calcutta but ironically also sharply pulls him back, so that relief comes only when the real is replaced by the imaginary.

Several scenes bear testimony to his predilection to turn inward. Just before his first interview, Siddhartha discovers a prominent tear in his pants. As he waits at the tailors, we suddenly see him occupying a different position in his self-imposed imaginary mise-en-scène: He is standing in a botanical garden, well attired in suit and tie, gazing pensively at the plants and flowers around him. The ex-botany student, whose studies in reality had to be abruptly abandoned because of his father's sudden demise, wistfully sees himself in this fantasy as the successful botanist, a few years down the road – a position he now knows he can never attain.

The constant escape into the imaginary enables Ray to articulate Siddhartha's acceptance of his castration, which is metamorphosed in his first nightmare. There he sees a guillotine being ominously drawn upward by a pair of muscular, hairy arms over his head, which is placed below it on the chopping block. The falling blade and the sickening splash of blood jerks the sleeping Siddhartha into wakefulness. Feverish and agitated, he is further shown disturbed by the raucous mating howls of the neighborhood cats. Hurling an old slipper to silence them, he falls asleep and soon has a new nightmare in which negative-shot images collide uneasily with positive ones in a strange surreal dream landscape wherein he sees himself primarily as a witness. Along a deserted shoreline, he sees members of his interviewing board (in negative) sitting behind a long table on which stand fetuses soaking in bottles. As the panning camera simulates Siddhartha's continuing dream gaze, the images slowly become positive to reveal, in succession: his sister Sutapa modeling and surrounded by a lot of men; a firing squad getting ready to execute his terrorist brother Tunu; a mob attacking a car; and his girlfriend Keya's sudden appearance as a nurse running to help the dying Tunu, then looking up with astonishment.

Siddhartha's nightmare both condenses and displaces the series of events that he has recently experienced in his daily struggles with his home and city. His victimization by one interview committee is condensed as one more fetus aborted by this ruthless patriarchy etched in predominant negatives in his subconscious. Sutapa's dancing lessons and popularity with her male boss, while carving out a successful position as a model surrounded by men in his dream-projected evaluation, is displaced beside the fearful projection of his politically subversive brother embracing death and punishment at the hands of the city's police. The nurse and part-time whore from whom Siddhartha had contemptuously walked away is both displaced by and condensed into his girlfriend Keya; but she seems to be ministering to the wrong brother, reaffirming Siddhartha's isolation and estrangement from his loved ones. The waves pounding the shore in his nightmare offer him no positive horizon. Hence, his real-life substitution of the familiar horizon of Calcutta by the new and temporarily assigned horizon of Bihar, where his new job as a traveling pharmaceutical salesman is taking him.

Northrop Frye's category of the low-mimetic code of realistic fiction, it seems to me, fits Siddhartha's character and predicament precisely. According to Frye:

If superior neither to other men nor to his environment, [this] hero [becomes] one of us: we respond to a sense of his common humanity, and demand from the [author] the same canons of probability that we [would] find in our own experience.[9]

Frustrated and overwhelmed by a city that offers him bombs exploding in moviehouses, drugged hippies eulogizing emaciated cows [Fig. 13], a medical student pilfering Red Cross donations, nurses moonlighting as whores, a sister flirting with sin, and a brother playing at revolution, the only viable response Siddhartha can conceive is "a machine gun to clean it all up." However, when given the opportunity to put this violent aesthetic into practice, he finds he cannot do it. Siddhartha's protest, as Ray insists on showing us, is always carried out on an impersonal level because he is continuously assailed by doubts and inner conflicts that leave him in a confused state of rage and frustration.

As we have seen, Ray always portrays Siddhartha as hesitant, groping, and inarticulate. Two crucial scenes bring all these qualities to the fore. The first depicts him at the house of his sister's boss, Ananta Sanyal. Siddhartha has gone there with the ostensible purpose of thrashing the daylights out of him; but when Sanyal actually appears before him as a very dignified looking and confident man, Siddhartha feels ashamed and defensive. Ray portrays most of the elderly men in the film, like Sanyal, either as a threat to Siddhartha or as useless. Among the latter is Narishda, who repulses Siddhartha with his empty rhetoric of the generation gap when the younger man goes to him for a job. The only thing that Siddhartha finds redeeming about Narishda is his "wonderful voice," and when Ray films Narishda, he never shows us the character's face: Instead, we hear a mellifluous voice (which I suspect is the filmmaker's) castigating poor Siddhartha's jobless state of being (and Siddhartha, in a voice-over, expressing his repugnance to us).

Siddhartha's ineffectuality is once again signified at the apartment of the whore-nurse Latika. When she lights a cigarette and parades before him in a bra, Siddhartha's disgust is articulated by switching the entire scene into negative. The impersonality of such a sexual contract between him and this unknown woman, who poses a significant challenge not only to his virginal manhood but more pointedly to his conventional Hindu upbringing, makes him get up and leave the room abruptly.

The sequence that best brings out his inability to act, however, is the Mercedes Benz scene, which the British critic, Tom Milne, has described very eloquently:

Charging blindly in to join an angry mob bent on revenge against the glossy chauffeur-driven limousine which has just knocked down a little girl, Siddhartha stops dead in his tracks. Facing him is not the abstract mask of expression, but another frightened helpless child sobbing in the backseat.[10]

In Frye's terms, we are presented here with a hero whose weakness appeals to our sympathy because it is pitched at our own level of experience. We sympathize with Siddhartha's dilemma here since, like him, we are aware of our own divided and confused feelings of empathy and rage: first for the poor little girl knocked down by the car; and second for that rich little girl inside the car who will very shortly become the unfortunate victim of this angry mob once they have finished beating up the car's driver. When Siddhartha plunges into the mob, he becomes a part of that audience wanting to participate in their collective rage; but when the moment comes for him to bloody his hands with a victim, he withdraws. The potency of his protest is nullified by this withdrawal since the question of *who* is the greater victim in this sordid episode is difficult to ascertain for someone with his vacillating but sensitive temperament. Overwhelmed by Calcutta's merciless reality, which is determined by a social majority he can never accept but can only escape, Siddhartha does not cave in or retreat like Conrad's Lord Jim into a narcissistically created Patusan universe. In the film's later stages, Ray in fact shows his hero ascending the ladder from a low-mimetic to a higher-mimetic status.

In the last frames of the film, Ray shows Siddhartha listening to a bird's song and writing to Keya. Milne describes this "superb final sequence":

Having contrived to remain true to himself by making the quixotic gesture of protest which ensures that he will lose his chance of a foot in the door of success, Siddhartha is banished to a remote village and a dead-end job as a pharmaceutical salesman. In a sordid little room he settles down to write a love letter

Figure 13. Siddhartha Choudhury (Dhritiman Chatterjee): frustrated by a city that offers him no job but an emaciated cow in Pratidwandi (The Adversary, *1970*). *(Photo by Nemai Ghosh; gift of Ben Nyce)*

to Keya. "I don't expect to be happy here," he writes, "but my worries are nothing to yours, and they'll vanish when I get your letter." And outside, somewhere amid the rice fields and ox carts of his childhood, the mysterious bird sings again, a bridge across time and space.[11]

Siddhartha's gesture of protest at the second interview, which Milne calls "quixotic" – yet which Ray, in an interview with Christian Brand Thomsen, calls "a marvelous thing because it comes from inside and not as an expression of political ideology"[12] – finds its culmination both in the writing of that love letter to Keya and in the mysterious bird's song to which he is listening in the film's final shot. Writing the love letter is also an act of commitment, the *only* one that Siddhartha is capable of performing.

There is, however, a third component that Milne seems to have missed. As Siddhartha is writing the letter and listening to the bird, its song draws him out to the terrace, whence he hears a funeral chant and sees a dead body being carried to the cremation grounds. The text of the letter is spoken by Siddhartha on the sound track (while we see him in the process of writing it), and as he signs off with a "yours, Siddhartha" and turns to face the camera, the frame finally freezes. Metonymically, the dead body becomes the death of Siddhartha's past in anticipation of the future, to which this letter and the bird's song point. The letter itself becomes a new kind of regenerative song for Siddhartha and Keya. Whereas, in the past, the bird's song had cruelly reminded Siddhartha of his estrangement from Sutapa and Tunu, that song (which Siddhartha continues to hear as the film ends) now permeates the words of this letter, infusing them with hope. Inherent in the new situation is the realization that it is such letters, metaphorically enveloping the bird's song, that will enable Siddhartha and Keya to overcome all their familial and professional problems before they finally come together.

Throughout the film, Ray uses the tantalizing and unfamiliar song of the bird to enunciate Siddhartha's hesitant efforts to define his alienated self in relation to his family at home and to the troubled city itself. When, in Calcutta, Sutapa pulls him to the terrace to demonstrate her dancing lessons for him, he balances the overwhelming anguish he feels while watching the display of her emancipation by plunging into a memory in which a bird's song figures positively. Siddhartha and Sutapa were children then; we see them share the same joyous feeling of rapture as they listen to that mysterious song, one morning, in the countryside. While Siddhartha has retained that memory, Sutapa seems to have abandoned it. For Siddhartha, his sister's dancing lessons become, at this critical juncture of their relationship, a crude substitute, not only replacing the memory of that bird's song but also indicating just how far she has moved away from him in the present. A few minutes later, when Siddhartha tries and fails to communicate with his younger brother, Tunu, the gap between the two is enunciated through another bird from the past: As Siddhartha watches the politically committed and sullen Tunu bandage a wounded leg, he slips into a memory of how he and Tunu as children had, one day in the countryside, suddenly witnessed a hen's neck being cut by a peasant. While the sensitive Siddhartha had turned away, he remembers how Tunu had stood by him and watched the entire act without flinching or covering his face. "Do you remember that bird?" Siddhartha asks Tunu, suddenly coming out of his reverie. When Tunu's responds with a vague "What bird?" Siddhartha acknowledges the total obliteration of such a memory for someone like Tunu by saying, "No, you wouldn't." For a political revolutionary like Tunu, the deliberate erasure of the past is necessary; all that matters is complete dedication to the cause in which he is presently involved. In Tunu's guerilla imagination of bombs, Che Guevara, Marx, fists, and manifestos, the memory of a slit hen's neck would be an expression of sentimentality. Through such interchanges, Ray makes us realize Siddhartha's painful estrangement from the two people he loves very much. Siddhartha still retains that mysterious bird's song, and the only other person who can reaffirm its validity for him is Keya, the woman he now loves.

Keya's father is marrying her dead mother's sister, and Keya, in protest, has decided to leave Calcutta and continue her studies in Delhi. Siddhartha, as we've seen, has also left Calcutta by the film's end to work in the neighboring state of Bihar. Since it is in this rustic landscape that he is shown once again hearing that bird's song, the indication is clear that if he and Keya are to meet in some harmonious future, it will have to be *away* from their city of Calcutta. In fact, as we have been repeatedly reminded by Ray, the bird had refused to sing in Calcutta: We had seen Siddhartha searching desperately and unsuccessfully for this bird in many of Calcutta's aviaries. It is, in fact, the positive potentialities of the bird's song that finally overcome Siddhartha's inertia and acedia. Through that song, the overwhelming presence of nature, the letter, and his love for Keya, we see him articulating a hope and renewed energy for the future – a future in which his Hindu acedia and frustration need not be repeated. The presence of nature, and of the singing bird as an agent of nature, is important and relevant to Siddhartha's liberated state of mind at the end of the film. In the words of Gilles Deleuze:

Nature is happy to renew what man has broken, she restores what man sees shattered. And when a character emerges from a family conflict . . . to contemplate the snow-covered mountain it is as if he were seeking to restore to order the series upset in his house but reinstated by an unchanging regular nature.[13]

Somnath's Response in *Jana Aranya* (1975)

In *Pratidwandi,* seventy-one young job aspirants sweated for survival under one ceiling fan. That was Calcutta in 1970. Five years later, in *Jana Aranya (The Middleman,* 1975), conditions have worsened for the Ray *purush,* Somnath. When we see him, along with other jobless youths of the city, mail a job application, Ray's ironic commentary informs us (as the letters are sorted in the post office) that there are one million applications for an advertised ten job openings! The faceless Narishda of *Pratidwandi* who repulsed Siddhartha with his empty rhetoric is savagely reprised in *Jana Aranya* as the Indian M.P. (Member of Parliament) who lectures Somnath first on the values of patience and then on select models of great Indian leaders, whom Somnath is asked to emulate.

Somnath's home, though devoid of homeyness, carries all the familiar signs of heaviness, listlessness, and dullness noted by Nirad Chaudhuri and sketched by Ray earlier in *Pratidwandi*. In addition, a power shortage has afflicted Calcutta's electricity with lengthy blackouts: Most of the time we see Somnath's family – his father, his eldest brother, Bhombol, and his brother's wife, Kamala – literally in the dark. Somnath yearns for every opportunity to escape from his home into whatever daylight the city has to offer, and the brightly illuminated operatic world of the middlemen *is*, in fact, granted to him as a refreshing contrast. The fatalistic and brooding tenor of Somnath's household – set primarily by his upright Brahmin father, who is clearly out of step with the world outside – is overturned by the cheerful, pragmatic, and cynical philosophy of the middlemen, who leave Somnath with this critical option: If you can't beat the city (and the system), join it. They then proceed to show him the ropes.

Somnath's area of darkness within the familiar space of his home presents us with a young man tired of scanning the want-ad columns of newspapers and typing scores of "Dear Sir" application letters every day. Persuaded by a middleman, Bishu, to try out the commercial world, Somnath immediately agrees. When Somnath enters Bishu's office, we see a remarkably different environment. His professional space is like a busy railway station. The mailboxes and desks of these middlemen may be crammed together, but there is a lot of animation and energy inhabiting their work area. Everyone is involved in the rat race, including the office "gofer," who is a fledgling pawnbroker in his own right on the side.

Somnath's at-home penumbral vision is rudely banished by this *Glengarry Glen Ross* vision spun from enthusiastic sales pitches. This is a robust world of confidence men who will go to elephantine lengths to make a sale. (An elephant actually figures in Bishu's tale of a middleman who tried to sell one to a hapless client!) The important thing, Somnath learns, is to understand the client's needs and spare no efforts in satisfying them. Thus, in trying to secure a pivotal order, Somnath takes a sample to Goenka, an important purchasing officer of a reputable Calcutta mill. When Goenka does not place the order, even after approving the sample with a laboratory check, Somnath is devastated. A coworker, Mitter, intimates that bribery may be necessary to clinch the deal.

The tension between Somnath's home and the middleman's world is cleverly asserted and maintained by Ray. Crucial scenes in the home, for example, are usually played out around the family dining table, just as important scenes in the other world are played out around the middlemen's desks or at a restaurant/café around a table. In one important scene, when the father learns that Somnath may have to taint himself by recourse to bribery, he sternly admonishes him not to do so. Ray frames the father at the end of the dining table, flanked by Somnath to his right and his older son, Bhombol, to his left; Kamala stands behind the old man. While Bhombol tries to convince his father that there is nothing wrong with bribery in the business world, the old man is unbending. Ray's mise-en-scène springs this moral conflict at us in a space that is plunged literally into darkness by a power failure. The powerful frontal lighting focused on the faces of the three men further highlights the troubling clash of morals at that table. Somnath emerges as passive and indecisive but leaning toward his father's moralistic views.

Somnath's position is rudely eroded and undermined, however, by the breakfast-table sequence that follows. Over tea and omelettes the next morning, the bribery angle is made more definite by Natabar Mitter, the sleazy, self-styled "public relations' expert." Mitter offers Somnath the valuable revelation of this important client's Achilles' heel: women. Goenka's wife has been an invalid for many years; he is sexually starved and can be bribed with an attractive woman in order to secure the contract. Thus if Somnath wishes to land a sale with Goenka, he will have to supply him with a prostitute. This proposition is made matter-of-factly in a busy restaurant bustling with customers in the bright cheerful light of morning.

Still burdened by his morals, Ray inserts Somnath into a third relevant scene at home with Kamala, his sister-in-law. We are once again around a table; again the electricity is out. Somnath is shown brooding in the dark when Kamala's hand intrudes into the frame and places a candle before him. His response is to move one of his fingers through the flame. Lest this action be mistaken for a trite metaphor, Ray quickly makes Kamala breach it. When she asks Somnath to unburden himself, Somnath tells her that his job involves bribery of a devious kind – pimping! He is seeking what Siddhartha in *Pratidwandi* had demanded of his interview board: an answer. Kamala, sensing his dilemma, does not offer him one; instead, she convinces him that she'll support him and approve of all his actions because she understands the conditions under which he will be forced to make them. What is astonishing is the candid way in which she validates the pimping she senses he will be forced to do. In a way she becomes the female version of Mitter here, offering Siddhartha the same kind of encouragement that his colleague had proposed earlier in the restaurant. The scene ends with Somnath wearily getting up and looking at himself in the mirror. It is the end of his innocence, and mercifully his image in the glass is dark. At this moment he becomes a middleman himself, reaching out to Mitter and Kamala in their separate worlds: He must receive approval from both of these worlds before diving into his first sin for success.

Somnath's predicament is more clearly crystallized when we insert him into Frye's ironic–mimetic frame of reference. In this category of Frye's, the protagonist functions in two ways: (1) by virtue of his isolation and (2) by his victimization. If such a hero, according to Frye, is "inferior in power or intelligence to ourselves . . . [then] we have the sense of looking down on a scene of bondage, frustration, or absurdity."[14]

The ironic tone in domestic tragedy deepens, Frye informs us, when the victim portrayed is either "typical" or "random." Frye calls such a person the *pharmakos* or "scapegoat," who

is neither innocent nor guilty. He is innocent in the sense that what happens to him is far greater than anything he has done or provokes, like the mountaineer whose shout brings down an avalanche. He is guilty in the sense that he is a member of a guilty society or living in a world where such injustices are an inescapable part of existence. The two facts do not come together; they remain ironically apart.[15]

In *Jana Aranya*, Somnath is established for us as a *pharmakos* from the very beginning. As a bright student, he fares badly in his B.A. exams: It appears that he is the victim of an irritable and nearsighted examiner who has assigned him an arbitrary passing grade instead of giving his papers the proper academic scrutiny they deserve. As a result, his standing in the employment market plummets, and he can't even apply for a decent job. The only alternative is to hunt for jobs by devious means with devious people. Thus, instead of questioning Mitter's proposed modus operandi, Somnath capitulates and agrees to find the appropriate whore for Goenka. The honest and upright Somnath, gradually sucked into the cesspool of shady businesses, ends up a worthless wheeler-dealer – one more in the nation's steadily growing tribe of successful middlemen. In Frye's terms, he is innocent, for when he shouts for a legitimate job, he gets buried under an avalanche he starts in spite of himself. Alan Brian describes this avalanche well, in which Somnath is beginning to

rent and hire out not only things but people, and there is a magnificent price in the search for a superior whore for his key client. Assignment completed, he returns home to his scholarly Brahmin father who innocently congratulates him on this important contract – "At last . . . what a relief!" A sour, witty, tough individual comedy ends.[16]

Somnath, however, is also guilty according to Frye's terms because he participates, not only in his own guilt, but also as a member of a guilty society. When Goenka's prostitute is finally located and arrives, Somnath is horrified to discover that she is the sister of one of his best friends. Again he is given an opportunity to back off from such a grimy contract. The girl, who knows him (and who is doing this for the sake of her starving family), pretends that she is not the *didi* or sister he knew once when he was a frequent visitor at their house. Somnath knows that she is lying, but rather than indulge in some kind of moral dialectic with her, he wordlessly plays the accessory and takes her to Goenka to clinch his contract at last.

Somnath's fall from grace is indicated very cleverly by Ray when one of the middlemen initially advises him that Somnath will do well in this profession because he "looks very appealing." "Helpless, you mean?" responds Somnath, to which he is given the proper cynical answer that "it won't last forever." What *will* last forever will be his middle position between the Somnath of the beginning of the film, victimized by the myopic graduate examiner, and the Somnath at the end of the film, who victimizes a friend's sister at Goenka's door. The man who received only a "pass" grade for all his honest academic endeavors *passes* the acid test of becoming a successful middleman. In time, perhaps he will become like the successful Shyamalendu, the room-at-the-top business protagonist of Ray's *Seemabaddha* (*Company Limited,* 1971), discussed later in this chapter.

Gangacharan's Response in *Ashani Sanket* (1973)

At one point in *Ashani Sanket* (*Distant Thunder*), Bhattacharjee – an old Brahmin from a neighboring village who is trying to exploit the young Gangacharan and is succeeding – fawns all over him, saying, "you have a lot of foresight." It is precisely through the clever use of his foresight *and* insight that Gangacharan establishes his hegemony in the village. When he and his young wife Ananga arrive at this remote Bengali village (sometime during 1942–3) of low-caste Hindu peasants, they are the sole upper-caste Brahmins. They even look different, and Ray's mise-en-scène enhances this effectively through their adoption of dress and postures. Gangacharan is tall and fair, just as Ananga is light-skinned and plump.

They possess all the Aryan features, which stand out quite conspicuously among the villagers, who are short, dark, and very Dravidian-looking. In fact, the villagers are proud of Gangacharan's and Ananga's Brahminical looks and bearing. Repeatedly we witness scenes in which the couple are *told* this by the grateful villagers. Their Brahminical presence seems to upgrade the status of the village itself. This assertion ripens Gangacharan's resolve to scapegoat the villagers and carve out a comfortable existence. Sensing the overall ignorance of the villagers and their blind acceptance of the Hindu caste hierarchy, Gangacharan, with calculated fore/insight, sets about exploiting them, often displaying his own limited intelligence against their naïve and collective stupidity. In Machiavellian terms, this Brahmin

knows how to make good use of the nature of the beast. From among the beasts he chooses the fox and the lion; for the lion cannot defend itself from traps and the fox cannot protect itself from wolves. It is therefore necessary to be a fox in order to recognize the traps and a lion in order to frighten the wolves.[17]

Let us see how Ray establishes Gangacharan's lion/fox personas. In addition to being Brahmin, Gangacharan wears several hats in the village: schoolmaster, doctor, village consultant, and officiating priest. His leoninity is first of all established through the Hindu hierarchical principle of actual and metaphorical *height*. As a Brahmin he has to be *taller* than the entire village, both in his actions as well as in his thinking. Whenever he visits a home, he always sits on an *elevated* level, usually on a small mat provided by the grateful host, while the rest of the villagers squat *below* him on the cow-dung floor. In one scene, Ray focuses on Gangacharan walking dignifiedly past a villager who is high up on a coconut palm tree. When Gangacharan passes him, the peasant salutes him deferentially, even from such a high position.

There are other leonine indicators: Whereas most of the male villagers are shown bare-chested, wearing only a flimsy garment around their waists, Gangacharan moves among them always fully clothed. (He bares his chest only in the courtyard of his own home.) His tortoiseshell spectacles give him the appropriate learned look, which can also become a stern look of disapproval when he chooses to glare over them at his victims. Ray also equips Gangacharan with other signifier-accesories that attest to his overwhelming appearance. The first is his umbrella, which he always places prominently as a scepterlike icon of his visible authority in every space that he enters. We see the umbrella prominently hanging on an awning before his students in his class or displayed conspicuously before the village council of elders when they come to him for advice. The other important icon is the hookah, or smoking pipe. The villagers rush to provide him with an untouched "clean pipe" every time he enters their courtyards; and when he wishes to portray his meditative persona to them, he gravely smokes over a problem before announcing its solution. Standing or sitting, vocal or silent, Gangacharan projects his lion persona very successfully.

The fox lurking inside Gangacharan also makes its presence felt, however, to complete his enterprise of exploitation and dominance. For all the services that he renders, "give me whatever you want" is Gangacharan's standard foxlike demand of recompense. To be obligated to a Brahmin carries with it both a sense of the thankfulness if he is paid in cash or kind *and* a sense of fear if he is not. The Brahmin's demands, blatant or implied, must be met; otherwise it's a "sin." Knowing this, the preliminary "whatever you want" in Gangacharan's litany of demands soon becomes more cunningly particularized to fit his, as well as his wife's, utilitarian needs. To the peasant suffering from diarrhea, Gangacharan offers free herbal medicine (he has jars of them stacked in his room) and demands "mustard seeds," which will make his evening curry more appetizing. For each student who comes to his school, he exacts "ten measures of rice" every month from their parents; from the aunt of one of his students, "tobacco and coal" for his hookah and his wife's kitchen stove; another's father is expected to "come and shave" him every morning. When asked to perform an exorcism for the seventy families of a nearby village recovering from a recent cholera epidemic, the fox in him excitedly asks Ananga to "make a list" quickly of all that she wants for herself and the house; he, of course, will offer his own list. While Gangacharan performs the ritual, Ray repeatedly zooms in to the plenitude of gifts and articles that the grateful villagers have spread around him.

While establishing the Brahmin as a Machiavellian, Ray time and again punctures Gangacharan's superiority by showing *us* his ignorance. Gangacharan admits to Ananga that he knows just the right number of Sanskrit *slokas,* or prayerful utterances, to carry him convincingly through any elaborate ritual or rite. His only claim to medicine is feeling his patients' pulse and ordering them to abstain from contaminated food or drink. As to Gangacharan's knowledge of current affairs, the old Brahmin Bhattacharjee knows more than he. For instance, since many Indian villages and cities have names ending in -*pur* (such as Sholapur, Kolapur, or Belapur), Gangacharan thinks that Singa*pur* (which "the Japanese have captured") is yet another Indian town "somewhere in the western provinces." Ray makes us feel a growing distaste for this caste-marked parasite who struts so proudly before the entire village and his wife. As he belches and pats his well-fed stomach, we wish that something drastic would happen to fracture his smugness.

Gangacharan's trauma and dislocation are enunciated through the arrival of the man-made famine that isolates him from the village and abrogates his Brahminic hold over it. He is rudely dislodged from his elevated subject-position as the village's *maha*, or most superior person. Gangacharan is now subjected to an endless series of images revealing to him his own greed and malevolence. The first warnings of all not being well in his well-ordered existence are given by Bhattacharjee, who tells him of the sudden spurt in rice prices "because of the war. Our government is fighting the Germans and the Japanese and so all the rice is being sent to our soldiers." Since both Brahmin and Dravidian depend on rice, there is now no question of Gangacharan getting even a palmful from the villagers. Frye, defining the functioning of this kind of protagonist in a tragic-ironic situation, maintains that such "a hero . . . is only somebody who gets isolated from his society."[18] The acquisition of rice at any cost for survival gradually reveals to Gangacharan his own gross nature; in addition, the man-made famine teaches him in a brutal way the Marxist truth that "peasants do all the work and we live off them." Aiding him in acknowledging this painful epiphany are Ananga and Bhattacharjee. While his wife liberates him from his selfish nature, the wily elder Brahmin reveals to Gangacharan a cunning reflection of his own exploitative foxlike nature.

Gangacharan's humbling is skillfully enunciated on two levels: through the villager's response to get rice, which results in a riot at the local grocer's store, and through Ananga's efforts to procure rice by working with the other women at rice cleaning and husking. Ananga initiates this process by telling Gangacharan that since the villagers have no measure of rice to offer them, she has decided to go and work with the women and get a hefty bundle of rice as payment for her day's labor. The haughty Gangacharan refuses: "We must not lower ourselves to their level," he tells his wife as he sets out to the market to buy rice himself at the new exorbitant rates. When he arrives, however, he sees a long line of villagers. Distancing himself from them, he hopes that some villager will sell him his share or, better still, volunteer to get the Brahmin's share as well; but no one comes forth. To make matters worse, a riot ensues, and when Gangacharan tries to intervene, he is knocked flat to the ground. With a shock he learns that hunger shows no respect for his Brahminical uprightness.

A palmful of rice is more important in these desperate times than all the caste marks on his forehead. Ray's editing here marvelously indicates the Brahmin's crushing defeat: In a series of quick cuts, Ray brings us closer to a recovering but stunned Gangacharan slumped dejectedly near a tree. The rhythms of these shots are orchestrated precisely to the thumping sounds of rice being husked. A quick cut establishes the rice being husked by Ananga. When Gangacharan returns home and mournfully tells his wife he was "unsuccessful" in his efforts to get rice, she surprises him by saying that she has managed to acquire it. Although Ray's visual presentation had already confirmed this for us, Ananga's admission is a cruel but necessary blow to Gangacharan's Brahminical ego. For a second time he is literally cut down to size – this time, in his own courtyard.

Bhattacharjee's intrusion into Gangacharan's home and his cunning manner of wheedling a meal (with all creature comforts attached), by playing upon the sensitivity of Ananga, further reveal to Gangacharan his own earlier Machiavellian self. While Gangacharan is teaching at his school, his household is entered and taken over by Bhattacharjee. Since he is an elderly Brahmin guest, tired and hungry, poor Ananga is forced to feed him, prepare his hookah, and even give him a mattress on which he can take his afternoon nap. When Gangacharan returns and finds his food, his pipe, and his afternoon sleeping place successively usurped, he is horrified. At first, he threatens to send the old Brahmin packing; but he subsequently relents in response to Ananga's pleas and allows the old man not only to share dinner with him but also spend the night. Much later in the film his generosity is repaid in a parallel situation at the house of the merchant Biswas. Biswas is rumored to have rice he is selling, so Gangacharan walks fourteen miles to buy it. When Biswas refuses to "sell rice – even to you, a Brahmin" and asks Gangacharan to leave, the tables are neatly turned. Still, as Gangacharan wearily prepares to walk homeward, a repentant Biswas calls him back and prepares to serve him a sumptuous meal of rice and fish and give him a night's shelter – the least he can do for a Brahmin guest. It is when he is about to eat that Gangacharan realizes that he has been thinking of only himself, not of others such as his wife or even that crafty Bhattacharjee, and is made to recognize the folly and pettiness of all his previous actions. He loses his appetite and cannot swallow this sumptuous meal.

Now, as he returns from Biswas's house, he is no longer the Gangacharan we saw in the first half of the film walking the familiar *pather panchalis* of his village completely absorbed in himself. We see him paying careful attention to the hard times around him. From his subjective point of view, we see the village women plucking *saal* leaves, tearing roots, and snatching snails as desperate food substitutes for their starving families. He sees the funeral exodus of emaciated peasants from nearby villages passing his household after staring imploringly at his courtyard. He has nothing to offer them – his own food jars are empty – but he shares their pain as well as their hunger.

In the final shots of the film, as Gangacharan readies to leave his home to make cremation arrangements for Moti, his wife's Untouchable friend who is lying in the open, dead from starvation, he is already redeemed, for this is a task a Brahmin would never do without polluting himself: Untouchables, alive or dead, are only to be cared for by their own people. Adding to Gangacharan's redemption is his readiness to open the gates of his own impoverished household to support the ten additional individuals, members of Bhattacharjee's family, rapidly descending on him. When Ananga corrects him, saying "not ten, but eleven," Gangacharan's fatherhood is celebrated emblematically as well as domestically. He will father a stranger's family as well as his own. He will dissolve his Brahminical status by cremating an Untouchable. The "distant" Brahmin has finally found his humanity and, therefore, come home despite the "thunder" all around him.

Shyamalendu's Response in *Seemabaddha* (1971)

In India, according to Nirad Chaudhuri, the "dominant minority" is

constituted by the Hindus of the Anglicized upper middle-class. . . . They can be divided into four groups: (1) The Officers of the Armed Forces; (2) The Bureaucratic, Managerial, and Professional Elite; (3) The Technicians; and (4) The Youth in Schools and Colleges.[19]

Siddhartha and Somnath clearly came from the fourth category, but Shyamalendu Chatterjee, Ray's protagonist of his 1971 *Seemabaddha* (*Company Limited*) belongs to the second. What is most conspicuous of this Indian *purush* is his calculated assimilation and display of Westernization. Ray's film endorses Chaudhuri's stinging critique of this class by showing how Westernization has created a masculine weakness and has become "a routine affair, where the influences (of westernization) have ceased to be stimulating."[20] What appears as an assertive, insolent, and self-confident caste, "strident in its contempt for Hinduism and Hindu ways," is from Chaudhuri's and Ray's point of view only a facade, an "egregious snobbery that is unaccompanied by the substance which could be assumed to have inspired it."[21] What Ray's film chooses to expose is what lies *behind* this facade – what Chaudhuri defines as "a dangerous void of faith, ideas, courage, and of course, energy."[22]

Pratidwandi and *Jana Aranya*, the first and third films in Ray's so-called City trilogy, open by plunging Siddhartha and Somnath into the rank and file of the unemployed. *Seemabaddha,* the second in that trilogy, begins with Shyamalendu confidently informing us that he has been successful in avoiding that trauma. "My future," he arrogantly maintains, "is completely tied to that of my firm" – Hindusthan Peters Ltd., which is British. Shyamalendu is a sales manager there, in charge of ceiling fans. His Calcutta is diametrically opposed to that of Siddhartha and Somnath: It is triumphantly vertical. Before Ray introduces us to his protagonist, his camera ascends slowly over the impressive high-rise building that houses the corporate empire of Hindusthan Peters (HP). To paraphrase Michel de Certeau's remarks from John Fiske's chapter on "Searing Towers":

To be lifted to the uppermost summit . . . is to be lifted out of the city (of Calcutta's) grasp. [His] body is no longer clasped by streets that turn and return it according to an anonymous law: nor is it possessed, whether as player or played, by the rumble of so many differences and by the nervousness of traffic.[23]

Since Shyamalendu acknowledges only one way – *up* – he has to create for himself multiple images as he ambitiously seeks to climb the corporate ladder. This small-town Patna boy is shown to be doing exactly that as he ascends the graph of success in the HP universe. In split-screen, during the credit sequences, Ray shows us how Shyamalendu sheds his small-town skin, gets married, moves into a luxury apartment, starts playing business-merger golf and, as the introductory orientation of this Anglicized Indian ends, winds up on his way to work in a chauffeur-driven car.

The Hindusthan Peters Calcutta of *Seemabadda* is, in Fiske's words, "the apogee of entrepreneurial capitalism, and in that role it attempts to control the meanings of the freedom it offers."[24] Shyamalendu endorses this principle by confessing to his sister-in-law, Sudharshana, "I like the risk and danger of my job. I'm like a jockey pressing for the finishing line. Who knows, I may even commit a foul accidentally" [Fig. 14]. The Calcutta of the small-time frauds and cheats of *Jana Aranya* is made to look positively innocent beside HP's "meritocratic society of (Bengali/Indian) yuppie capitalism (where) *up* is the reward for those who most successfully conform to its ground rules."[25]

After a brilliant academic career in Patna (in the state of Bihar), Shyamalendu Chatterjee and his wife, Dolan, shift to Calcutta, where he joins the British manufacturing company Hindusthan Peters Ltd. Soon promoted to sales manager, Shyamalendu now works hard to achieve his highest goal: to become a director of this company. Meanwhile, Dolan's younger sister, Sudharshana, comes to pay them a visit. In Patna, Sudharshana had admired and liked Shyamalendu even before he had married her sister. During her Calcutta visit, this admiration develops into a mutual attraction. At this point, Shyamalendu is confronted with a major crisis at the office: A consignment of ceiling fans, intended for export, is rejected on final inspection. A delay in shipment would mean heavy losses in money and prestige for the company and himself. With the help of the personnel officer, Shyamalendu causes a strike in the factory, in which a watchman is seriously injured. The lockout that follows justifies the delay in shipment, and the crisis is averted. For his actions, Shyamalendu is inducted into the board of directors. His happiness is shared by all, except a terribly disillusioned Sudharshana. Unable to forgive him for what he has done, she returns to Patna, leaving a crestfallen and dejected Shyamalendu behind.

Are Shyamalendu's actions in engineering a strike justifiable or not? Are they an act of desperation when he feels threatened in his role of the socially aspiring, upwardly mobile executive? Or does he do it to upstage his other sales rivals, vying for the same position of director?

There are two centers from which Shyamalendu's actions must be evaluated: the company's management world and the world of personal ethics. If the Hindusthan Peters world has caused a significant change in Shyamalendu's thoughts and feelings, then his actions in creating a strike to save the money and prestige of his company are justifiable in relation to that world. His "goodness," then, has to be measured *not* in moral terms but in professional terms; and, as an HP sales manager, Shyamalendu acts with all the company's interests at heart and saves it from the disgrace and ruin that would have befallen it had the important consignment deal fallen through. There is a buried irony here, however: What has the company done for our Anglicized professional hero to have deserved from him such loyalty? The rewards are made very clear by Ray: Shyamalendu has an apartment whose "covered area is 2780 square feet." He has two servants, a Persian carpet, and can afford to send his son to an exclusive, British boarding school at a hill station, with the company bearing all the expenses. To earn these rewards, he has agreed to play by the rules: He has modeled his life according to the dictates of the English, corporate, executive world, stifling his own nature and essentially Indian identity. Ray has faithfully translated novelist Sankar's wry observations of these instances of conformism. In the opening scenes, we see Shyamalendu:

Figure 14. Shyamalendu (Barun Chanda) confessing to Sudharshana (Sharmila Tagore) that he "likes the risks and dangers of my job" in Seemabaddha *(Company Limited, 1971). (Photo by Nemai Ghosh; gift of Ben Nyce)*

walk back gravely along the corridor. On this familiar walk he never looked at anyone. High placed officers had to cultivate this particular habit with special effort. They must be able to walk through a crowd without letting anyone know where they were looking.[26]

We always see him smoking foreign cigarettes. "It was unthinkable for a senior executive of Hindusthan Peters to puff any native brand openly."[27] From someone who was once an aspiring academic in small-town Patna, Shyamalendu operates like an HP clone: "all the comforts of this household – this air-conditioning, carpet, fridge, telephone, bearer, cook, car – they are all tied to invisible wires of the Peters' fan."[28] The sellout is complete.

Sudharshana, on the other hand, seems to view Shyamalendu's engineering of the strike exclusively as a moral issue. She fails to take into account the context in relation to which the action of the "strike" is ordered by the man she admires so much. At the end, when she rejects Shyamalendu by returning the expensive watch he had given her as a gift, it amounts to an emotional gesture rather than an ideological one. This is further complicated by the fact that vaguely, unseen, there hovers the figure of "the revolutionary" to whom Sudharshana is committed in Patna. It is not made very clear whether or not she wants to marry him once she returns to Patna after being disillusioned by her other hero, Shyamalendu. Although we are never shown this revolutionary character (an original addition by Ray) in the film, it *is* hinted that Sudharshana's union with him will not be a very rewarding or fulfilling one. Revolutionaries, even more than sales executives, are prone to committing extreme acts in the espousal of their social beliefs and ideologies. The "killing" of a parasite, for instance, may be defined by a revolutionary as "an act of social justice," or the murder of a vacillating comrade as "an act of mercy," or the death of a targeted enemy as "a necessary ideological step." Would Sudharshana condemn all of *these* actions from her overriding, moral center, the contextual base once again not coming into play, and would her rejection occur only on the individual and emotional level?

Ray seems to be noncommittal here. In his interview with Christian Brand Thomsen, he had these comments to offer on his film's protagonist:

It is certainly the system that makes Shyamalendu what he is. He is part of a bureaucratic and commercial machine which has no place for one single man. If you want to live in a society, you immediately become part of the pattern. And that drives you into something you may not have been. This man clearly has two sides: he has his private feelings and his conscience, but the system forces him to dissemble them and think only of security and advancement. But it's an open film and doesn't make any final statement.[29]

But the statements in the development of the narrative and the characters are indeed there. Like Sudharshana, Ray does pass a definitive value judgment on this company man. There is a scene where he shows Shyamalendu raucously laughing with the personnel officer at the possibility of the death of their watchman (who had incurred serious injuries during the strike). Hilarity ensues as they visualize how they would have gone to his funeral, sent his widow wreaths and compensation, provided for his children's education, and so on. Somehow, it fails to convince: It seems totally out of character with Shyamalendu, who is otherwise always shown as struggling with his private feelings while being overwhelmed by the machinations of this highly competitive, cutthroat, professional world.

What is very convincing, however, is the sheer weariness of soul that overtakes Shyamalendu when, on the day he is made a director, the elevator in his apartment complex stops functioning, and he literally has to climb the hundred stairs to his abode of bliss – only to be permanently exiled from Sudharshana's affections and estimation. Ray registers this condemnation by having her get up, hand him the expensive watch, and then suddenly vanish from the screen. The last shot of the film has our Anglicized hero slumped on his chair, left with nothing but the material artifacts of his success. Life at the top is going to be very exhausting and very lonely.

The Responses of the Forest-Bound Male Quartet of *Aranyer Din Ratri* (1970)

The Ray *purush* quartet of Ashim, Sanjoy, Hari, and Shekar of the 1970 *Aranyer Din Ratri* (*Days and Nights in the Forest*) resolve to break all the bonds that tie them to the city of Calcutta. Leaving the city, they embark on a reckless holiday in the forests of Palamau in the adjoining state of Bihar. Two are professionals: Ashim is a successful executive, and Sanjoy is a high-ranking labor official in a jute mill. They are old friends who have even worked together on a literary journal they once used to publish. Hari is a famous cricket player. Shekar is the group's self-appointed clown; he is a gambler and a parasite with no steady profession. Each of the four men project a need to renounce Calcutta and replace it with the ambience of the forest they choose to enter. Ashim finds his professional success hollow and boring; Sanjoy is tired of hiding his middle-class timidity behind his Marxist rhetoric; Hari has been jilted (and slapped) by Atasi, his sophisticated Calcutta girlfriend; and Shekar, who had nothing really important to do in Calcutta (the advent of the horseracing season being a week away), has his gambling racebook thrown out of the speeding car in the film's opening moments.

The retreat into the forest has a rich tradition in Indian thought and philosophy. Indian historian Richard Lannoy points out that, in the period between the sixth and third centuries B.C.,

when society became increasingly differentiated, . . . the new urban man felt increasingly alienated from nature; social discipline called for by new productive techniques created a sense of anxiety among the more individualistic nonconformists. At such periods of inner crisis and difficulty, man retreated into the forest to test his own strength and recover the sense of identity with his surroundings.[30]

What attracts Ray's male quartet from Calcutta to the forest culture of Bihar is what Lannoy rightly categorizes as "envy" for "the surviving tribal life with its sense of collective unity." All four men come from a rigid, introverted, caste-ridden, Calcutta-centered society. Penetrating the forest, they hope to encounter "a carefree, colorful, joyous, extroverted tribal way of life in this refreshing environment of the forest." In Bakhtinian terms, the men are determined to plunge into the "less organized, less rationalized, even the relatively lawless state" of the carnivalesque.[31] Ray indicates their preparation for the carnivalesque during the credits of the film itself. Sanjoy is giving his male buddies a titillating description of the beautiful pastoral setting as well as of the tribal women who wear "no blouses," move like "amazons" through the forest, and freely cohabit with their men in "fun and games." Such a description arouses in them a desire to escape from the antagonistic forces of a Hindu and Westernized culture of Calcutta, with its personal and professional demands, and emulate these tribals, who seem to be free of nine-to-five labor and to balance work effectively with fun.

When Ray shows Ashim and Sanjoy lounging in the forest bungalow, one of them murmurs, "it adds years to your life," watching the horizontal expanse of the forest stretching infinitely into the horizon before them. In terms of space, the tribals themselves personify this horizontal thrust into plenitude and communal bonding. They defeat the vertical dialectic by which success in the city is always measured. "The higher you rise," Ashim announces in his first drunken soliloquy, "the greater you fall." The tribals, both men and women, are always shown either sitting in a circle or linked to each other as a long horizontal chain, especially when they are dancing. The male quartet tries to mimic this when they sit down at the long wooden table to drink the tribal country hooch. However, despite this assumed horizontality, each of them is too isolated by his own privatized trauma to forge an integrated chain. They are therefore attracted to the rustic principles of harmony and community that these tribals display. In Richard Lannoy's terms:

the tribes emphasize equality in social behaviour within the ethnic group, greater equality of status for women, more liberal relations between the sexes. . . . The absence of puritanism, frank indulgence in pleasure, and a strong sense of corporate identity all favour the tribal passion for music and dance, at which many tribes excel.[32]

Duli and her tribe of tribal women endorse this by drinking with their men. Later we see Duli provocatively encouraging the voyeuristic gaze of these city men when she cleans their room. When the tribals are shown dancing, they move as one presence and one being, unlike our drunken urban quartet clumsily doing the "tribal twist" on the forest road and announcing to the gleeful Tripathi women that they are "V.I.P.'s – very important persons." In reality, of course, they are very insecure persons.

The carnivalesque, in the idiom of Bakhtin, offers our Calcutta male quartet "the true feast of time, the feast of becoming, change and renewal. It is hostile to all that is immortalized and completed."[33] The Hindu caste system and the Westernized Bengali city of Calcutta have "immortalized" these four men and "completed" their individualized freedoms. Their movements have been restricted into predictable spheres of activity and stasis: Ashim lives his life trapped between executive decisions and cocktail parties. Sanjoy survives between fighting management in the professional sphere and getting his brothers and sisters settled in the domestic one. Hari's life is restricted to the runs he piles up on the cricket pitch, and Shekar rolls aimlessly between dice on a gambling table and money spent on the racing turf. "The spirit of carnival," Bakhtin says, "preaches the joyous relativity of all things."[34] This is exactly what these men are seeking on this holiday. They want to liberate themselves from all caste and class compartmentalizations that their Hinduism and Western preferences have imposed on them in the city.

They begin by unanimously agreeing that they will not shave. Like the tribals, they decide to bathe publicly at the well near their bungalow. They will use the well's cold water and not ask the caretaker to heat it for them. They will get up every morning not to the alarm clock but to the cowbells' ringing drifting in from the fields. Finally, they will get drunk not on imported Scotch but on country hooch. When Shekar sets fire to the Calcutta newspaper and proclaims, "all links with civilization are severed," he speaks for all of them; and yet, this severance is not easy for them to effect. For instance, their passage to the local bar from their bungalow involves a short walk through a dense forest. Every time our quartet find themselves within this forest, Ray shows them trying, in the true Bakhtian sense, to "enter the spirit of utopian freedom."[35] It is in this spirit that we see Ashim and Sanjoy leading their urban tribe, followed by Hari and Shekar. Since Hari is the most traditionally masculine of the four, he displays his "joyous relativity" by first miming a fast bowler in cricket (which as a sportsman he is *not* – he is a batsman who scores runs) and then echoing Johnny Weissmuller's familiar Tarzan cry. When Sanjoy asks everybody to be quiet and experience "a real sunset," Shekar ruminates that this sunset reminds him of the one in a "Burt Lancaster western." In spite of these urbanized echoes, the forest grants them a temporary relief from their city-bred "prohibitions and hierarchic barriers,"[36] which trap them once they leave the forest. Their bungalow pretends to be a pastoral retreat but in reality has all of civilization's trappings. It does have an ancient *punkah* (hanging fan) that one of the tribal women is employed to pull, but otherwise it provides them with all the modern amenities. The first thing Shekar does when he enters his room in the bungalow is to check whether the toilet is working.

The men are in a mood deliberately to defy established laws. When Aparna asks Ashim why they did not reserve the bungalow in advance to avoid all the hostile confrontations they are having with the government forest officials, Ashim tells her they wanted to disobey all laws and regulations. By transgressing laws and rules, the men hope to regain a primitive kind of masculinity that they feel they have lost because of living within the laws in the city. They want to replace their sober, lawful state with an intoxicating, lawless one. Pointing to this are the film's two drunken scenes.

The first drunken scene starts with the camera scrutinizing each of the three men lost in the welcoming coils of tribal alcohol. Shekar, who refuses to drink anything but "imported Scotch" (which they don't have), is the only one who is sober. The scene begins with a drunken Ashim proclaiming "what a life" thrice. In a quick flashback, he sees himself at a cocktail party, sober, confident, and charming: That is the cultivated persona of the executive that he is trying to explode. Alcohol forces the troubled Ashim to crawl out of that persona and exclaim, "the higher you rise, the greater you fall." Not wanting to be alone in his misery, he now sets out to make the timid Sanjoy into a *pharmakos* or scapegoat. "Go ahead, stay in your rut," he taunts him (in the same way Tunu mocks Siddhartha's stasis in *Pratidwandi*) "and be a cent per-cent Bengali, middle-class, conventional good boy." Sanjoy's laughter is an acknowledgment of this critique. Ray shoots the drunken scenes in what Bakhtin refers to as "the antique tradition of free, often improper, but at the same time philosophical table talk."[37] Ashim centers this table talk around Sanjoy's inability to "score" with his boss's daughter because of his sexual timidity and his domestic responsibilities, getting his younger siblings' lives settled at the expense of his own.

The true brotherhood of drinkers also links up the sober Shekar with the drunken Hari. Shekar wants to heal Hari's broken heart: He wants to replace Hari's sophisticated Calcutta girlfriend, Atasi, with the sensuous tribal Duli, whom he affectionately nicknames "Miss India." He succeeds in letting Hari pay for Duli's drinks, and the next morning he invites her and her tribal girlfriends to serve as domestics in the bungalow.

At this stage, one should delineate Shekar from his three friends. Shekar does not fall, and therefore is not inhibited by the conventional frameworks of caste, class, profession, and the truths that these men personify. He is not trapped by these truths, as are the other three men. Hence he becomes "The lawless herald of the objectively abstract truth."[38]

It is Shekar who insists that "we'll all be hippies" and burns the newspaper, delinking the men "from civilization"; but it is also he who ushers the men *back* into civilization when he spies the sophisticated Tripathi women taking a walk under "their umbrellas in their scarves and slacks." When these women later surprise Ashim, Sanjoy, and Shekar bathing like tribals in their underwear near the well, it is Shekar who approaches their car to recover Hari's wallet without any trace of shame and embarrassment. This incident, in fact, is central to the film's second drunken scene: Ashim feels he has lost his dignity before the Tripathi women because they caught him bathing. The carefully groomed executive had been exposed like a tribal – "a soapy fellow" whom Hari laughingly mocks when Ashim tries to castigate him for losing his wallet. Shekar, who has this time been forced to drink the hooch, is afraid that Hari might assault Ashim; but at this critical juncture, Hari explodes into laughter, miming the dignified way Shekar had retrieved the wallet for him. When all the men join in this laughter, Ashim's, Hari's, and Sanjoy's hurt is dissolved and in a sense parodied. Their laughter reaffirms the foursome.

For these men, Calcutta had insisted on the drama of their individual bodies and their private materialistic way of life. Hinduism had further particularized their thoughts and actions. The medieval forest and the liquor now act as two signifiers to the contrary, liberating them from Calcutta and Hinduism. The integrative laughter that erupts comes from the quartet as whole, a *unified body* of friends, and offers them "a loophole of hope" [Fig. 15].[39] It liberates the men from the fears of their assumed selves of the executive, the Marxist, the sportsman, and the parasite. It opens their eyes to their future. By uncovering the truth of who they are, or their being, it readies them for a becoming. It liberates them not only from the external censorship of Calcutta and Hinduism but, more important, from their own fears of what Bakhtin calls "the great interior censor."[40] That is why Hari, despite having his head broken by the vengeful tribal domestic Lokha, a man he had falsely accused of stealing his wallet, is in the end able to laugh and recognize his own folly that led to his injury. Shekar, who loses his racing privileges at the film's beginning, laughingly accepts the boiled eggs left by the Tripathi women at the end. Sanjoy will have to live with his rejection of the widow Jaya, and Ashim could

Figure 15. The laughter that offers Ashim (Soumitra Chatterjee), Hari (Samit Bhanja), Shekar (Robi Ghosh), and Sanjoy (Shubhendu Chatterjee) "a loophole of hope" in Aranyer Din Ratri (Days and Nights in the Forest, *1970). (Photo by Nemai Ghosh; gift of Ben Nyce)*

very well laugh at the way Aparna had undermined his confidence and then vindicated him with all his honor intact. Laughter, in the final analysis, returns with them to Calcutta as a useful and free weapon they can now use against all the forces that had victimized them (or might one day) in the city.

Fearsome Fathers and Traumatized Sons

Before scrutinizing the various kinds of conflicts that erupt between fathers and sons in some of Ray's films, one must understand what Richard Lannoy defines as the "special bond which unites father and son" within the Hindu family hierarchy.[41] Lannoy calls this bonding a "relationship of *mutual dependence.*" What is crucial to this relationship, forged as it is out of "the rigid formal system of obligations, is its culturally prescribed alienation (on a personal level) between father and son which not only acts as a control on the son's unconscious oedipal wishes," but also reveals that "the aloofness of the father suggests an unconscious resentment of the son" as well.[42]

Sudhir Kakar offers us an interesting explanation of how the Hindu father and son arrive at this state of mutual dependence fueled with feelings of ambivalence toward each other. The Indian son, according to Kakar, experiences two births: After his first biological birth, his early years find him "overpowered by his mother's protective nurturing and love."[43] Once he comes into his youthful years, however, the son is ejected out of "the intimate cocoon of maternal protection" and plunged into "the unfamiliar masculine network woven by the demands and tensions, the comings and goings of the men in the family." This second birth, for which he is totally unprepared, often leaves the son "bewildered, uprooted and misunderstood."[44] As a result of this "narcissistic injury" caused by the removal of the mother's adoration and support, the son seeks "reinforcement" by trying to identify with his father. Here he is hampered, though, by "the ambiguous role played by the Indian father."[45] Instead of offering his son physical confirmations of his love and a guiding, reassuring presence, the distant and aloof father exposes his son to a bewildering pattern of hesitant love and calculated restraint. In Kakar's words:

[T]he principles of Indian family life demand that a father be restrained in the presence of his own son and divide his interest and support equally among his own and his brothers' sons. The culturally prescribed pattern of restraint between fathers and sons is widespread in India, sufficiently so to constitute a societal norm. In autobiographical accounts, fathers, whether strict or indulgent, cold or affectionate, are invariably distant.[46]

In Ray's *Devi* and *Nayak,* the heroes are subject to a symbolic assault by a series of oppressive father figures. Umaprasad, in *Devi,* opposes his father Kalikinkar by deliberately adopting a rational and liberal stance against his father's superstitious and feudal one. In *Nayak,* the aspiring actor Arindam opposes his two formidable, theatrical elders, the thespian father figures Shankarda and Mukanda Lahiri, to establish his celebrated matinee-idol status in films. By maneuvering the very father figures who had traumatized them, Umaprasad, and Arindam try to gain their respective places in the symbolic order.

In Ray's *Jana Aranya,* Somnath's conflict with his father is developed by means of the careful opposition maintained between renunciation and worldliness. The father's severe renunciation of the world forces Somnath to embrace the conflicting norms of worldliness. The ethical ideology of the father is found wanting before the son's practical maneuverings that pay the bills and put food on the table. In *Kanchanjungha,* however, Ray confronts us with the symbolic and idealized father figure in Indranath Choudhury, whose principles of worldliness are politely heeded and then determinedly dismissed by Ashok, the young tutor desperately looking for a job.

In all these films, the fate the fathers and sons ultimately attain is a negative one. Ray certainly makes the father's impending defeat and despair very evident; yet, in the words of Ravi Vasudevan, "restitution is never made possible for the son as well. Faced to live out the drama of 'lack' (of the mother, of the true as opposed to the bad father, of social positioning) the son presents the illusion of control, but in a way which reasserts lack."[47]

In *Devi (The Goddess,* 1960), Kalikinkar Roy has two sons. The elder, Tarapada, conveys the power of the father when he drunkenly informs his wife, "to please the father is to please the gods." When his wife berates him for obeying his father – who had asked Tarapada to bow down and kiss the feet of seventeen-year-old Doya because she was no longer his sister-in-law but a reincarnated version of the goddess Durga – Tarapada had done so. He sees no reason in defying his father. "All belongs to father here. This house, this property, money, everything." Ray now cuts to a theatrical comedy being watched in Calcutta by Kalikinkar's younger son, Umaprasad: Onstage, we see a group of young men reproving their father for their illegitimate status. Following the play is a scene of Uma and his friend Bhudib riding home in a carriage. Bhudib has made up his mind to marry a widow and is worried about his father's wrath descending upon him when he hears of this intention. Uma agrees to argue his friend's case before the father. He feels he has "all the current arguments" that will convince Bhudib's father to agree to the marriage.

These scenes act as a prelude, establishing Uma as a young man determined to set himself up in the Westernized city of Calcutta in deliberate opposition to his feudal Hindu father, who commands obedience in his rural surroundings of Chandipur. The play's accusation bears a direct reference to what Kalikinkar, unbeknownst to Uma, has done to his son's wife, Doya. Inscribing her illegitimately as a goddess, he has deprived her of her legitimacy as Uma's wife. This becomes the first site of confrontation between Umaprasad and his father when, returning home, Uma finds he cannot gain access to his own wife because of her recent apotheosis.

Uma's English-style training in Calcutta demands a rationalist answer from Kalikinkar's recent mad behavior toward his wife. Kalikinkar tries to dissolve Uma's anger by lapsing into a Sanskrit *sloka*, which he translates as "a son offering absolute respect to one's father." Kalikinkar is so blinded and bound by this *sloka* of unremitting obedience that he refuses to see how it has instigated him to the breaking up of his son's marriage. When Uma demands "proof" of his wife's apotheosis, Kalikinkar can only offer an explanation of his alleged "dream" in which the goddess has rewarded his years of service to her by actually coming into his household as Doya.

A prominent four-poster separates the rationalist son from the dream-entranced father in the mise-en-scène here. While, from one side of the bed, Ray has Uma offering his father intimate knowledge of his wife's physical being to break the old man's supernatural illusions of her as a goddess, the bed itself powerfully inscribes the reversal of the myth of Oedipus in which the father and the son are clearly revealed fighting for possession of the same woman. Geeta Kapur explains the "predatory" nature of the father–son conflict:

> The desire of Kalikinkar is quite obviously cast in the mould of the Oedipus Complex. But there is an inversion which makes the desire more predatory. . . . In the Oedipal story, and its re-enactment in every male child's psyche, there is a desire to murder the father in revenge for the sense of castration he produces in the boy. In *Devi*, it is the father who, coveting the daughter-in-law, wishes to castrate the son.[48]

Uma loses in this first confrontation with his father because Kalikinkar, in addition to the "dream," offers Uma proof of Doya's apotheosis by referring to "the miracle" that has just occurred. A beggar had placed his dying child at Doya's feet, and it is miraculously restored to life. The irony of Doya's humanness dying before Kalikinkar and her husband because of her false sanctification, and the whole town of Chandipur turning up before her to gain her blessings, is of course lost on the old man – but *not* on poor Uma. He rushes out of that doomed house to inhale deep gulps of rational air. He needs the normality of a boatman's song to drown out the hysterical chime of bells in which his goddess/wife is trapped.

Unable to fight his father's so-called miracles and dreams that have enslaved Doya and separated her from him, a bewildered Uma finds a father substitute in one of his teachers, a Professor Sarkar, to whom he goes for guidance and help. Sarkar, however, is unable to help the young man. Listening to Uma's conflict, Sarkar offers, as an example to be emulated, a conflict he once had with his own father. "Stand up for your rights" is the only advice he can offer. Even though Uma does so in his final encounter with his father, when he accuses Kalikinkar of nearly killing his wife and his elder brother's son Khoka, Uma presents only the illusion of control: His father, by this stage, has slipped into senility. When Kalikinkar hears that Doya's goddess powers had been unable to cure Khoka's sickness (as she had the beggar's child's), all he can utter is, "she didn't give him back." By deflecting the blame onto Doya, he provokes poor Doya to go mad and drown herself. While Ray shows Kalikinkar falling at his son's feet, whatever sense of victory Uma would have felt at this moment is immediately undercut by Doya's suicide, which her husband is forced to witness. Doya's madness turns her into an unrecognizable "other," mortifying Uma and preventing him from saving her. The film ends by confirming the lacks of both father and son, although Ray clearly takes the side of the son.

When we are first introduced to Arindam Mukherjee, the thirty-six-year-old popular film star of Ray's 1966 *Nayak* (*The Hero*), he has authority, passions, and powers of expression. As Frye describes such a hero:

If superior in degree to other men but not to his natural environment the hero is a leader. He has authority, passions, and powers of expression far greater than ours, but what he does is subject both to social criticism and to the order of nature. This is the hero of the high mimetic mode. . . .[49]

But Arindam is constantly subject to the criticism of his peers, namely his mentor and first father figure, Shankarda, the "real dictator" and "leading light" of the drama troupe in which "the role of the hero," as Arindam tells Aditi (the journalist to whom he reveals his past), "was always kept for me." In the film, a crisis occurs when Arindam wants to make the inevitable transition from playing the high-mimetic hero on the stage to playing that hero in films. Shankarda opposes Arindam's desire to find fame and fortune in films because he feels that once Arindam abandons the stage he will *lose* his high-mimetic status. In a revealing speech, he warns Arindam:

Listen, Arindam, I know there is a lot of glamour in films, but they have no connection with art. An actor in film couldn't possibly build up a sustained part. I know this for certain. I have made a study of it. One is a puppet in the hands of the director, of the cameraman, of the sound recordist; then there is the man who cuts the film and sticks it together again – a puppet in his hands too; the main source of inspiration for an actor are the spectators – all those dark heads you see behind the footlights. That's where your energy comes from – what happens when you take them away? Where's the thrill, then? How can the film give you that?

While Arindam is agonizing over his "rebirth" in the world of films, Jyoti, his manager, encourages him by asserting, "this is the age of Freud and Marx, Arindam. No rebirth, no providence." Shankarda has to be disobeyed. Then Arindam has a dream, in which Freud and Marx are both invoked: It begins with a rain of banknotes falling around Arindam. He sees himself running through this paper-currency landscape thoroughly enjoying its mint ambience. Suddenly the dreamspace darkens; the Marxian plenitude of cash is now overtaken by Freudian echoes of guilt. He hears the loud strident sound of a telephone. A large skeleton hand, holding the telephone, now appears prominently in his dreamframe. Then more hands appear. He sees himself fleeing from them. Finally he collapses into a quagmire of currency. It begins to suck him in. Suddenly, Shankarda appears, sitting on a heap of money. Arindam tries to reach out to him, but Shankarda remains impassively seated. He can't help him. He's made out of paper like the money itself. Arindam sees himself going under.

In Marxian terms, his dream content inscribes his "exchange value." He has defied Shankarda by exchanging his value as theatrical actor for stardom, but his guilt, in Freudian terms, follows him around. The dead Shankarda's warning is disguised in the phone's urgent ringing: The son is still "connected" to the father. As Arindam succumbs to success, however, he sees himself dragged down by it. Shankarda, as his ego-ideal, is unable to help him. In fact, the ego-ideal of the father mocks the son by being made of the money that is sucking Arindam down. The chintzy format of his dream presentation reveals very suggestively Arindam's commercially tainted imagination as well. The melodramatic mise-en-scène of the dream shows how impoverished Arindam's thoughts have become: Even in his dreams, he continues to perform in the cheap artificial world of the commercial Bengali film industry. Arindam's "providence" has been financially rewarding, but his "rebirth" as an artist has been stillborn.

Arindam becomes a popular film star, but only by sacrificing his status as a stage actor. In his confessions to magazine editor Aditi Sengupta, he displays signs of Aristotle's hamartia ("tragic flaw") [Fig. 16], emerging (in Frye's words) as

a strong character in an exposed position. . . . The exposed position is usually the place of leadership in which a character is exceptional and isolated at the same time, giving us a curious blend of the inevitable and the incongruous which is peculiar to tragedy.[50]

It was inevitable that, with his "voice and looks" and his ambition, this
350-*rupee* stage actor was bound to succeed in that fierce supply-and-
demand, 35,000-*rupee* film-actor world; but the personal loss involved,
as Arindam admits to Aditi, is shameful. His migration from authentic
stage actor to tinsel film star (via the role of "the hero," Brojeshwar, that
he has been offered in his very first film, *Devi Choudrani*) occurs, in Arindam's mind, before Shankarda's funeral pyre. Ray's mise-en-scène brilliantly articulates Arindam's conflict at this critical moment. While the
body of his idealist father figure and mentor is being cremated behind
him, the face of Jyoti looms largely over him in the foreground, enticing
him to make that inevitable plunge into the glitter of the commercial film
world. Jyoti's Mephistophelian plea is expressed in clear economic terms.
"As a stage actor," he tells Arindam, "you earn three hundred and forty
rupees a month with an annual increment of ten *rupees*. As a puppet in
film, you can get thirty thousand *rupees* per film." By assenting, Arindam
breaks all his links not only with the stage but with his mentor as well.
On the very first day of shooting, however, Arindam finds out how right
Shankarda had been all along as to the status of the film actor.

At first, Arindam is given an actor's acknowledgment by his costar, the
renowned character actor Mukanda Lahiri, who is playing the role of his
"father" in Arindam's very first film. (In Ray's film, he plays the second,
pivotal role of surrogate father as well!) Arindam's first meeting with
Lahiri is itself staged as a father–son encounter. We see Lahiri being cos-
tumed for his role as "father" before a stage-lit makeup mirror, which
frames a timid Arindam quietly entering Lahiri's room. Cut to Arindam
now making his way shyly, haltingly, to pay the elder actor his respects.
When Arindam tries to introduce himself, Lahiri cuts him off by insisting
that he'll only call him Brojeshwar (i.e., the name of the son character).
Although Lahiri insists that Arindam "should not call him Father," since
his theatrical vanity does not think much of these young stage actors trying to revolutionize theater and film by their newly acquired "Hollywood
mutterings," Lahiri displays a lot of fatherly attributes in a series of instructions that he barks out at Arindam, like "mind you, don't smoke,"
and so on. When he complains of a "stiff neck," Arindam dutifully steps
forward, like a son, to massage it and remove the pain. Lahiri, now in a
manner most reminiscent of Shankarda, offers Arindam a professional father's advice: "Remember – there is only one indispensable person on the
set: the actor. If he is not there, the work has to stop." However, when
Arindam sees the director, the cameraman, the sound recordist – all giving
him directions on how to stand on the chalk marks, how to face the cam-

Figure 16. Arindam (Uttam Kumar) displaying his "tragic flaw" to Aditi (Sharmila Tagore) in Nayak (The Hero, 1966). *(Photo by Nemai Ghosh; gift of Ben Nyce)*

era, how to speak the lines toward the mike – he realizes the validity of Shankarda's remarks about the film actor being nothing more than a mere "puppet" on the set as opposed to Lahiri's assertion of the film actor's alleged indispensability. When Arindam muffs a take, and Lahiri learns that he has come fresh from the world of the stage, the old man humiliates him before the assembled cast. Arindam swallows the veteran's insults about his "voice" and his "phrasing," knowing that the old man's acting days are numbered in this world of the cinema, in which to exist one must adjust to the wishes of technicians. This is confirmed years later when we see (in Arindam's next flashback) the broken-down, alcoholic Lahiri visiting Arindam's posh apartment and begging for any kind of job, even a nonacting one, because Arindam's "word counts these days. Couldn't you find me anything . . . doorman . . . something?"

Arindam, however, has not forgotten that day of humiliation. Appropriately, we see him take his revenge. When this old man, who had once lectured him about his "voice," is suddenly overtaken by a nasty fit of coughing, Arindam sinks the dagger he has kept sheathed all these years by reminding the old veteran that he can't do anything for him because, "You need something more than a voice these days, you know." Looking back now, however, he realizes the cruelty implicit in his conduct, and painfully accepts Aditi's scornful judgment on the way he had acted toward Lahiri. His vulnerability is revealed to us at this moment as he pours out a résumé of his callous acts to this refreshingly honest, young, woman journalist. In his relentless drive to become the *nayak* or hero, the darling of the masses, he has arrived simultaneously at a private loneliness and exposure that he makes known only to Aditi. It is this self-exposure that Arindam realizes when Biresh, his trade-union friend, tries to exploit it.

In their college days, while Arindam was memorizing his lines, Biresh would be busy addressing a group of striking workers outside a nearby factory. On their way home, the two friends would argue about their goals:

> BIRESH: You know why I bring you here, don't you?
> ARINDAM: You don't bring me. I come because I like to come.
> BIRESH: It's no good just coming. I want you to get involved a bit more. The trouble with you is – all these plays and things keep you in a world of make-believe. You never get a chance to get to know the real world.
> ARINDAM: You think so?
> BIRESH: If only I could get you to feel these things a little more – that would be good.
> ARINDAM: What do you mean good?
> BIRESH: With a voice and a personality like yours, if I could only get you to stand and speak!
> ARINDAM: In front of that gate?
> BIRESH: Yes.

Five years after this conversation, Biresh makes good his promise. In those five years, Arindam has become a famous film star, and Biresh seems to have completely disappeared. One day, he suddenly turns up at Arindam's house and requests that his old friend drive him to an unknown destination. Arindam complies, but is horrified when that destination turns out to be yet another factory gate before which are assembled a horde of striking workers to whom Biresh wants Arindam to speak. When a displeased Arindam demands an explanation, Biresh points to his ability as a famous film star to raise the morale of these strikers. Arindam must now exploit his role as "hero" to speak of himself and his feelings for them:

BIRESH: It'll cheer them up to see you. They've been on strike for twenty four days. They've been expecting you. They're also your public.

As Arindam drives away, refusing all of Biresh's demands, we see how
cleverly Ray has made clear to us Arindam's fallen status: The theater audience, which was once the source of Arindam's energy, has now become
in these striking workers an emaciated crowd into which our hero is expected to pour some energy by exposing his inner self to them. Again and
again, we are made to see Arindam's entrapment as he is prompted to expose it to Aditi, who serves in a way as a devil's advocate, bringing our
"hero" face-to-face with his own dispossessed and unheroic condition.

In the film, we often see Arindam trying very hard to fracture his own
high-mimetic status as a hero – sometimes succeeding, but mostly failing
because his audience won't allow him to make that surrender even when
"fathers" no longer figure in this audience. When the film opens, we see
Arindam in a deep-focus shot tying, with a flourish, the laces of his stylish black-and-white shoes. Later, as a drunken Arindam stumbles into his
train compartment and sprawls on his berth, he laughs contemptuously
at himself when he is unable to undo that simple gesture and untie his
laces. His laughter is cut short, however, when the businessman's wife,
Manorama Bose, instantly gets up and takes off his shoes like a loyal and
obedient fan. On the other hand, when his audience is a seven-year-old
girl, whom he happens to meet in the train's corridor, he does indeed succeed in making himself anonymous:

ARINDAM: *(in Hindi)* What is your name, my pretty miss?
GIRL: Rita. And what is yours?
ARINDAM: Arindam.

Delighted at *not* being recognized and acknowledged as the film star Arindam Mukherjee, he confidently offers only his first name, as he would to
a close friend. For the first time he feels the separation of his name from
his image: If her name is Rita, his is Arindam. However, the moment recognition of his image creeps into his name, the hero overpowers the man
in him, bringing to the fore what Nirad Chaudhuri characterizes as the
modern Hindu's "inactive bad temper and . . . corrosive sense of grievance." This is illustrated further in the scenes that occur between the film
star and his private audience, the Bose family, who share his first-class
train compartment during his journey from Calcutta to Delhi.

From the moment Arindam enters the compartment he shares with the
Boses, he is treated not as a fellow passenger but as *the* famous film star.
Although Haren Bose, in his own circles a well-known industrialist, is in-

dignant at sharing the same space with this "notorious" film star, whose latest "scandal" with somebody's "wife" has been splashed all over the newspapers, his wife and teen-aged daughter, Manorama and Bulbul (ardent Arindam fans), are absolutely delighted. In voicing his objections, Mr. Bose is acting very much like a father figure here. Bulbul, meanwhile, sick and running a fever, has been consigned to the upper berth, from which she can blissfully stare at her idol as he sits and sleeps on the lower berth facing her. Manorama, of course, can't stare or flirt with him because of her Hindu wifely status and the overriding presence of her stuffy husband; but we do see her sneaking a hundred looks at her idol while pretending to do up her face in a small compact makeup mirror.

As Arindam enters the compartment, we see Mr. Bose having a lot of trouble opening a bottle of cough syrup for Bulbul that Manorama has just handed him. Like the proverbial tinsel hero, Arindam volunteers his assistance, and with a sharp, strong twist manages to unscrew the stubborn cap. Ray cuts to Bulbul's eyes and then to Manorama's, glistening with awe and admiration at this stupendous feat: The gleeful "son" has succeeded in upsetting the "father" again. Arindam, however, suddenly recognizing the unfortunate resurgence of his heroic status, with wry humor and honesty tries to help the embarrassed and fatherly industrialist from losing face – and patriarchal authority – before his wife and daughter:

> ARINDAM: (handing the bottle to Mr. Bose) Here you are. It's not so easy if your hands . . .
> BOSE: Yes . . . perspiration . . .
> MANORAMA: Congratulations.
> ARINDAM: For opening the bottle?
> MANORAMA: No, for the prize you're going to get in Delhi.

Arindam senses that it is the hero's power of action, even if it be something as minor and inconsequential as opening a bottle's cap, that has prompted the adoring gaze in the woman's as well as the sick girl's eyes. Although Manorama is ostensibly congratulating him for the "prize," he knows (as do we) that this bottle incident is in itself a "prize" that will long figure in the memory of both these women. So in the end, as the train is pulling into Delhi, Arindam asks Manorama about Bulbul's fever; and her reply, in keeping with his high-mimetic status, is totally predictable:

> MANORAMA: Temperature's down this morning. She thinks it's due to your magical presence.
> ARINDAM: I didn't know I had such powers of healing.

The pointed sarcasm in that last line reveals a mockery aimed at both himself and his admirers, who want him never to surrender that mode in which he has long been a prisoner. To reiterate Biresh's words, *they* are also his public, and it is most fitting that Ray ends his film with our hero adjusting his tie and rehearsing his smile for his fans who have come to greet him at the Delhi station.

Kanchanjungha (1962) reveals Indranath Choudhury as a fearsome father lording it over his predominantly female household. He has tyrannized not only his wife and two daughters but also his brooding son-in-law Shankar and his foolish son Anil. As a result, these two men had retreated – the former into gambling and drinking and the latter into an awkward Don Juanism – but in no way had they challenged Indranath or even dared to confront him as rebellious sons. Ray, however, presents Indranath with an important moment in the film where he plays the additional role of the "symbolic" father by trying to use his influence in granting Ashok, a likable young man, steady employment in Calcutta.

The scene between Indranath and Ashok begins with a mist enshrouding both men as they are seen, in long shot, slowly strolling toward the camera. As they converse, with Indranath doing most of the talking (actually, pontificating), we see the mist dissolving around them; its clearing gradually revealing to Ashok the layers of falsity that cling to this elderly scion, lost as he is in the importance of his own position and glory. "I have lived," Indranath pronounces with confident finality. "I exist. I have a title from my former masters of which I'm very proud." Here is an elderly Indian boasting to Ashok that because he was loyal to his colonial masters, the British, he now enjoys what he officiously terms as "the fruits of independence" or, in Indian terms, his *pravritti* (worldliness).

Indranath's strength flows only from the British persona he has constructed out of his deliberately self-terminated Bengali self. When he sends Ashok off to get the woolen scarf that he has forgotten in his room, it is done with the command of an English aristocrat. When Ashok returns, Indranath lectures him on emulating the "true sporting spirit" of the British. He "takes himself," in Deleuze's words, "to be a *higher man* who claims to judge life by his own standard, by his own authority . . . without law."[51]

By revealing himself in this pro-British, non-Bengali way, Indranath succeeds in creating, in his symbolic son, Ashok, the strong desire to transgress and challenge Indranath's power over him as idealized father. Ashok finds it easy to do this because Indranath has already revealed his blind spot: the betrayal on which his Indian identity rests.[52] Why should Ashok offer any respect to an Indian father who insists on worshiping the white-skinned colonizer? When Indranath asks Ashok if he wants him to put in a word on his behalf, the young man responds, "I don't need your help, sir. I'll make it on my own." Ashok's *navritti* (renunciation) shocks Indranath. It is the only moment in Ray's films in which the renouncing "son" walks away fulfilled, having triumphed over the "father"'s lack, displayed so arrogantly in all its worldly or *pravitti* trappings.

In his 1975 *Jana Aranya (The Middleman)*, Ray returns to an examination of worldliness and renunciation, though this time the roles played by father and son are reversed. The retired father is seen in the very first shot of the film, entering his flat. Widowed prematurely, he has renounced the world and lapsed into a brooding solipsism. His life revolves around his two sons, Bhombol and Somnath; the dining table, where the family meets at the end of every hard day; and the radio, which broadcasts news and Rabindra Sangeet. His eldest son, Bhombol, is shown to be already in conflict with him when we enter the narrative: The father clings to ethical values that, in Bhombol's eyes, have already become obsolete. It is easy for someone who has renounced the world to cling to high standards of morality. Worldliness, Bhombol insists, demands a tougher, immoral response. The father, having lost his elder son to the harsh demands of survival, tries to perpetuate his moral tradition through Somnath, the younger one; but here too he fails, because, like Willy Loman, he is completely out of step with the world around him. He reveals the same "tired eyes" as the examiner who did not evaluate Somnath's examination paper properly because he lacked "the proper spectacles."

Ray presents the father as a man sinking more and more into blind renunciation. No attempt is made by him to dispel the darkness around him. The renunciation that has set in pushes Somnath into the opposite direction. Gaining no wisdom from a shadowy father, he becomes the willing apprentice of the middlemen who show him a way out of this darkness. The film's ending is very poignant: Somnath enters his house and announces to his father that he has finally landed the contract with Goenka. As he quietly breaks this news to his father – with no mention of what it has cost Somnath personally – we see the old man wiping a tear from his eye and uttering, "At last . . . what a relief!" Then he bends toward the radio, from which we hear a Tagore lyric, "darkness is gathering over the forest." The old man, literally in the dark because of another power blackout, will be *kept* in the dark metaphorically as well by Somnath's embrace of worldliness. The only way by which his sons will keep his *navritti*

Figure 17. Somnath (Pradip Mukherjee) announces to his father (Satya Bando-padhyaya) that he has finally landed the contract, before the eclipse overcomes both in Jana Aranya (The Middleman, *1975). (Photo by Nemai Ghosh; gift of Ben Nyce)*

(renunciation) alive is, as the song suggests, by piling up a whole forest of shadows around him. Ray shoots this scene of the father down a long corridor, completely isolating him in his illusions. As the father moves toward the radio, Ray's camera slowly tracks in toward him, and the frame gradually fades into black. The tired eyes of the renouncing father are, cinematically, permanently blinded. Somnath's face, when we see him convey his news to his father, is also framed in partial eclipse: half shadow and half light [Fig. 17]; but the eclipse that Ray makes father and son embrace is, of course, total.

Concluding Remarks

As defined by these films, Ray's position indicates an incisive criticism of the contemporary male Hindu or Bengali's "common lack of faith, energy and courage." His indictment reveals "a whole [male] order in a state of premature debility."[53] While indecisiveness prevents young men like

Siddhartha and Somnath from passionately pursuing or preserving any ideals, an easygoing and affluent materialism distorts values and moral schemas for men like Shyamalendu and the Calcutta quartet of Ashim and his friends. Men like Arindam and Gangacharan will never recover from the exhaustion in which the human condition has placed them. As we saw in Chapter 2, Ray has given his Indian woman a voice to signify her process of *becoming* the New Indian Woman. Ray's Indian man, by contrast, has become so defeated by this process of becoming that he seems to have lost his voice altogether.

4

Satyajit Ray's Political
Vision of the Doubly
Colonized

*To the private Bombay Ray
circle who, along with
me, were colonized
convincingly by Ray:
Rafique Baghdadi,
Rashid Irani, Derek Antao,
the late Abdullah Abbas,
and Viji & Ahmed
Bungalowalla*

The Tradition of the Doubly Colonized in India: A Critical Introduction to the Hegemonic Structures of Hinduism and Colonialism

Ray was often criticized for averting his face from political issues in India. When a critic suggested to him that he did not sufficiently commit himself in his films, Ray responded that he committed himself to human beings and making statements, and that, he thought, was a good enough commitment for him.[1]

In 1976, Ray decided to make his first non-Bengali film, *Shantranj-ke-Khilari (The Chess Players)*. This project was in many ways a major departure for him. Professionally, it was a step into unknown territory: the language (a mixture of Hindi [India's national language] and Urdu), the milieu (Lucknow), the period (the 1856 annexation of Oudh by the British), and the scale (his biggest budget). Structurally, it was also a radical departure, with its simultaneous unfolding of strands of fiction adapted from Premchand's famous Hindi short story and historical facts painstakingly researched and re-created from Indian archives and British/Muslim documents and sources. Here was a Bengali filmmaker setting out to portray Indian aristocratic feudalism and British colonialism through the conflict that developed between two very distinct and different cultures: the effete and ineffectual Indian versus the vigorous and malevolent British. Ray returned to similar political concerns when he made his second Hindi film, *Sadgati (Deliverance)*, for television in 1981. Again, the literary source was a Premchand short story and the language Hindi; but now the milieu was a small, Indian village outside Bengal, and the theme was racism and exploitation within the dominant and complex framework of the Hindu caste system.

177

Both of these films are watersheds in Ray's cinema. They established a filmmaker whose vision was not limited and bound by the contours of his native state of Bengal. They revealed an artist remarkably at ease in a different language, an alien milieu, and confident in his political exposition of historical/religious themes. They also demonstrated that his creative powers did not suffer as a result of his exposure to the commercialized world of the Hindi film and television industry. In spite of the big budgets and popular Hindi film stars of the two films, he managed to bring his personal vision to a high standard of creative fruition.

In this chapter, I try to establish how Ray elected to become a historical filmmaker. In *Shantranj-ke-Khilari* and *Sadgati*, the two films to be examined, he offers us a political examination of Indian history. What interests Ray in both films is how power works in the oppressive society that was created by Hinduism when the Aryans invaded India around 1750 B.C., and how this tradition was continued and perpetuated by the elaborate network of colonialism that was established and implemented by the British when they came to the Indian shores under the pretense of being "traders" in 1700 and stayed on as "imperialist rulers" till 1947.

Ray's political explorations center around the struggles between predominant and minority cultures. In *Sadgati*, he reveals a poisonous Hindu caste/class hierarchy at work that separates the privileged Brahmin from both the low-caste Sudra and the outcaste Untouchable. In *Shantranj-ke-Khilari*, he examines how the British takeover of the Indian kingdom of Oudh was first aided by Oudh's Muslim aristocrats and justified by the British on the grounds that the Indians, as an inferior race, were unfit to administer law and order.

In order to make the political struggles of *Sadgati* and *Shantranj-ke-Khilari* historically specific and visible in his work, Ray makes quite subservient the "aesthetic effects" and "essential human values" for which he has been often lauded and praised. In fact there has been a tendency to read many of Ray's films exclusively from an aesthetic and/or humanistic perspective; these, in fact, are the labels that have been stuck on Ray to prove his political noninvolvement. My intent, in this chapter, is to offer a counterbalancing critical evaluation of these two films as primary political-historical texts.

The Hindu Hegemony

The Aryans appeared to have entered India in several distinct waves, the earliest being c. 1750 B.C. and the last between 1300 and 1000 B.C. According to historian Richard Lannoy, many non-Aryan tribes were Aryanized, and this process was conducted not by the original Aryan tribes but by the Aryanized indigenes, who were the products of intermarriage. The Aryan word for the indigenes was *dasa*, which in classical Sanskrit meant "slave," "bondsman," or "helot." This servile class was incorporated into the new Aryan social order under the name *sudra*, which meant "laborer" or "cultivator." As a result, a new type of social organization emerged, developed by the Aryan overlords and modified by the Aryanized indigenes. It was based on the four *varnas* ("colors"), classes or estates: Brahmin (priest), Kshatriya (warrior), Vaisya (trader), and Sudra (cultivator). This fourfold order gave birth to the Hindu caste system, whose predominant characteristic lay intrinsically in the determining of who could be "initiated" into it and who could be "excluded" from it. The first three classes/castes were the privileged ones; the *dasas*, or the Sudras, were not. What was now set up was a hierarchical gradation of status in which the Brahmin (priest) represented the apex of power and generated a downward spiral of fear and hegemony emulated by the other two.[2]

Complicating this *varna* division was the *jati* system of further classification and division of castes and subcastes according to the degree of "purity" and "impurity," and how the sources of pollution determined a specific structure within the caste system itself. Richard Lannoy underlines the basic assumptions of such a system when he observes:

[Because] pollution was regarded as being so dangerous to social well-being, its elimination was an essential task which could be performed only by specialists [to whom the caste system gave the name Untouchables]. Without untouchables to take upon themselves the societies' impurity there could be no Brahmin and therefore no purity.[3]

What the caste system stressed, we note, was a characteristic division of labor. The Brahmin interpreted the scriptures and granted religious sanctions; the Kshatriya fought and protected; the Vaisya planned and generated the economy; the Sudra labored on the farm; and all that was considered impure was designated to the Untouchable, whose job was to clean and remove it. However, the most important structural aspect of this social order, as Lannoy points out, was

the role of the dominant caste. . . . In almost all Indian villages one caste, either through numbers, riches, or hereditary status, is dominant. . . . All other castes are dependent and their relations with the dominant caste are *personal*.[4]

This enabled the dominant caste to possess and practice absolute economic, political, and religious power, especially in the Indian village, where the tenets of Hinduism were strictly followed and unquestionably obeyed. The dominant caste's role was that of the patron in relation to all the other castes in the village. It monitored all the disputes, administered justice, rewarded the obedient, punished the rebellious – and exploited the weak, the gullible, and the ignorant. Premchand's short story "Sadgati" ("Deliverance") dramatically particularizes the effective and monstrous way in which the Hindu caste system was put into practice.

Premchand's "Sadgati" (1931): The Dialectic of Sweat, Toil, and Silence

Let us commence with critic Govind Narain:

[T]he Hindu religion . . . [was] utterly incapable of giving spiritual sustenance or moral guidance either to the individual or to society. The social structure it gave sanction to was based on exploitation, injustice, and a complete disregard of the individual's right as a human being. . . . For Premchand, the value of an institution – religious, social or political depended on what it had done to improve the lot of the common man. "The greatness and distinction of any religion," he said, "consists in these: to what extent does it make a man more sympathetic to another man; how exalted is the ideal of humanity which it protects; and to what extent is this ideal translated as action."[5]

In another essay, entitled "Mahajani Sabhyata, Commercial Civilization," Premchand discusses the theory of bondage and labor that Hinduism sanctions and that is illustrated so strikingly in his story "Sadgati":

Human society has been split up into two groups. The larger proportion consists of those who toil and sweat; a very small proportion of those who, by virtue of their power and influence, exercise control over the large mass. The first group has no sympathy, not the least consideration of any kind for this large mass. The sole purpose of its existence is to sweat for its masters, to shed blood in their service and one day to say goodbye to the world in silence.[6]

Even the names of his principal characters symbolize the oppressed conditions of these villages. Dukhi, the name of the central protagonist, means "one who is always in pain." There is no way that this tanner/Untouchable is ever going to transcend his caste, class, or social/professional position. His wife's name, Jhuriya, means "wrinkles." She is a woman born with them. She can never escape their imprint: They live on her skin as permanent reminders of her exploited condition. The Brahmin priest is named Ghasiram – a mock-heroic name that literally translates as "lord [ram] of grass [ghas]" but that, in this caste-bound world, carries enormous weight. He cannot be addressed by his name, however, because of his exalted status; hence, he is always to be addressed by the title of Baba or Panditjee. The former means "most holy and respected sir"; the latter, "a man of learning and wisdom."[7]

Food becomes Premchand's next important item of caste distinction, leading to rules of pollution and purity. When Jhuriya tells Dukhi that "we will have to offer the Pandit some food he can take home and cook . . . I'll put it in my dish," Dukhi cries out that she should not commit such sacrilege: "Baba will just pick up the dish and dump it," since for the Brahmin, this food would have become polluted, having been touched by an Untouchable.[8] Nothing should be done, Dukhi tells his wife, to antagonize the Pandit, who is well known for his violent rages. "When he is in a rage, he doesn't even spare his wife, and he beat his son so badly that even now the boy goes around with a broken hand."[9] Venting his rage, as Premchand reminds us, is the Brahmin's second nature since his religion and his hierarchical standing give him the liberty to perpetuate abuse, not only on his own family members, but also on all the members of other Hindu castes subservient to him. Physical punishment for the culprit may be justified if the Brahmin's life practices, endorsed by the Hindu religion, are in any way undermined. To the Brahmin priest, Hinduism gives the privilege to deform and disfigure.

In such a totalitarian existence of "mutual bondage . . . the reification of social bonds through formal, stereotyped, part–object relationships" are very important to exercise and maintain.[10] Dukhi enunciates this when he picks up his stick, takes a bundle of grass, and goes to make his request to the Pandit:

He couldn't go emptyhanded to ask a favour of the Pandit; he had nothing except grass for a present. If Panditjee ever saw him coming without an offering, he'd shout abuse at him from far away.[11]

It is not that the priest needs animal grass fodder from this poor farmer. What the Pandit expects is the reinforcement of the *ritual of giving*, as sanctioned by the codes of his Brahminical standing.

Ritualization, then, plays a conspicuous role in the Hindu world, and Premchand evokes the narcissism of the Pandit when he introduces him through the ritual of early morning *puja* or prayers that are a priest's first function after awakening. Premchand ironically begins with these words: "Pandit Ghasiram was completely devoted to God." However, as we read through the paragraph in which the Pandit goes through all the intricate preparations of the ritual, we are suddenly made aware of the determined narcissism of the man as he embellishes himself into a godhead figure. He applies sandalwood paste with a straw to his forehead before the mirror, draws a red circle between the two lines of sandalwood paste, and inscribes perfect circles on his chest and arms *before* applying himself in devotion to the images of the lord before him. By creating this sanctified Brahminical persona, the Pandit visibly defines and reaffirms his power over the other castes, especially the Untouchables. Premchand skillfully navigates us to this realization by having us look at the Pandit's caste-marked form from a prostrate Dukhi's point of view. From such a subservient perspective, "the Pandit's glorious figure [fills] Dukhi's heart with reverence." Nevertheless, when Premchand resumes his omniscient narration, the priest emerges as a rather short, roly-poly fellow with a bald, shiny skull, chubby cheeks, and eyes aglow, waiting for his daily assembly of victims.[12]

Once Dukhi makes the plea for his "lordship to help fix an auspicious date for our Bitya's [i.e., daughter's] proposal," the stage is set for the Untouchable's exploitation.[13] This takes the form of several *tasks* which this poor farmer must perform as *his* ritual of gratitude to the Pandit for the sanctioning of his daughter's future happiness. If he fails at a single task, the Pandit will refuse to come or grant him that crucial favor. It is poor Dukhi who is really going to be held responsible for his daughter's future. Since he will not be given a second chance, he has to make the best of it. What we have here is a cruel blackmail practiced by the privileged caste, which strengthens, in Nandy's words, the "perception of the colonized as the gullible children who must be impressed with conspicuous machismo." The tasks, orchestrated by the Pandit, assume "the given format of a play," in which Dukhi is forced to multiply his own downtrodden status as Untouchable for the sake of the Pandit's imposing and arrogant identity.[14] Dukhi has to sweep the floor of the Pandit's dusty cowshed; plaster it with cow dung; carry heavy sacks of hay from the storeroom and deposit them into the fodder bin; and, finally, split the wood of a fairly thick tree trunk into neat small bits for the Pandit's domestic needs – for which job he is given an old, blunt ax. The signifiers of "dust," "cow dung," and "fodder," metonymically comment on Dukhi's own reduction at the hands of this roly-poly monster.

When Dukhi has the temerity to appear at the Brahmin's house to ask the latter's wife (the Panditayin) for a light with which to light his *bidi* (a local smoking herb), he has verbal abuse and burning coals flung at him. What is specified most categorically by Premchand in this exchange is the repeated passivity and guilt with which Dukhi accepts this abuse. Guilt is built into the ruthless machinery of the caste system itself. Since Brahminism practices so relentlessly the negation of the Untouchables, in Franz Fanon's words, "a furious determination to deny [to these people] all attributes of humanity . . . forces the people it dominates to ask themselves the question: in reality, who am I?"[15] When Dukhi finds himself on the receiving end of the Panditayin's verbally flung abuses, he reacts passively:

She was speaking the truth – how could a tanner ever come into a Brahmin's house? These people were clean and holy, that was why the whole world worshipped them and respected them. A mere tanner was absolutely nothing.[16]

When actual coals are flung at him and he is nearly burned, his reactions remain the same. In fact he accepts his own punishment unconditionally: "To himself he said, 'This is what comes of dirtying a clean Brahmin's house. How quickly God pays you back for it! That is why everybody is afraid of the Pandits.'"[17] We see how this ratio of fear is kept incandescently alive by a bond that reduces the castebound victims into absolute nothings, not only in the eyes and breaths of their privileged masters but even in their own.

When the Pandit wakes up after his nap and goes outside to check on Dukhi, he is horrified to find the wood lying just the way it was, with the exhausted Dukhi fast asleep nearby. The blackmail that the Pandit now unleashes on the tanner to get the impossible task finished is established by Premchand through the verbal power of the Pandit's priestly "voice," which is supposed to have the power to please deities and destroy demons. In this case, all it accomplishes is inciting a poor Untouchable to his death. The thunderous ax strokes Dukhi is made to deliver on the tree trunk are juxtaposed with the Pandit's goading words descending like harsh judgments from the oracle of religion itself on the exploited tanner:

"If you don't find an auspicious day for your daughter's marriage, don't blame me. That's right, give it a real hard stroke, a real hard one. Come on now, really hit it! Don't you have any strength in your arm? Smash it, what's the point of standing there thinking about it? That's it, it's going to split, there's a crack in it."[18]

Finally, Dukhi falls senseless to the ground. The Pandit, unmoved, goes inside, drinks some *bhang* (an intoxicant), empties his bowels, bathes, and comes forth attired in full pandit regalia to claim his victim.

When the news of the tanner's death spreads, a new threat crops up – contamination:

"Who would come to draw water with a tanner's corpse near by?" one old woman said to Panditjee. "Why don't you get his body thrown away? Is anybody in the village going to be able to drink water or not?"[19]

Dukhi's dead body very significantly becomes "the corrosive element, destroying all that comes near him; he is the depository of maleficent powers, the unconscious and irretrievable instrument of blind forces."[20]

These are not Premchand's words but Fanon's, painfully anchored in this crucial moment in Premchand's story. Premchand now piles on the pollution signifiers to evoke the sheer barbarity of Brahminic consciousness. Thus muses the Pandit: "How could a Brahmin lift up an untouchable's body? It was expressively forbidden in the scriptures and no one could deny it." A little later when his wife insists that the body "is beginning to stink," her husband reminds her, "Wasn't the bastard a tanner? These people eat anything, clean or not, without worrying about it. They are all polluted."[21]

Premchand now juxtaposes pollution and purification signifiers with deadly irony. After the Pandit has made a "noose" and managed to drag the dead body by its feet to a scavengering heap, he goes home, immediately bathes, reads out prayers to the goddess Durga for purification, and sprinkles Ganges water around the house. Ritual and the priest's participation in it conveniently wipe away all traces of this heinous crime. The Pandit is shown doing all the "right actions," as demanded by his religion's scriptures, to purify what amounts to murder. It is priestly privilege as endorsed by Hinduism's cruel laws that triumphs over the weak and suppressed, who lose in life as well as in death.

The British Hegemony

Ray's original contribution in his film *Shantranj-ke-Khilari* was to add the two important historical figures of Wajid Ali Shah, the Muslim Indian ruler of Oudh, and General James Outram, the British Resident to whom Wajid is forced to surrender his crown. In this fascinating subtext (conspicuously absent in Premchand's short story), Ray shows us not only Outram's prejudicial authority but also what critics Bill Ashcroft, Gareth Griffiths, and Helen Tiffin point out in their excellent study *The Empire Writes Back:*

a trace of ambivalence or anxiety about its own authority. In order to maintain authority over the Other in a colonial situation, imperial discourse strives to delineate the Other as radically different from the self, yet at the same time tries to maintain sufficient identity with the Other to valorize control over it.[22]

Whereas Premchand's story "Chess Players" depicts only the collaboration and competition between the native elites of Oudh's aristocracy, Ray adds to this the struggle between Wajid Ali Shah and Outram, who follow their own ideologies in the ruling of the state of Oudh itself. Let us look closer at Premchand's short story to decipher how the two Indian elites of Oudh participated in this game of overt competition and covert collaboration with the English colonizer.

Premchand's "Shatranj-ke-Khilari" (1924): A Chronicle of Idleness, Irresponsibility, and Indulgence

Since Premchand's 1924 short story "Shatranj-ke-Khilari" ("The Chess Players") deals with an actual historical event – the takeover of the Kingdom of Oudh and its capital city of Lucknow by the British – and since the history of Lucknow itself is reflected through the obsessions of his two main characters (both Lucknowi aristocrats during the reign of their *nawab*, King Wajid Ali Shah), it is important to know Premchand's own approach to Indian history and the themes he wished to articulate in stories like this one. As Govind Narain writes:

Premchand was a keen student of history, and like many thoughtful Indians who were engaged in intense self-examination to find out why their great country had become a victim of foreign domination, he reflected on the rise and fall of nations. But unlike most of his countrymen who, to escape from the painful reality of the present, were taking shelter in a sentimental glorification of the past, he tried to look at the past in a critical way. He regarded the past not as an ideal but as a starting point to discover our roots. History to him was not something to be idealized but to be learned from: "From history we ought to learn not what we were but also what we could have been. Often we have to forget history. The past cannot become the custodian of our future" (Premchand's *Kuch Vichar or Some Thoughts*).[23]

Before focusing on the two *nawabs* (aristocrats), Premchand's short story begins with a historical look at Wajid Ali Shah's Lucknow, a veritable "cauldron of pleasures," in which the *three I's* of a self-obsessed culture dominate: "idleness, irresponsibility, indulgence are everywhere." All of these arise from a society dedicated primarily to so-called noble pleasures, such as the appreciation of the arts, and a sybaritic excess in which both the *nawab* and the *fakir* (holy man), the Raja (King) as well as the beggar, "participate, fascinated." It is a decadent society, adept at solving "complex dilemmas," arising from the various *games* that are played endlessly in this "merry-go-round" universe "of merrymaking like dice, chess, and a ninety-six-pack game called *ganjifa*."24 It is a myopic world, completely indifferent to what is happening outside.

Having established this Dionysian world, Premchand now focuses on his two chess-addicted *nawabs*, Mirza Sajjad Ali and Mir Roshan Ali (hereafter referred to as Mirza and Mir). Since both have "hereditary *jagirs*" (inherited property) and don't have to earn a living, chess becomes a consuming passion to pass their idle hours. Both are involved, day in, day out, in mock "war manoeuvres" on the chess board, and Premchand's censure of this abnormal obsession is first shown to us by the dissatisfaction it creates within the twin families of the *nawabs* (in which their *begums*, or wives, figure prominently). Premchand's critique spirals downward: spreading from the wives inside their bedrooms to the servants inside the *nawabs' havelis* (mansions), and finally, to the locality's residents outside the *haveli* walls. Another kind of war is declared by their wives, the local residents, the servants, and the retainers against the two *nawabs'* consummate neglect of their persons and their hereditary *jagirs*.

Premchand intensifies his critique by showing, first, how their chess addiction renders them significantly impotent before their respective wives; and second, how it transforms Mirza's *begum* Khurshid into a virago and Mir's *begum* Nafeesa into an adulteress. Faced by a consistent connubial neglect, Mirza's *begum* feigns a headache to capture her chess-besotted husband's sexual attentions. When Mirza (after having failed to satisfy his wife's passions) meekly tries "to foist all the blame on Mir Sahib," this high-spirited woman thunders at her defensive husband, "Why don't you tell him straight that he is not wanted and be done with it!" But when the cowardly Mirza refuses on grounds of Lucknowi etiquette codes of hospitality *and* the likelihood of physical retaliation, since Mir is a "full two feet taller" than him, this fierce woman resolves to personally take this matter into her own hands. "In that case," she informs her reluctant spouse, "let me handle him. . . . When I need my husband, I'll have my husband."25 Such a remark clearly inscribes the reversal of sexual roles in this household. This is reaffirmed by her deciding, at this very moment, to step out from behind her traditional Islamic seclusion of the *purdah* (literally: curtain) and stride openly and brazenly into "the hall of audience" – the traditionally endorsed Islamic male space where both *nawabs* usually play their chess and where the presence of any woman is *not* permitted. She astonishes both her rivals by daring to intrude into their masculine arena, where she proceeds to overturn the chessboard in a fiery rage. While her husband watches nonplused, trembling from the wings, Mir, having heard the clatter of the chess pieces and the jingle of Khurshid's bangles from his position in the hall where he has been lounging, quickly slinks away toward home.

If Mirza's wife, Khurshid, has been transformed into a strident virago, resorting to both stratagems and direct actions to gain what is left of her husband's sexual favors, Mir's wife, Nafeesa, has pursued a different solution by actually taking on a virile lover:

The Mir Sahib's wife prefers her husband to be as far away from home as possible. . . . But the change of plans [now that they can't play at Mirza's house, they have started to play at Mir's house], with Mir Sahib sprawling at chess all day long at home, acutely distresses her. It restricts her freedom: it prevents her from longingly lingering at the window.[26]

Having established the *nawabs'* domestic upheavals caused by such a chess-mania, Premchand consolidates his indictment by offering further warning signs. Inside the *havelis*, the *nawabs'* servants complain to the *begums* about blisters and warn them of the impending ruin that could visit their homes. Outside the *havelis*, a few of the locality's residents with Old World views begin prognosticating dire and inauspicious happenings: "There's no hope left. If our rich folk behave like this, then God help the country."[27] Such choruslike remarks allow Premchand to depict the preparation for the systematic takeover of the city of Lucknow (and the state of Oudh) being planned by the British:

The kingdom's in utter chaos. . . . The wealth of the countryside is sucked into Lucknow. . . . Debts to the British company keep mounting. A creeping uglification starts taking over. The annual taxes can't be collected, because the economy is going to the dogs. The British Resident issues repeated warnings, but in the welter of ubiquitous dissolution there's no one to listen to them.[28]

At this stage, Premchand introduces the character of a virile Muslim Royal Cavalry officer. The officer has been sent to Mir by Wajid Ali Shah, king of Oudh, with a request for a supply of soldiers and to prepare for a military involvement should the British Resident invade Lucknow. To escape this call of duty, Mir decides not to be at home. He finds a lonely spot on the other side of the River Gomti where they can resume their chess games uninterrupted. This provides Mir's *begum* with an excellent opportunity to fulfill her sexual longings, which had been, of late, rudely frustrated by the brain and brawn of her husband soused in chess at home. Thus, Mir's masculinity is *twice* challenged by Premchand: on the battlefield and in the bedroom. In both areas, the triumph belongs to this cavalry officer, who soon emerges as the dashing warrior and the better lover,

especially in Mir's *begum*'s eyes. She confirms this by congratulating her
lover on his swift disposal of the *nawabs* who, frightened by his belliger-
ent demands, now always make themselves scarce. In fact, the officer is
free to come and go as he pleases in Mir's house and ravish (or be ravished
by) the house's mistress, since it is *Mir* who will never be caught staying
home – a neat reversal in the moves of the husband–lover–wife combination of the love triangle that Premchand makes his characters achieve.

In the next section, Premchand skillfully juxtaposes the chess moves of
the two *nawabs* with the historical moves of the British involved in Lucknow's inevitable takeover. Their faces cloaked, our two noblemen play
their game. "Check" and "checkmate" are the only words that escape
their lips. So engrossed are they in their moves that they fail to see their
city and country visibly collapsing on the other side of the river. Their vision does not stray beyond the rigid square of their chessboard. The historical process, which they fail to notice all around them, is commented
on and supplied by the author:

> In the meanwhile, the country is collapsing. The soldiers of the East India Com-
> pany march on Lucknow. Commotion and panic everywhere. The townsmen
> evacuate their wives and children to the countryside. But our two good friends,
> the chess players, remain blissfully unaffected. . . . Their one fear is they will
> be spotted and reported by an official retainer.[29]

Each of them subsequently *does* express fear, but here again, the *nawabs*
are made to empathize with Lucknow's tragic political fate only when
each one finds himself at a losing side on the chessboard itself.

When Mirza keeps repeatedly checkmating Mir, the defeated Mir corroborates his humiliation by offering a continuous and alarming historical commentary of Lucknow itself being checkmated by the superior
forces of the British army. He hysterically yelps at Mirza that there must
be at least five thousand soldiers coming, and they seem to be all young,
strapping specimens with pink, baboon faces. Mirza shows no interest in
what Mir is saying. (The fact that there is also a youthful, strapping Indian soldier enjoying his wife at home highlights Mir's emasculation for
a third time in the story.) When they begin another game, it is Mirza who
takes over as hysterical commentator, as it is now he on the losing side
of the board. Mir, on the other hand, has relapsed into his normal indifference, unmoved by the news that the *nawab* Sahib has been taken prisoner:

> "My God," says Mirza-ji, "you *are* heartless. If such a calamity doesn't move
> you, what will?" To which the Mir replies: "First save your king, then think of
> the Nawab Sahib. Checkmate! I win."[30]

Their sense of responsibility does not extend to their own ruler or to their feudal lands, which have brought them thousands of *rupees,* the favors of patronage, and all kinds of luxury and comfort every year. Their patriotism, in fact, is only a fiction evoked during losses and gains at the chessboard. Thus it is appropriate that their final quarrel, which results in each killing the other, erupts from the game of chess itself.

The last section of the story begins with Mirza accusing Mir of cheating. Tempers flare up, and wild words are exchanged. Most of the insults, embedded in these wild words, refer to each man's pedigree: Each reviles the other's most ancient Muslim ancestors. In a typically racist and reductive pattern, Mirza's ancestors are reduced to "farmers who all cut grass" and Mir's to "the original cooks . . . in the house of Gazi-uddin-Hyder."[31] Each uses the other's family tree as a convenient scapegoat to gloss over his own impotence and inadequacy in the present. When eventually they kill each other, we feel no sympathy: They have died defending the (fictitious) honor of their chess rulers instead of really defending their (lifeblood) sovereign Wajid Ali Shah against a foreign invader. They have invited their own doom and the collapse of their beloved city by displaying a completely futile and reckless whim of aristocratic excess. In fact, they have helped to weaken their homes and the structure of domestic and community life involving their wives, servants, and retainers. The foreign power, whose work is facilitated by such an internal rot, has only to enter the fray and drag away what Premchand describes, with resounding irony, in his last line: the two men's "companionate corpses." In the final analysis, such an end befits this pair – as useless in death as they were in life.

The Colonized Artist's Response: Ray's *Sadgati* (1981) and *Shatranj-ke-Khilari* (1977)

In their roles as colonized artists *and* historical spokesmen, both Premchand and Ray endeavor, through their respective talents, to indict the forces of colonialism and racism as they existed, not only between the two cultures of the British and the Indian, but also within Hinduism itself, by showing that both were antihuman and persistent hegemonic doctrines, and that their all-pervasive influence still persists in the India of today.

Ray's Sadgati *(1981): The Deviant Politics of Liberation*

In the Hindu philosophical tradition, the concept of *dharma* plays a very essential role. As psychoanalyst Sudhir Kakar defines it:

Today, *dharma* is variously translated as "law," "moral duty," "right action," or "conformity with the truth of things." But in each of its various patterns . . . there runs a common thread: *Dharma* is the means through which a man approaches the desired goal of human life. As the *Vaisesikasutra* has it, *dharma* is "that from which results happiness and final beatitude."[32]

In addition to its philosophical role, *dharma* has an important social function to perform as well, especially in a Hindu society. In this context, Kakar defines *dharma* as

a social cement; it holds the individual and society together. . . . *Dharma* is both the principle and the vision of an organic society in which all the participating members are interdependent, the roles complimentary. . . . Moreover, it is generally believed that social conflict, oppression and unrest do not stem from the organization of social relations, but originate in the *adharma* [not *dharma*] of those in positions of power.[33]

Ray's film *Sadgati* (*Deliverance*) powerfully indicts *adharma*, or that which is *not* dutiful, as practiced by the caste system. It is the Brahmin priest's *adharma* that ultimately brings about the death of the Untouchable tanner in the form of his *sadgati*, or deliverance.

The word *sadgati* itself is interesting since it comes perilously close in meaning to the important Hindu word *moksha,* which has been taken to mean "self-realization, transcendence, salvation, a release from worldly involvement, a release from 'coming' and 'going.'" To attain *moksha* becomes, therefore, the ultimate goal of all Hindus. It is that final stage in the Hindu's life in which he is able to free himself from all worldly attachments and merge with *brahman* (the infinite). There is, however, a second meaning of *moksha* in Hindu philosophy: "the state in which all distinctions between subject and object have been transcended."[34]

Since *moksha* encourages the breaking down of barriers and distinctions and inspires a steady advance to fundamental unity, not only *within* a human being but also *between* humans, the "deliverance" achieved because of this practice is supposed to be ennobling and blissful. However, *moksha* acquired a disturbingly practical meaning, where "deliverance" could be attained by a stubborn *adherence* to barriers and distinctions. This was done by those castes who stood to gain privilege and power, which they eventually used to reduce their victims to a state of complete inertia and death. It is this distorted version of *moksha* that Ray's film attempts to show by demonstrating the *adharma* doctrines preached by the Hindu priest to his oppressed constituents of Untouchables.

"For many," Kakar tells us, "the essence of *moksha* can be grasped . . . through vivid visual symbols, such as the Hindi image of *shakti* and *shakta* – the energy and the inert."[35] These become the predominant images that Ray employs to demonstrate the processes of caste exploitation. The Brahmin priest's *shakti* or energy is spent, on the one hand, on the over-articulation of ritual toward a *shakta* or inert god as the object of its worship; on the other hand, it is spent in the ruthless subjugation of all other castes, *their* inert state being the object of its hegemony. Conversely, the exploited castes expend all their energy in satisfying the perverse whims of the Brahmins and finally become *shakta* or inert, and so receive their *sadgati* or deliverance as a punishment. Two other sanctioned means of release or *moksha* that Ray enunciates in this powerful parable of exploitation are *bhakti* ("intense devotion") and *karma yoga* ("selfless work"). The Pandit instigates the Untouchable to work by calling upon the sanctified principle of *karma yoga*: If the Untouchable does not complete the "tasks" assigned to him, his daughter's future is in jeopardy, as the Pandit may not specify a date for the daughter's marriage. The Pandit impresses upon the Untouchable to interpret this kind of labor as "devotion" or *bhakti*. "Devotion" to a priest as sacred as himself is a special privilege granted to the Untouchable, for which the latter should be grateful. This perverse logic, in turn, leads us to the complicated issue of right and wrong actions as defined by the doctrine of "duty" or *dharma*.

Right actions and wrong actions in Hindu culture are relative, as Kakar points out:

They emerge as clear distinctions only out of the total configuration of the four "co-ordinates" of action. Hindu philosophy and ethics teach that "right action" for an individual depends on *desa*, the culture in which he is born; on *kala*, the period or historical time in which he lives; on *srama*, the efforts required of him at different stages of life; and on *gunas*, the innate psychological traits which are the heritage of an individual's previous lives.[36]

In the film, Ray shows how each of these four coordinates function, and how the evil actions of the Pandit are justified and upheld within the dominant framework of Hinduism; but we the spectators, outside this framework, clearly see the patterns of exploitation, excess, and victimization.

Ray's film faithfully adheres to the plot and spirit of Premchand's narrative. By dramatically depicting the pollution taboos arising from the sharing of food and physical proximity, Ray demonstrates the miserable condition of the outcast, in this case, Dukhi. The Pandit's narcissistic self-

preparation, his ritualized utterances, and the religious sanctions underlying these lead to the creation of a persona whose control over the lower
caste is unquestioned. It is a persona that Ray actually articulates as that
of Ravana, the demon king of the giants from the epic *Ramayana*. As
Dukhi comes into the Pandit's courtyard, Ray pans from him very slowly
to frame him as diminutive beside a large papier-mâché statue of Ravana
(which will be burnt on the important Hindu festival day of Dassera to
signify the victory of good over evil). Then he cuts to the Pandit, who is
shown calculatedly absorbed in his prayers, but at the same time, keenly
aware of his day's first victim. The metonymic association of Ravana with
the Pandit is most accurate. In the *Ramayana*, Ravana is described as "a
breaker of all laws; tall as a mountain peak, he stopped with his arms the
sun and the moon in their course, and prevented them rising."[37] Our Pandit generates the same kind of terror: He is a breaker of all ethical laws
since he is a law to himself; his sacred authority, as endorsed by the caste
system, makes him *appear* as tall as a mountain peak; and he petrifies the
other castes into obedience by a complex network of customs and social
observances.

In Part I of the film (the first of five), the use of labor is a crucial idea
articulated by Ray to bring out the distinction between the two castes: the
exploiter and the exploited. In Dukhi's world, the man, his wife, and his
daughter labor to prepare gifts for their "god" – this fat and well-fed Pandit. In the Pandit's space, his labor ritualistically arranges itself around
the gods placed on the alter before him. While Dukhi's family toils with
primitive creativity and urgent desperation in the making of their gifts for
the Pandit, no creativity or any kind of authentic passion is discerned in
the actions of the Pandit. In his sacred mise-en-scène, Ray shows him as
being more obsessed with his *own* caste-marked reflections in the mirror
than with the gods before whom he performs these daily rituals of *puja*.
On the sound track, Ray cleverly mixes the sounds accompanying the
Pandit's prayer rituals with the sounds of Dukhi's daughter breaking twigs
and leaves as she, with her parents, prepares a bundle of grass for the
Pandit's cows. The wheezing of the sick Dukhi, hurrying with his bundles
to the Pandit, are now intermixed with the harsh sounds made by the
latter's wooden clogs as he makes his way to his swing in the courtyard.
Part I ends with Dukhi pleading for his daughter's sake and the Pandit
agreeing, provided the tanner finishes numerous "tasks."

Ray very poignantly etches for us in Part I a picture of Hindu stratifi-
cation and exclusivity. The *desa* (culture) in which each has been born;
the *kala* (historical times) in which they live; and the *sramas* (efforts) re-

quired of them – all endorse the calculated process of exploitation in the caste system. Even their *gunus* (psychological states) assert very deviously here that, in this life, the Untouchable is suffering and the Pandit enjoying because of their evil or good actions in a *previous* one. Since both the Pandit and the Untouchable *believe* in these coordinates, each is bound to the other and has to play, to the best of his ability, his designated/chosen role as oppressor or victim. This is consistent with what Hindu culture constantly emphasizes: that "as long as a person stays true to the ground-plan of life and fulfills his own particular *svardharma* or life task, he is travelling on the path towards *moksha*" – or, as Ray's film clearly shows, toward *sadgati,* the "other" or *deviant* form of *moksha* as deliverance.[38]

In Part II, Ray concentrates on Dukhi's trapped condition as he sets about doing his assigned labor for the Pandit. Ray visually depicts this Untouchable as being constricted by the space all around him: We see him framed within narrow enclosures of the cowshed or gazing through the confining areas of windows and doors. Ray's camerawork highlights the tanner's victimization. We see Dukhi constantly passing under two predominant gazes: one of the papier-mâché demon Ravana and the other of this village's flesh-and-blood incarnation of Ravana, the Pandit. Ray adds to this surveillance an additional, ironic twist, as we observe our earthly Ravana lazily relaxing on his swing and delivering a lecture on generosity from the *Gita* to a select group of devotees while, within his own courtyard, a man has been reduced to a beast of burden.

When Dukhi asks for an ax to cut the gnarled and obstinate tree trunk, he is given an old and blunted one by the Pandit. Dukhi has to moisten its blade constantly with the dirty water of a puddle nearby. The more he tries to hack the tree, not making any palpable progress, the closer we see him approach his own extinction. The blunt ax is a reminder of how this Pandit is deliberately misusing the Untouchable's *shakti* (energy) in order to reduce him to an inert *shakta* state, like the bark of that very tree.

While defining the relationship between the Pandit and the Untouchable, Ray makes us aware of a conspicuous exhibitionism on the part of the Pandit, which is to remind the tanner who is master here. By doing so, the Pandit arouses in Dukhi (in Fanon's terms) "the native's muscular tension [that] can find an outlet" in some kind of an explosive activity, whereby the cutting of trunk now gets invested with the spirit of death itself.[39] Dukhi works on the tree trunk like a man possessed – either he will kill that tree or that tree will kill him – and Ray's skillful editing juxtaposes the Untouchable's furious assault on the tree outside with shots of the Pandit, calmly enjoying his meals, inside his home. The verbal invectives that Dukhi is shown hurling at the tree trunk are clearly aimed at the Pandit himself. Ray's crosscutting between the exterior and interior spaces makes this very clear: "You son of a bitch. I'll rip you apart. I really will. Even if it costs my life." But when all his efforts fail to make even a dent on the tree trunk, Dukhi flings his ax away in anger. It lands, unfortunately, at the startled Pandit's feet. The priest has just finished his meal and come out to survey the tanner's progress. Dukhi is so mortified by what his anger has made him accomplish that he falls to his knees and grovels before his benefactor like a whimpering animal. Before this arrogant caste-marked figure who has come to inspect his labor, the form and content of Dukhi's *shakti* is dramatically emptied.[40] His devalued self is forced to accept his own disintegration. It is something he cannot fight since it is ordained by his oppressor, who now stands towering over him. Dukhi is warned. This task must be finished by sunset; otherwise, he will not be granted any favors.

In Part III of the film, liberation is achieved. Aghast at finding Dukhi slumped over the tree trunk, the Pandit rudely wakes him up and, using his famous "voice," exhorts the exhausted laborer to "break this *lakdi* [wood]," or he would end up "breaking your *ladki's* [daughter's] heart." Goaded ruthlessly by such puns and taunts, Dukhi's emaciated body suddenly erupts in an orgy of activity that finally cleaves that recalcitrant wood into two; yet as the wood splits, so does the Untouchable's heart. Ray's cinematic language powerfully articulates death's overwhelming entrance into the trapped being of the Untouchable here. Ray lets his camera move closer and closer into Dukhi, like death itself. Tight close-ups of Dukhi's straining body proliferate as he unleashes his last flood of energy – the downward descent of the ax; the gloating face of the Pandit feeding whispered insults into his victim's ears; the gradual setting of the sun behind the hill; and the tree trunk about to be split. This tableau ends as we see Dukhi achieve his goal, then collapse and succumb to death.

To understand the essence of *moksha* in the Pandit–Untouchable relationship as enunciated by Ray, it is important first to grasp the kind of bonding that occurs between the two selves, or "I's," of the Hindu personalities involved in this unfortunate contract. As Sudhir Kakar informs us:

[M]oksha can best be understood to mean that a person living in this state has an all pervasive current of "I," "I" as the centre of awareness and existence in all experienced situations and in all possible selves. . . . *Moksha*, however, is not limited to gaining this awareness of "I" in a composite self. Rather it is held that this ultimate "man's meaning" is not realized until a person has a similar feeling of "I" in the selves of others, an empathy amplified to the point of complete identification. Until and unless this awareness of "I" in the composite self and in the generalized "other" is established and maintained, man, Hindus would say, is living in *avidya* [ignorance or false consciousness].[41]

Ray's film enunciates *and* indicts the *avidya* conduct of the Pandit. As we have seen, by his immersion in his own "I," the Pandit cuts himself off from the "I" in the Untouchable. By driving Dukhi into a frenzy of misdirected *shakti,* the Pandit has made the Untouchable "other" achieve not his *moksha* (liberative transcendence) but rather the mere *sadgati* (deliverance) sanctioned by a malignant caste system.

The Pandit's *avidya* conduct becomes even more apparent if we evaluate his actions against the fourth coordinate of action, known as the *gunas.* In historian Richard Lannoy's definition:

Sattvas [pertains to light, spirituality, subtlety], *rajas* [pertains to passions, energy, physical vitality, and strength], *tamas* [pertains to darkness, lethargy, stupidity, heaviness]. The three categories are called *gunas,* a philosophical concept for the triple quality inherent in *all* matter . . . including the body, the temperament, and food. In fact, the three are traditionally associated with the *varnas* [castes]: Brahmins [*sattva*], Kshatriyas and Vaishyas [*rajas*], Sudras and Untouchables [*tamas*]. . . . The human organism . . . exists in a state of equilibrium between "upward" and "downward" gravitation. Downward all things gravitate towards darkness, differentiation, decay, and dissolution [*tamas*]. . . . Upward all things move in the direction of light, undifferentiation, unity, spirituality [*sattva*].[42]

The Pandit's *avidya* becomes apparent because he is constantly shown by Ray not as exhibiting the *sattva guna* but as exercising the *tamas guna.* By directing his *shakti downward* through all his words and actions, the Pandit moves *away* from his traditionally recognized *sattvic* state. Instead of exemplifying light, unity, and spirituality, he becomes, through the exertions of his hegemony, the *tamasic* bearer of darkness, decay, and dissolution. He uses his religiously established *sattvic* status to terrorize the Untouchable and bring about his demise. Even his *rajas* state of physical vitality and health is one that he can maintain only by exploiting the other castes. The Untouchable becomes the easiest to transform into a state of absolute nothingness because, according to the harsh edicts of the Hindu caste structure, he *already exists* in a permanent *tamasic* state of darkness and decay.

Having claimed the life of the Untouchable tanner, the Pandit in Part IV decides to convey this news personally to the victim's widow, Jhuriya.

Her collapse and subsequent protest are evoked by Ray very poignantly. Occurring as the only positive moments in the film, they momentarily overwhelm the arrogance of this Brahmadatta ("man of God"), who has to flee her moving presence and outburst of grief. When the Pandit, immaculately dressed in white, comes to give her the news, she is shown bringing in a herd of cattle from pasture. As his harsh words regarding Dukhi's death hit her, she collapses among her animals, starting a mini-stampede. Ray then, however, shows her rising like a magnificent wounded animal to face him. Tearing the air with her wailing, she stuns the Pandit to awed silence and disbelief. He had expected her to grovel at his feet; instead, her screams cause panic among her animals, who knock the Pandit down, sullying his impressive white priestly regalia. He is forced to beat a hasty retreat, his clothes and dignity in tatters. Previously, we had the Pandit and his wife talk, from their superior and anointed point of view, about "the stink" of these poor people's dwellings, their "foulness," their "bestial" nature in everything that characterizes their caste. Now the very animals of the Untouchable and his wife knock our Pandit down and "pollute" his white clothes and his carefully created persona.

Ray begins Part V of his film by showing the Pandit sleeping calmly in his room under the framed image of his many gods. In this way, the director reaffirms the priest's identification with that *rakshasa* (giant) Ravana, since he is now shown resting, as giants are apt to do, after having consumed his latest victim. This idea is slyly emphasized when Ray cuts from the sleeping Pandit inside to Dukhi's corpse as it lies outside in the rain. Jhuriya now enters that literally Untouchable space and starts berating her dead husband for leaving her and her daughter. As the storm gathers momentum around her lamentations, her situation seems increasingly hopeless [Fig. 18].

Ray's camera now moves inside the domestic/religious space of the Pandit's house. His own wife enters and, paralleling the weeping woman outside, starts to scold her husband for not doing anything about the Untouchable's dead body, which is "polluting" the environment and preventing the Brahmins of the village from fetching water from the well. Both women focus on a future in which each feels victimized by her own spouse. Their condition can change only if their men use their *shaktis* or energies properly – which, in Dukhi's case, cannot happen because his *shakti* has already transformed him into a *shakta* or inert object. The Pandit's *shakti*, however, can be revived to get rid of the pollution that has descended on his house and this village. The metaphor of "labor," therefore, is ironically reversed by Ray and transferred from the exploited na-

Figure 18. Jhuriya (Smita Patil) berating her dead husband's corpse (Om Puri) for leaving her and her daughter all alone in her lamentable and Untouchable space in Sadgati (Deliverance, 1981). *(Photo by Nemai Ghosh; gift of Ben Nyce)*

tive (Dukhi) to the exploitative Pandit as he decides, early the next day, to use his energy and drag this corpse to a distant dung heap. As the body is thrown among the skeletons of already eaten animals, the metaphor of one caste having devoured another is, in itself, powerfully conveyed. This is reaffirmed not only by the stunning visuals that accompany the painful scene of Dukhi's last journey, but also by the steady drum roll on the sound track.

In the film's final scene, we see the Pandit purifying, with mantras and holy water, the "polluted" spots where the Untouchable's body had lain. This he does to increase his sense of psychological security, by acting as his ancestors would have in the past *and* as his Brahminic peers would in the present. To him, *right* action and his own *individual dharma* come to mean *traditional* action and *caste dharma*. In this light, his occupational activity and social actions would be considered "right" and "good," since they conform to the traditional pattern prevalent in his kinship and caste group.[43] On this shattering revelation of injustice, the film ends.

Between the Burdens of the White Man and the Whims of the
Chess-Besotted Lucknowi Aristocrats: The Representation and
Presentation of Colonialism and Nationalist Elitism in Ray's
Shatranj-ke-Khilari *(1977)*

As mentioned earlier, Ray's 1977 film is not merely a literary adaptation
of Premchand's famous 1924 short story. By employing a variety of different narrative discourses, Ray tries to define British colonialism and Indian
nationalist elitism, in the terms of Ranajit Guha, as "a function of stim-
ulus and response, representing nationalism as the sum of activities and
ideas by which the Indian elite responded to the institutions, the opportunities, resources, etc., generated by colonialism."[44] To Premchand's original story, in which only the two Lucknowi chess-besotted *jagirdars* or
landlords figure as reciprocating their "responses" to the overriding "stim-
ulus" of chess offered by the British, Ray adds the two important historical figures of Wajid Ali Shah, the king of Oudh, and General Outram,
the British Resident (sent by then–Governor General Lord Dalhousie), to
whom Wajid is ordered to surrender his crown. The narrative moves of
the two chess players as they function in Premchand's story are now put
into a particular historical context. The complex problems that emerge
from the players' chessboard are paralleled in Ray's text by the complicated contradictions that arise in the power play that develops between the
two elites of Wajid and Outram in their struggle for control over Oudh.

   In the "Preface" to the published script of *Shantranj-ke-Khilari*, Ray defines three primary reasons he was drawn to the story: "My interest in
chess, the Raj period, and the city of Lucknow itself."[45] Chess already figured strongly in Premchand's story, but Ray's research in the other two
areas revealed interesting facts about the deposed King Wajid and the British Resident Outram. The former, according to Ray:

> was an extraordinary character. Outram describes him as a worthless King,
> which he probably was, but this was compensated for by a genuine gift for mu-
> sic. He was a composer, singer, poet and dancer. He also wrote and produced
> plays on Hindu themes (he was a Muslim himself) in which he acted the main
> part. All this made the King a figure worthy of film treatment. As for the char-
> acter of Outram, I was struck by the fact that he had qualms about the task he
> had been asked to perform. This was revealed in a couple of Dalhousie letters.
> Thus both the King and Outram were complex three dimensional characters.[46]

   Many of the sources he consulted while preparing the film were cited
by Ray in the 31 December 1978 issue of *The Illustrated Weekly of India*

after an Indian critic, in the 22 October 1978 issue of the same magazine, attacked Ray for a very "Orientalist" approach in his depiction of Wajid as a weak, ineffectual, and effeminate monarch. To defend his position and authenticate his re-creation of these two figures, Ray listed (among others) the following sources for his research (the remarks and comments are Ray's):

1. *Blue Book on Oude:* It contains, among other things, a verbatim account of Outram's last interview with Wajid, and describes Wajid's taking off his turban and handing it to Outram as a parting gesture.
2. *Abdul Halim Sharar's Guzesta Luknow* (translated into English by E. S. Harcourt and Fakhir Hussain as *Lucknow: The Last Phase of an Oriental Culture*): Sharar provided most of the sociocultural details, as well as a fairly extended portrait of Wajid both in Lucknow and his Calcutta periods.
3. The Indian Histories of Mill and Beveridge, both critical of the Annexation.
4. *The Letters of Lord Dalhousie:* One of these letters provided the information that Outram grumbled about the new treaty and apprehended that Wajid would refuse to sign it.
5. The biographies of Outram (by Trotter and by Goldschmid).
6. *The Indian Mutiny Diary* by Howard Russell, who was on the spot when the British troops ransacked the Kaiserbaugh Palace. He gives the only description of the interior of the palace I have come across.
7. The young Wajid's personal diary, *Mahal Khana Shahi.* This turned out to be an unending account of his amours.
8. The text of Wajid Ali Shah's *Rajas* (where he plays Krishna).
9. *Umrao Jan Ada (A Courtesan of Pleasure)*, which gives a fascinating and authentic picture of Lucknow in Wajid's time.
10. All English and Bengali newspapers and journals of the period preserved in the National Library in Calcutta.
11. I was also closely in touch with Professor Kaukabh of Aligarh University. He happens to be a great grandson of Wajid Ali Shah and is considered one of the best authorities in India on Wajid.[47]

The reason for such a historical immersion on Ray's part becomes very clear in the film's prologue. Before entering the narrative proper, Ray sets up the historical framework within which his filmic text is going to operate. He does this "to educate," in Andrew Robinson's terms,

the (Indian as well as the Western) audience's widespread ignorance of the facts of the relationship between the British and Oudh in the century leading to the Annexation – in India as much as elsewhere: to which the film's ten minute prologue seemed the only solution.[48]

While an invisible narrator in a voice-over paints for us the historical background against which the fictive narrative scenes will stand out, the prologue visually provides (1) a presentation of the two chess players absorbed in their game, followed by (2) several characteristic vignettes of Wajid Ali Shah. This is completed by (3) a cartoon sequence sketching the British takeover of Oudh as a large "cake" swallowed by the Governor General, Lord Dalhousie.

Ray begins his historical exposé with a close-up of a chessboard. From the right side of the frame a hand enters, hovers over the pieces, and moves a white bishop. From the left side of the frame another hand enters, moves a black knight in response, and captures a white pawn. In a voice-over, the prologue's invisible narrator tells us to

Look at the hands of the mighty generals deploying their troops on the battle-field. We do not know if these hands ever held real weapons. But this is not a real battle where blood is shed and the fate of empire decided.

The camera pulls back and we now see the two Lucknowi landlords, Mir Roshan Ali and Mirza Sajjad Ali. As Ray's camera frames them playing chess with rapt concentration, the narrator intones:

It has been like this ever since the day the two friends discovered this noble game. You may ask: have they no work to do? Of course not! Whoever heard of the landed gentry working? These are noblemen of the capital of Oudh, or Lucknow.

A close-up of a Mogul arch now fills the screen. The camera slowly pulls back, and images of domes and minarets rapidly accumulate in the frame. A group of noblemen from a nearby rooftop are now shown watching pigeons wheeling in the sky. In the next shot we see gaily colored paper kites fighting airborne duels with each other. Such innocent pastimes are next juxtaposed beside a crueler one, in which a brutal and insensitive crowd is shown in feverish animation at a cockfight. Then Ray inserts a close-up of a throne. The camera pulls back to reveal that it is empty. The voice-over informs us in mocking tones:

This is the throne of King Wajid, who ruled over Oudh. But the King had other interests too.

Wajid is now introduced playing the Hindu god Krishna in his play *Rajas,* where he is surrounded by an adoring female conglomerate (the proverbial *goopiyaas,* or Krishna's consorts). The accompanying song we hear is a love song composed by Wajid himself. More vignettes of the protean

Wajid follow: A Muslim Wajid, surrounded by a crowd, plays the *tasha* (drum) at the grand Islamic festival of Mohurrum. We then see him at night, reclining in his harem with his favorite concubines. Next comes a close-up of Wajid and, as the camera pulls back, we see him finally sitting on his throne. The irony, of course, is not lost on the narrator, who promptly advises us: "Nevertheless, there were times when the King sat on the throne."

Such an introduction skillfully summarizes the sad part played by the aristocratic class of landlord and king in facilitating Oudh's annexation by the British colonial rulers. Their blinkered absorption in games and arts and their ensuing neglect of state affairs created not only a native political impotence but also gave the imperialist aggressor the *justification* to step in and set things right. This is indicated by the final portion of the prologue, in which the British colonizer makes his appearance. This section begins with Wajid sitting in his *durbar* (court). The camera moves in toward the crown on his head. The narrator, on cue, informs us:

If he was not overfond of ruling, he was certainly proud of his crown. Only five years ago, in 1851, he had sent it to London to be displayed at the Great Exhibition. But listen to what an Englishman had to say about it.

A close-up of a letter written by Lord Dalhousie fills the screen, accompanied by an English voice reading from the letter:

The wretch in Lucknow who has sent his crown to the Exhibition would have done his people and us a great service if he had sent his head in it – and he would never have missed it. That is a cherry which will drop into our mouths one day.

An animated sequence follows showing cherries and their crowns being knocked off by Dalhousie. As the last cherry is swallowed up, the narrator tells us, with historical solemnity, which Indian states each of those swallowed cherries represents:

Punjab, Burma, Nagpur, Satara, Jhansi. The only one left is the cherry of Oudh, whose friendship with Britain goes back to the reign of Nawab Siraj-ud-Daula. [The nawab] had been unwise to pit his forces against the British. No wonder he was defeated. But the British did not dethrone him. All that they did was to make him sign a treaty pledging eternal friendship and five million rupees compensation. Ever since, the Nawabs of Oudh have maintained this friendship. When British campaigns needed money, the Nawabs opened their coffers.

The ensuing animated sequence illustrates this colonial process of political and economical exchange. We see a *nawab* asleep on the throne. Next to him is a cake with OUDH written boldly over it. In struts GG (the Governor General). He taps the sleeping *nawab* on the shoulder. The *nawab* wakes and hangs his head in shame. The GG points angrily at OUDH. The *nawab* takes out a knife and slices off a piece of OUDH and hands it to the GG, who gulps it down and struts away. Concludes our ever-vigilant narrator:

Poor Wajid! If only you knew what was in the mind of the Resident of Lucknow, General Outram.

With this, the prologue ends.

The grand doctrine of British "efficiency" that Joseph Conrad castigated in the opening pages of *The Heart of Darkness,* and which the British so often used to justify their "takeovers" of those Indian states ruled by inefficient monarchs like Wajid, was nurtured, as Ray's prologue so accurately indicates, by the very lassitude of its natives – men like the two chess players and their ruler, Wajid. The prologue thus sets the tone and the direction Ray's film is going to take. The characters in this animated strip critically point to the caricatured figures of the two chess players themselves. In addition, the stylization represented in the prologue is in keeping with the stylized tone and setting of the film itself. It reflects the film's accurate vision of a Lucknowi elitist culture in which aesthetics, calligraphy, dance, games, music, poetry, role-playing, decorum, manners, style of dress and mode of address, customs and costumes, all took precedence over history's realpolitik trends. The mocking commentary and the lush visuals constitute a cultural attack on Oudh's elite itself and lay bare the hollowness of its elites and of their brand of native nationalism.

In addition to the prologue, Ray adds to his filmic text three crucial scenes that do not figure in Premchand's original short story. The first is between the chess players and the city's garrulous and gracious *munshi* (secretary/interpreter – as Premchand himself was called), a Hindu character created by Ray to establish the harmony that existed between the Muslims and Hindus in Wajid's Oudh; the second has King Wajid Ali Shah accepting, in a long monologue before his ministers, the hopelessness of his political position; and the third occurs in the study of the British Resident, where General Outram, in a compelling political exchange with a junior officer, Captain Weston, tries to justify the judgment that the Indian ruler of Oudh is unfit to rule. Let us deal with each in the order indicated.

One day, the chess players are about to commence their game when the city's *munshi* arrives to see them. Annoyed by this intrusion, but in keeping with the *nawabi* code of hospitality, they receive him most graciously in their "hall of audience." In the conversation that ensues among them, the two main topics discussed are "chess" and "the British." The *munshi*, at first, elaborates on the "rumours" he has heard of the British speculating some sort of "a takeover" of Oudh; but finding the two *nawabs* casting wistful glances at the chessboard, and realizing his own untimely intrusion, he very skillfully steers his remaining remarks to "the history of chess" to capture their bored and straying attention. Also wanting to retain the "British" in his conversation, however, the *munshi* now cleverly proceeds to teach them the rudiments of playing chess "the British way," its main contribution lying in the "Englishman's ability to produce quick decisions" in the game. Reacting strongly to this, the *nawabs* (who play chess at a more leisurely and languid Indian pace) launch a mighty tirade against similar British qualities that they detest. These include the British obsession with "speed," "communications," and "actions"; their insatiable "desire for wealth"; their "confounded efficiency" in administration, and so on. So animated does Mir become that he snatches an ancient cutlass from the wall and brags about the martial eminence of his ancestors. Since Mir has never handled a weapon before, he cuts a very clumsy figure, ventilating empty rhetoric with this ancient relic in his unaccustomed hands.

This scene is crucial for two reasons. First, it points to similar actions that will be performed by *both nawabs* at the end of the film. Second, it allows Ray to presage the irony and hollowness of what they profess, as will become apparent in the end of the film. Mir's inability to handle a hereditary weapon when confronted by mere *notions* of British "efficiency" is reflected at the film's end by Mir's clumsy firing of his ancient gun when he is labeled a cuckold. The martial eminence of his ancestors truly rings hollow when Mir fires at Mirza instead of aiming his weapon at his real enemies – the *gori palton* (white troops) of the British, which are at that very moment riding into Oudh. Although these two *nawabs* rant and rave against the efficiency ethics of the British, it is here they meet their own downfall. In fact, their willingness to "now play chess according to British rules" in the film's last shot exposes their mock-heroic attitudes as well as justifies their collaboration with the British.

Throughout the film, Ray is very unsympathetic to the two Lucknowi chess players, constantly undermining their points of view. This enables him to exhibit their characteristic blindness to everything around them because of their obsession with chess. When Mir remarks that "whatever happens, the British can't stop us playing chess," Mirza retaliates, "We are talking of war and he thinks only of chess." However, the fact that

Mirza is also infected with the same chess virus is indicated by Ray in the
marvelously orchestrated connubial scene that follows between Mirza and
his *begum* (wife), Khurshid, who has become the unfortunate victim of
her husband's cruel neglect. Mirza's view of chess is repeatedly subverted
by Khurshid, who becomes, as it were, the spokeswoman for Ray. The
scene opens in Khurshid's bedroom, where we see her feigning a migraine
headache so that Mirza is forced to abandon his chess game with Mir and
hurry to her *zenana* (boudoir), where she will try to seduce him. As he
ministers to her, she snaps out at "that stupid game" which keeps him
so preoccupied. Mirza's response is characteristic: "why, it's the king of
games. Ever since I started to play chess . . . my power of thinking has
grown a hundredfold." But Mirza's thinking outside the realm of chess
has not grown at all! It has, in fact, narrowed to such an extent that, in
Khurshid's undermining retort, the game only makes her husband "sit
hunched over that stupid piece of cloth and jiggle around those stupid
ivory pieces." Khurshid further indicates the dangers of such an obsession,
which has forced his friend's (i.e., Mir's) wife to take a lover. "All Lucknow knows that his wife is carrying on with another man. Only you
and your friend don't know."

Having surprised him on a verbal level, Khurshid orders her husband
to lie down on the bed. When he meekly complies, she boldly sits above
him. Khurshid wants him, "especially your eyes, red from staring at those
stupid chess pieces" to look "at me." She sets herself up as his flesh-and-
blood wife in opposition to those ivory representations of women he fingers on the chessboard. She is using all her feminine wiles to arouse his
dormant passions. As this sexual game begins and she pulls a coverlet over
them, Ray cuts to the drawing room, where Mir wonders about the prolonged absence of his friend. He tiptoes to the door, listens to the sounds
of lovemaking, then tiptoes back. A reverse traveling shot follows. As the
foreground is darkened by the two ends of a curtain drawn together, Mir's
hand suddenly appears in the middle, and with a deft but casual movement, he shifts one of his pawns to a more advantageous position on the
chessboard.

Ray cuts back to the Mirza–Khurshid sexual site in the *zenana*, where
the uncomfortable silence between the two, after Khurshid's failure to
arouse Mirza, is accentuated by the distant barking of dogs and passing
of horse carriages in the night outside. Khurshid finally releases him and
sits on the edge of the bed looking away. Ray's mise-en-scène makes it very
apparent that although her sexual game has failed, Mirza's responses are
very nonaristocratic. He is agitated, not so much by his sexual impotence

but by his prolonged absence from the chessboard. He is anxious to get back to his abandoned game. He excuses his sexual nonperformance by stating to his *begum* that "my mind was elsewhere. It was with Mir waiting and the game half-finished." He is completely oblivious to his wife's perpetual waiting and *her* half-finished or never-satiated games of passion. Ray also has him sing a love song to cover up his romantic awkwardness, but the intrusion of his song at such a delicate moment ironically deflates the masculine lover he is trying to play in his wife's presence. As he hurriedly exits, Khurshid, like a betrayed Scheherazade, angrily calls for Hiria, her faithful old maidservant, and demands that "you tell me a story. I want to stay awake all night."

Ray now focuses on the drawing room. Mirza slowly walks in and assumes a solemn air. Mir, guessing by his disheveled appearance what must have transpired, solicitously inquires about the *begum:*

MIR: A bad headache?
MIRZA: Very bad.
MIR: Tch. Tch. *(Signs ostentatiously, then moves a piece)* Check!

Ray's narration, as I have tried to show from the above scene, is very ironic in relation to the two chess players, because they are, in E. M. Forster's celebrated definition, "flat characters endowed with a single trait" – their consuming obsession for chess.[49] Because of this, their behavior is highly predictable. Having witnessed Mirza's indifferent behavior in a sexual/domestic situation, we can certainly anticipate what his (as well as his friend's) actions will amount to when they are finally confronted with the alarming political changes taking place around them in Oudh. "Rounded characters," to extend Forster's definition, are on the other end of the spectrum. In Chatman's accurate description, "they possess a variety of traits, some of them conflicting or even contradictory; their behavior is not predictable – they are capable of changing, of surprising us. They inspire a strong sense of intimacy."[50] We see this intimacy very clearly established through the character of Wajid Ali Shah, whom Ray presents in ways that are always capable of surprising not only the British Resident General Outram, with his limited and fixed notions of Occidental masculinity, but also us. Ray's narration creates in us the strong anticipatory need "to demand the possibilities of discovering new and unsuspected traits" in Wajid; he very skillfully modulates Wajid's functions "as open constructs, susceptible to further insights." Wajid Ali Shah becomes for us, and for the director, "virtually inexhaustible . . . for contemplation."[51]

Before Wajid Ali Shah actually *speaks* his monologue, Ray depicts the
monarch's characteristics through purely *visual* means. In the visual résumé of Ray's prologue, we see Wajid adopting several *roles* and expressing
several *abhinayas* (gestures). Ray frames him first as Lord Krishna, playing the flute and assuming the stance of the eternal lover. Then we see
him leading a Mohurrum procession, dressed resplendently as a Muslim
prophet. This is followed by a shot of Wajid stroking his cat, in a style
very reminiscent of a James Bond villain, while enjoying the sensuous
glances of the *kathak* dancer at a lavishly performed *jalsa*. Next, we see
Wajid composing a poem and reciting it loudly to his court during a trial
when he is expected to render a judicial verdict. These expressions of Wajid's eccentric personality are crucial indices of his effort to transcend his
position as king by adopting all these varied roles of dancer, flute-player,
prophet, lover, and poet. His confidence in himself is fueled by his imaginative life, in which all this role-playing enhances the traditional image of
the royal administrator and ruler. Furthermore, his ministers, his courtiers,
and even the ordinary citizens of Oudh accept this: When Wajid comes
out with a poem instead of a judicial verdict at a trial, they are not in the
least surprised.

This peculiarity of Wajid, which Ray cites here, has an analogue in Forster's *A Passage to India*. Aziz (also a Muslim, like Wajid), who is lying ill
in bed and has some quarrelsome Muslim friends visit him, suddenly decides to recite a poem. Immediately, all squabbling in that narrow, dirty
room stops. The imaginative life celebrated in the poem casts its spell over
the speaker and the listeners, and the day-to-day existence, with its dullness and squalor, is wonderfully transcended:

[The poem] had no connection with anything that had gone before, but it came
from his heart and spoke to theirs. . . . The squalid bedroom grew quiet; the
silly intrigues, the gossip, the shallow discontent were stilled, while words accepted as immortal filled the air. . . . The poem had done no "good" to anyone,
but it was a passing reminder, a breath from the divine lips of beauty, a nightingale between two worlds of dust.[52]

Wajid's recitation, though having no connection with the trial, is an unspoken appeal for his recognition: first as a poet and only then as a law-
giver and king. The poem, though of no practical value, forces the king's
audience to experience the poet's imaginative life. Similarly, at the end of
the *kathak* recital, when Wajid learns from his weeping prime minister,
Ali Naqui, that the British Resident General Outram is due to arrive and
ask for Wajid's peaceful surrender to the British government, Wajid's first

reaction is to upbraid Ali Naqui for such "unmanly" display of emotion in public. "Only poetry and music should bring tears to a man's eyes," he tells him, once again subjugating politics to poetry. Even with his historical fate sealed, Wajid clings to his uniquely offered claim to kingship. In the monologue that follows, he demands from his ministers, with amazing rhetoric, the answer (if there could be one) to the following syllogism: If the British think that he is unfit to rule, could they produce a single English monarch who could compose poetry and music of such a high order? "The common people sing my songs," he concludes, "and they love my poetry because of its candor."

It is precisely these bewildering aspects of Wajid's personality that intrigues the British Resident, General Outram. In Outram's view, Wajid is a ruler completely lacking in masculinity. Instead of ruling like a man, Wajid loves to dance. Instead of administering and rendering verdicts, Wajid composes poetry and songs. These are unkingly, decadent, and unmanly qualities for a ruler. The scene in which Wajid is analyzed by General Outram for the benefit of Captain Weston, one of his assistants, is played out very skillfully.

We are in Outram's study. As we come into the scene, Ray shows Outram reading aloud to Weston from an official document that gives "an hour by hour account of the King's (Wajid's) activities, dated the 24th of January." What we get here is the official description of Wajid. Weston's responses, however, offer resistance to the damaging portrait of the king that Outram's discourse is trying to build. Moreover, Ray works out this dialectic like a chess game, with appropriate moves and countermoves between the two officials, adding a further richness to Premchand's original story.

"Did you know," Outram informs Weston at the outset, "that the King prayed five times a day?" The implication is that instead of ruling and administering Wajid is more interested in trivial and nonmonarchial activities like "praying." Weston's response to this is, "Five is the number prescribed by the Koran, sir." This categorically affirms Outram's ignorance of Islamic religion and culture. Acknowledging Weston's move, Outram dips into the official document to come up with the following damaging fissures in Wajid's personality:

"His Majesty listened to a new singer, Mushtrari Bai, and afterwards amused himself by flying kites on the palace roof." That's at 4 P.M. Then the King goes to sleep for an hour but he's up in time for the third prayer at 5 P.M. And then in the evening – now where is it? – "His Majesty recited a new poem on the loves of the *bulbul* [a Persian nightingale]."

Outram expects Weston to come up with the damaging adjectives and epithets to typify Wajid as the inappropriate ruler. "Tell me Weston . . . What kind of poet is the King? Is he any good, or is it simply because he is the King they say he is good?" But Weston, using his own authority – for he knows the Urdu language and the people and culture of Oudh firsthand – informs Outram that, as a poet, Wajid "I think is rather good." To prove this he not only recites a Wajid poem in translation but also interprets it for him. To Outram's narrow, militaristic British mind, the poem "doesn't amount to much," but when he informs Weston of this, the latter quickly counters by indicating that the poem "doesn't translate very well, sir."

Checked again, Outram's next gambit is to target the perplexing image cast by Wajid's bizarre masculinity. The nonviolent Wajid challenges not only Outram's concept of the virile and masculine ruler but also (as Ashis Nandy observes in his brilliant review of the film) "the dominant concept of kingship in Indian Islam as well as the Hindu Kshatriya or soldier tradition."[53] We can see very clearly here why that Indian critic was so upset about Ray's "effeminate portrait" of Wajid. When Weston insists that Wajid is "really gifted" as a composer of songs, poems, *and* as a dancer, Outram's colonial ire rises. "Yes, so I understand," he fires back at Weston, "with bells on his feet, like naked nautch-girls [professional female dancers]." We see very clearly here the colonial intent: How can you call Wajid a king when in addition to wearing a crown on his head he also wears bells on his feet? Arriving rapidly at this conclusion, Outram demands: "And what kind of King do you think that all this makes him, Weston? All these various accomplishments?" When Weston slyly responds, "Rather a special kind, sir," Outram stops pacing, stiffens, and erupts: "Special? I would have used a much stronger word than that Weston. I would have said a bad King. A frivolous, effeminate, irresponsible, worthless King." When Weston tries to protest, Outram, pulling rank as British Resident, warns Weston that "any suspicion that you hold a brief for the King" would ruin Weston's chance for any future promotions "once we take over" Oudh. It is a lamentable victory on Outram's part, but the struggle between the two men adds an important layer to Premchand's excellent short story.

The scene above shows Outram in his official garb, but Ray later humanizes him by portraying him as a victim of his own government's policies as well. On this level Ray shows Outram privately expressing his anger at the British government for endorsing Oudh's annexation without any justification. In this scene, Outram interestingly offers his doubts to Dr. Joseph Fayrer, a young resident physician, who, unlike Weston, is not Outram's inferior. Outram tells him that "we have even less justification

Figure 19. General James Outram (Richard Attenborough) reluctantly doing "his damnedest" to get Wajid Ali Shah (Amjad Khan) "to sign and abdicate" in Shatranj-ke-Khilari (The Chess Players, *1977). (Photo by Nemai Ghosh; gift of Ben Nyce)*

for confiscation here. . . . The administration here is execrable. I don't like our fat King either. But a treaty is a treaty." This refers to the early treaty Wajid had signed with Outram's predecessor, in which the British government had insisted that Wajid disband his army and turn over most administrative problems to the British forces that would thereby guard his borders and maintain law and order in his kingdom. When that treaty was conveniently abrogated in 1837, Wajid, in Outram's words, "was not informed." In giving expression to his doubts and ire, Ray makes Outram a scapegoat of history and realpolitik as well. As a servant of Her Majesty's government, "the soldier" Outram has to obey the wishes of the Crown. "I'm called upon to do my damnedest to get him to sign and abdicate." Outram feels uneasy to face Wajid and dishonor him a second time. When the treaty earlier was abrogated without the king's knowledge or consent, it was administratively broken; to appropriate his kingdom now without his consent is again to commit administrative treachery! The fate that he had spelled out for Weston would have embraced Outram himself if had he failed to carry out his duties. Although Ray shows him ultimately obeying "the soldier" in him, it is a very reluctant Outram who finally emerges as the winner of this duel [Fig. 19].

Another significant departure is the completely new ending worked out by Ray to bring his study of colonialism to a satisfying end. Premchand's ending resolves the question: What will happen to these two chess players who are so ignorant about the changes taking place all around them? In Ray's ending, the emphasis is not on resolution at all. Finding the peace of Oudh threatened by the military presence of the British, the two chess players decide to play chess outdoors for a change. Mir finds a deserted mosque in the countryside, where we see them resume their games. Into this sylvan setting Ray introduces Kaloo, a young and impressionable Hindu boy. He is the only villager who has stayed behind to see the colorful and impressive uniforms of the British troops moving into Oudh. As a child, he is obviously fascinated by the pomp and the pageantry.

While he goes to fetch food, the *nawabs* start squabbling. At the precise moment Mir points an ancient gun at Mirza, Kaloo rushes in loudly announcing the arrival of the *gori palton* (white troops). Unnerved by this, Mir fires the gun, and Ray crosscuts from shots of the majestic British troops to the stunned faces of the two *nawabs*. For the first time, the intention of the British to annex their kingdom finally dawns on them. When Kaloo chooses this moment to ask his all-important question: "Why is nobody fighting the Angrez [British]?" he becomes, very appropriately, the historical spokesman of the Indian Nationalist Movement itself, which ninety years later would successfully drive out the British from India on 15 August 1947.

While pointing to India's political future through the figure of Kaloo, Ray at the same time exposes the two *nawabs*' cowardly collaboration with the enemy. This is different from Premchand's ending, in which the two *nawabs* kill each other. Ray's masterful irony is indicated by keeping them alive and by making them immediately adopt the British style of chess playing now that Oudh has a *gora* or "white" ruler on its throne. His trenchant criticism of such a betrayal is firmly underlined by the film's last shot, in which these two silly caricatures (for that is how he wants history to "fix" them) are seen swatting mosquitoes and bursting into roars of laughter as they begin their first chess game according to their colonial masters' "new rules."

Concluding Remarks

If Ray had often been accused by his critics for being an aloof artist and not a committed one, the fault lay not with Ray, but with his critics, who often confused commitment with propaganda. As an artist, Ray did not want to be a propagandist because he felt he was not in a position to give "answers to social problems."[54] He wanted to present these problems and let the audience come to some kind of a realization after having witnessed the artist's presentation of them. Of course, the artist's sympathy predicted a certain taking of sides (as both his overtly political films illustrate), but even here Ray was taken to task for trying to humanize characters like an Outram or a Wajid or turning his cinematic gaze away from strife, wickedness, and violence. Ray's definition of struggle eschewed the blatant signifiers of social violence (or, for that matter, waving red flags and filling the screen with images of balled fists) and replaced them with the struggle of an inadequate person trying to become someone. He was not interested in the character of the "heroic mold." For Ray, the ordinary people you meet every day in the street were more challenging subjects; and yet when he dealt with them, he politicized not only them, but also the issues and conflicts they faced.

Another thought to bear in mind is that beneath the aesthetics of his richly textured craft, there was always a strong moral attitude running through his cinematic oeuvre. In his earlier, *rasa*-inspired work, especially in *The Apu Trilogy*, Ray was involved with a cinema whose primary function was to arouse in the spectator a peculiar form of pleasurable excitement that accompanies the mysterious and wonderful process of growing up; but moral attitudes never deserted his characters even in these early films. Apu's breaking away from his mother and his final reconciliation with his neglected son, for example, were both achieved on a moral level.

Even a complex subject like the death of feudalism in *Jalsaghar* (*The Music Room*) became intensely vivid because of its presentation through the ancient form of *rasa*. Even here, however, Ray's attitude toward the *zamindar* was sympathetic: In spite of his recklessness, Biswambhar Roy was shown to display a stubborn, almost moral attachment to his music. From among his newer work, *Pratidwandi* (*The Adversary*) exemplifies Ray's position very pointedly. There are two brothers in the film: Tunu, the younger one, has embraced the Naxalite cause (a radical, leftist movement that was started in rural Bengal in 1967). Siddhartha, the elder, although ideologically conscious, cannot quite make up his mind; yet it is the latter's vacillating attitude that attracted Ray. Tunu did not interest Ray as a person: Since all his actions and thoughts were determined by his leftist ideology, he became for Ray a predictable and one-dimensional character. Siddhartha, assailed by doubts, became for Ray the more interesting character, especially when all his thoughts and actions were exposed and tested in challenging situations.

One of the aims of this chapter has been to put the poetry of Ray's early work and the politics of his later work under the rubric of his moral consciousness. What greater expression of commitment could critics expect than that demonstrated in film after film as Ray dealt with the social, human, and ethical issues in the role of a creative artist?

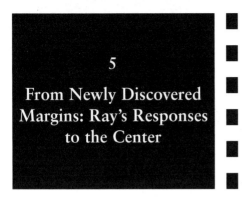

5

From Newly Discovered Margins: Ray's Responses to the Center

*To
the late but perennially alive
Larry Schwartz,
who loved India and Ray;
Cuthbert Lethbridge,
the finest individual Ray
archivist; and the late
Jason Fernandes,
for fun-filled M.A. "Ray"
Days at The Aakashvani*

Introduction

Ray's humanism was endorsed by the *bhadralok* "center" (i.e., the Bengali middle class) to which he belonged. However, as the climate of India in general and Bengal in particular deteriorated in the 1990s on all fronts – political, cultural, social – and as this deterioration was felt in an everyday experience of "marginality," Ray was forced into a search for an alternative authenticity to the notions of *bhadralok* centrality.

He started off by questioning the powerful fundamental beliefs of Hinduism, sanctioned by conniving *bhadralok* bureaucrats and fanatical religious zealots in *Ganashatru* (*An Enemy of the People*, 1989). This start was not auspicious, however, because the character chosen to question these "centrist" tendencies was not very convincing. Critic Asoke S. Viswanathan identifies accurately the confusions in Ray's characterization of Dr. Ashoke Gupta: "Where indeed is the cinematic isolation of the good doctor struggling to convince an insensitive, brute majority of the dangers of blind faith?"[1] The characterization lacked conviction because the doctor's isolation emerged from living in an idealist's fool paradise. The same complaint may be leveled against Ray's depiction of Ananda Majumdar, the ailing father and founder of Anandnagar in his next film, *Shakha Proshaka*: Both men work in the public sphere of contemporary India, yet both seem completely unaware of the excesses that are ubiquitous there. Dr. Gupta works in a public hospital in Chandipur owned and run by a capitalist and his hand-picked "Hindu" coterie, which controls every civic, public, and religious activity. They have the temple, the newspapers, the hospital, the commercial facilities, the municipality, even the public meeting halls comfortably in their pockets. Confronted by the center's effective capacity to brand him "an enemy of the people," Dr. Gupta's misguided idealism and his inept use of the spoken and written word seem to make him terribly unfit for the job of facing the centrists. His antagonists, as well as those who throw their lot with him, are also portrayed in a very problematic way. Finally, there is the optimistic ending, which seems less a convincing critique of the corrupt center than a wish fulfillment on Ray's part.

In *Shakha Proshaka* (*Branches of the Tree,* 1990), the challenge to the center is articulated more confidently. The film falls into some of the traps that undermine *Ganashatru,* but what saves it is Ray's use of the spoken word, which functions in this film to expose and critique the centrist values of the Bengali middle class.

It is *Agantuk* (*The Stranger,* 1991), however, that decisively abrogates the *bhadralok* center. In his essay "Satyajit Ray's Secret Guide to Exquisite Murders," Ashis Nandy eloquently characterizes the film's distancing strategy:

In *Agantuk,* Ray defies the conventions of his own thought and his self-definition as a chosen carrier of the European Enlightenment in India even more dramatically than he usually does in his more ambitious movies. The defiance comes through a painful process of self-transcendence and self-negation; he has to set up a formidable anti-self in the form of a truant anthropologist who rejects all progressive definitions of civilization and gracefully lives out his faith.[2]

Middle-class Indians (and their *bhadralok* Bengali counterparts) cling to a carefully constructed self-image that they consistently try to define, in historian Richard Lannoy's terms, "as industrious, orderly, adult and socially organized."[3] They do so by holding "responsible" jobs, marrying into and rearing "educated" families, and contributing aesthetically and socially to the culture circulating around them, usually in the metropolitan centers of India. In 1955, Ray's "truant anthropologist," Manmohan Mitra, defiantly left his family and abandoned the "center" of Calcutta. Thirty-five years later, being, in Geza Roheim's words, "free, untrammeled and truly self-reliant,"[4] he suddenly chooses to visit his niece, Anila Bose, who lives with her husband, Sudhendu, and son, Satyaki, in an upper-middle-class Bengali suburb. His letter heralding his impending arrival offers no apology for his long absence from his family nor any explanation for his plan to generate belatedly some kind of bond with his "only niece." His letter raises a turbulent storm in the placid teacup existence of the Bose family. Manmohan Mitra, as *Agantuk* or "the stranger," is Ray's most successful "other" simply because his "otherness" is constructed by his niece, her husband, and their *bhadralok* friends. In order to try to claim their authority over his slippery identity (he could be Chhoto Mama [Younger Uncle] or a clever fraud pretending to be one), they take great pains to define him as "radically different" from themselves, deliberately asserting their "geographical and social distance" as *bhadraloks* from this truant stranger masquerading as uncle. Nonetheless, Ray's narrative relentlessly makes them arrive at a transformation of their own inauthentic selves. Not only do they become displaced from the center, but their eyes are forced open to witness their own selfishness, greed, and misplaced cunning by a man who comfortably and proudly resides on the margins.[5]

From "Zero" to "Captain Nemo": Ray's Problematic Alphabet of 1990s Indians

The biggest lapse of *Ganashatru* (*An Enemy of the People*), it seems to me, emerges through Ray's characterizations of his main dramatis personae: The idealistic Dr. Gupta and his black-sheep conservative younger brother, Nisith, who is the ambitious chairman of the Chandipur Municipality. What could have developed as an interesting clash of ideologies between them never materializes because Nisith is very poorly developed as a character.

Nisith's Machiavellian conservatism doesn't seem to interest Ray; it is the idealism of his brother upon which he is more focused. All Nisith wants, we are told, is money and power, and Ray proposes to illuminate this through Nisith's preference for Westernized values. Instead of offering a critique, Ray offers a stereotype via Nisith's fondness for flashy bureaucratic occidental attire and constant smoking of imported cigarillos. Five years earlier, in *Ghare-Baire* (*The Home and the World*), Ray had shrewdly castigated Sandip's nationalistic duplicity by showing us his preference for expensive British cigarettes over the cheap and badly made Indian ones, even when espousing his "Indian-only" Swadeshi cause. Surely Nisith's conservative ideology emerges from a troubled psyche, but this does not seem to interest Ray. Nisith is repeatedly described as "dangerous," both as a family member and as a reactionary opportunist, but we are never shown the tremendous power he is capable of wielding. In Ray's narrative, he appears more like a mere prankster. By taking too many shortcuts, Ray short-circuits his analysis of Nisith's character. The same can be said of the two women: Mother and daughter have no roles to play in the film except to wait on the sidelines and, from time to time, intervene in the circulating male discourse as occasional voices of hope and reason; but very seldom are they heard or even listened to by the men.

Ray's dramatization of Haridas Bagchi, the two-faced editor of the town's most prominent "progressive" newspaper, is equally problematic. Initially, we see him agreeing to publish Dr. Gupta's controversial findings about the polluted temple water. When he later declines, the reason offered by Ray is surprising: Haridas, it transpires, had previously published a lot of Dr. Gupta's liberal-minded essays not because he believed in them but because he was smitten by Indrani, the good doctor's equally liberal-minded daughter. Inserting this clumsy romantic plot, especially at a crucial climactic stage of the conflict, sidesteps the political dimension of Haridas's duplicity.

Similarly, Indrani's boyfriend, Ranen – editor of the incendiary literary journal *Torch* and founder and guiding spirit of the town's progressive theater group – is clichéd as well. Ranen sits out most of the film until Ray suddenly transforms him into an intervening agent. The very day both Dr. Gupta and Indrani are fired from their jobs and face eviction from their family home, Ranen steps into the breach and, under the admiring gaze of his sweetheart, announces theatrically to the doctor that his theater group will support him and that his literary group will publish his scientific findings as pamphlets and distribute them within the temple's precincts. Ranen himself, Ray seems to suggest, becomes "the torch" whose beam of light will lead the Gupta family out of the darkness that has so suddenly descended on them. However, this theatrical intervention fails to convince, since neither Ranen's credentials nor his character had been properly established.

Heartbeats on a monitor accurately establish *Shakha Proshaka*'s thesis as the credits extend horizontally across the screen like "branches of a tree." The film's title refers more specifically to the Majumdar family tree. The "center" is the aged patriarch Ananda Majumdar, and the film opens with a bouquet of flowers the grateful citizens of Anandnagar have sent him on his seventieth birthday. In his sprawling rural house he lives with two senile "branches": his ninety-three-year-old "mad" father and Proshanto, one of his sons, reduced from "the most gifted one in the family" to his unfortunate "idiot" state by a near-fatal accident in England. The three other sons, who left their father in search of success, live in the modern city of Calcutta. Ashoke, the eldest, is a wealthy business executive; the second, Probir, is a prosperous "self-made" businessman; and Protap, the youngest, is in advertising. Uma and Tapti are the two daughters-in-law, and finally there is Dingo, Tapti and Probir's eight-year-old son.

The father's phenomenal success in rising from an ordinary provincial clerk to the owner of a mica mine and eventually builder of the entire township of Anandnagar, has cast a gigantic shadow over all his sons. Whereas his ascent to the top was achieved by virtue of Gandhi's and Nehru's principles of "honesty is the best policy" and "work is worship," the sons (with the exception of Proshanto) have pursued their versions of success by other avenues, primarily in the urban center of Calcutta, where they were able to escape their father's puritanical shadow. The eldest, Ashoke, has carved a life of luxury out of black-money hoardings and cleverly manipulated tax evasions. Probir has chosen to follow Dionysus – he drinks heavily, smokes constantly, and is a compulsive gambler – yet his private business is doing very well because he knows how to play the game of greasing palms. A loveless marriage and many affairs have not dulled his appetite, nor soured his cheerfully cynical disposition. Ananda Majumdar's utilitarian work ethic, inherited from his own father, "a poor but honest schoolmaster," survives only in his "idiot" son, Proshanto – although, ultimately, it resurfaces in his youngest son, Protap, who resigns his highly paid position as an advertising executive, having discovered that two of his closest associates were cooking up an enormous swindle, and chooses to join a poor theater group to pursue his love of acting.

The father's heart attack on his seventieth birthday summons the three prodigal sons and their families from Calcutta to his bedside in rural Anandnagar. The stage is set for a reexamination of the *bhadralok* values that the Majumdar family espouse, whether they choose to inhabit the margins or the center. On one side, Ray defines a curious moral order that seems to prevail only among the "injured" in the Majumdar household, from the senile grandfather who has reverted to a childlike purity; to Ananda, the patriarch, whose moral uprightness is brought crashing down by his heart attack; to Proshanto, the "idiot" son who finds salvation only in the Western classical music that incessantly flows from his room; and finally Protap, who resolves to stay as far away as he can from the corrupt world of commerce. On the other side, Ray assembles the *proven* success makers, namely Probir and his elder brother Ashoke. There is something rotten in this state of Majumdar, and Ray is determined to prune the rotting branches from this family tree standing in the winter of modern India's discontent.

In *Agantuk*, a similar division of characters is wonderfully achieved by means of the uncle's letter, which arrives like a missile in the Bose household one Saturday morning and is pounced upon and savagely critiqued by the parochial couple in the film's very first scene. While Anila wonders about the authenticity of this strange man proclaiming himself her Chhoto Mama or younger uncle, her husband strengthens her skepticism by declaring, "whether or not he is your real uncle, I just hope the man is civilized and well mannered. Otherwise, the next ten days are going to be difficult indeed."[6] The marginal outsider daring to invade their respectable family circle is immediately labeled as an uncivilized "other," and everything stemming from him is ridiculed: from his usage of the Bengali language – "a very florid style" – to his impertinent request, "I hope you don't mind offering your hospitality to a complete stranger." (From the husband's insular perspective, the stranger is not "asking" for hospitality but "extorting it.") The wife, astonished that her missing uncle can "actually write" a letter in Bengali, is surprised even more at his occasional use of the English language, a talent that only *bhadraloks* are supposed to display. "Look," she tells her husband, "he's written the date in English and used other English words. Here it is – 'unnecessarily'"! Instead of rejoicing at the prospect of meeting a lost blood relation, the husband and wife are unnecessarily alarmed, and they project their own insecurity by casting aspersions on him. "He hasn't had much education. He's led the life of a vagabond without any discipline," murmurs the outraged husband. "Obviously he left home only to avoid responsibilities. People like him are parasites," the wife chimes in. The husband promptly advises his wife to lock all her cupboards and conceal the most valuable art object in the house – a bronze statuette – in case this stranger decides to steal it.

Their ten-year-old son's reaction, however, is completely different. Being a stranger to the *bhadralok* sensibility that is forming inside his own psyche, Satyaki finds the impending arrival of the "fake uncle" very welcome. For the boy, he is a figure of compelling mystery, someone who promises to be exotic and *different* from his dull and predictable parents. It's the middle of his summer holidays; he needs an exciting diversion, and it will be fun to have a strange man in the house. The boy's name, in fact, clues us to the immediate bonding that will take place when the uncle arrives, since Satyaki was one of Krishna's most faithful disciples. In fact, the uncle, on first meeting him, inquires, "Which Satyaki are you, the disciple of Krishna or the son of Sudhendu Bose?" Satyaki responds by opting to play the role of the former, thereby imposing on the uncle the mythical identity of the "trickster" god, who, "like Dionysus, was a god of transgression, and his divinity was all the more numerous and potent because he rejected the rule of reason."[7] By making Satyaki his uncle's faithful disciple, Ray moves him away from his parents' *bhadralok* indoctrination, thereby making him take his first crucial steps in the forging of his own individuality.

The stage is now set for an interesting exchange of dichotomies: Every positive action that the uncle performs is thereafter given a negative interpretation, usually by Sudhendu, since it is he who wears the *bhadralok* trousers in this household. The rare coins that the uncle offers as a gift to Satyaki are genuine (having been collected during his nomadic travels); yet Satyaki's father feels he could have easily purchased them in Calcutta before coming here. The uncle's fluent command of the German language, including his correct pronunciation of the word *Wanderlust* (which he uses to explain to Anila the puzzling nature of his footloose existence) is dismissed by her husband, who maintains that any *bhadralok* Bengali can learn German by taking classes at the Max Müller German-language center in Calcutta. Sudhendu's narrow vision doesn't seem to extend beyond the "center" of Calcutta. Rare coins and European languages, as far as he is concerned, are to be found and acquired only in urbanized settings: All numismatists and linguists who come from outside the center are to be regarded with suspicion, conclusively labeled as fakes, and then banished.

The (T)issues of Language: Ray's Principal Instrument of *Bhadralok* Censure

Ray's last three films are heavily reliant on the spoken word. *Ganashatru,* his adaptation of Henrik Ibsen's play *An Enemy of the People*, was a curious departure for Ray, since the play is so dependent on speech, and Ray is known for the lyrical progression of his images – especially those memorable "wordless" moments he has so often inscribed in his works. When asked, in an interview with Jayanti Sen, to comment on his choice of material, Ray replied:

In regard to the problem of being dominated by too much dialogue, I feel that in this particular play the dialogues and even monologues would never weigh on the audience, and good cinema could always result from good speech delivery. An important element which has drawn so much to the play is the fact that it is based very much on "human action" . . . action in the sense of inter-action and reaction between one another and with the society at large, the varied levels of these relationships between Man and Society. This is a very important element in the play which I feel is the essence of good cinema.[8]

In Ray's 1990s trilogy, the spoken word becomes the most prominent "signifier of the social, political and cultural struggle" in which his characters are embroiled. The "words and propositions" expressed by the speakers "change their meanings according to the positions the characters are shown holding" either at the center or at the margins; and it is in "reference to their positions" and through their utterances that Ray finally makes his characters arrive at their own meanings of being and becoming.[9]

In *Ganashatru,* language becomes most critical in the scene showing the public debate between the two brothers [Fig. 20], for it explicitly spells out the opposition between Dr. Ashoke Gupta's scientific bent of mind, his reliance on logic and reason, and Nisith's manipulative rhetoric, fed and fueled as it is by calculated appeals to the fundamentalist forces supporting him. The debate is rudely cut off, however, just when it is becoming interesting: Doctors in India are often faced with the dilemma of being obedient to their scientific training or to the demands of their religion; Hinduism, for example, insists that water coming from a holy source can never be contaminated, since God purifies it through the inclusion of a mysterious property within it. Knowing this cannot be proved scientifically, Nisith asks Dr. Gupta, "Do you call yourself a Hindu?" "Of course I do," he stammers, "but there are certain Hindu religious customs I don't follow because of my scientific training." Nisith, as a result, does not have to work very hard to triumph over his brother. The latter's defensiveness regarding his scientific position often teeters on the brink of unbelievable naïveté.

Money is at the center of many debates in *Shakha Proshaka.* In the very first scene, the patriarchal Ananda Majumdar defines two types of money for Proshanto: "One is 'white' which you can account for and one is 'black' which you cannot account for." Proshanto, the wise fool, does not agree; for him both kinds of money amount to a "zero." In the next scene, when the father is being eulogized at his birthday celebration, Proshanto's summation is visually reaffirmed by Ray's camera, which focuses conspicuously on the "0" behind the speaker's head – actually, part of the lettering on a banner congratulating Ananda for having lived "70" years. From Proshanto's perspective, money exacts a fatal accountability: It can either reduce an honest man like his father to a "zero" before the horrified eyes of Anandnagar's marginal audience, or it can inflate the status and respectability of his corrupt brothers in the affluent "center" of Calcutta by adding "zeroes" to their bank accounts.

Proshanto's strength as a consistent critic of his brothers' *bhadralok* practices arises out of the authority of his voice. Most of the time, he lives in the margins of his own cavelike room; yet, when he emerges from it, as he does when he participates in the ritualistic family meals, his utter-

Figure 20. The language war between Nisith's (Dhritiman Chatterjee) manipulative rhetoric and Dr. Ashoke Gupta's (Soumitra Chatterjee) scientific logic in Ganashatru (An Enemy of the People, *1989*). *(Photo courtesy the Ray Archives, University of California at Santa Cruz)*

ances resoundingly silence those of his acquisitive brothers. Every time Ray makes Proshanto a visible part of the mise-en-scène, we know he is going to speak with moral authority. This forces a peculiar didacticism on Proshanto's character: Where does his lunacy end and his lucidity, as a keeper of the moral flame in the Majumdar family, begin? There are, for instance, his curious prophetic utterances: On his father's birthday, he tells him to "be prepared" for a heart attack. Later, at the dining table, after the heart specialist has left, he suddenly announces to the family that "father will get well." Do his powers as a seer give Proshanto the right to be his father's only moral guardian? Or is his father's heart attack somehow willed by Proshanto, to "open" his father's eyes to the venal natures of his citified *bhadralok* sons?

Proshanto evades all normal conversation (of which he is quite capable) with his brothers. Instead, in their presence, he constantly hums passages of Western classical music. At the dining table, when the two elder brothers are busy exposing each other's deviant ways of making and spending money, Proshanto silences them by loudly banging his hands on the table. In an earlier dining scene, he insists that one of his sisters-in-law put food in his plate only when he bangs on it. Both gestures astonishingly work in silencing the *bhadralok* discourse; his "lunacy" has found a theatrical language that makes the "sane" family members suddenly conscious of their moral lapses. His banging, metonymically suggesting a judge's gavel, signals a "guilty" verdict, not once, not twice, but many times over. His humming, on the other hand, seems to purify the space, which is infested by phrases and gestures that always come wrapped in the language of profit and loss.

When Protap strays into Proshanto's room, the Western religious music playing there inspires him to confess to his "idiot" brother his pure act of resignation. Proshanto not only approves but applauds Protap's actions by suggesting that Protap should consider himself fortunate in having sidestepped the Majumdar family tradition, which, in his estimation, only amounts to "a zero." This "zero" is then measured by Proshanto against the "seven colors of the rainbow," "the green of the grass," "the blue of the sky," "the red of the rose," and "the seven pure notes of music." Even though Proshanto tells Protap that he is alone in his salvation, this cathartic assertion supports Protap in his newly chosen vocation of the theater.

In *Agantuk*, Manmohan Mitra practices the clever process of "appropriation" in his verbal dealings with Satyaki and the boy's friends: His language, when he tells them stories, remolds the children's thinking and plays an important role in separating their thoughts from the privileged site of their *bhadralok* center.[10] When he first meets Satyaki, the uncle tells him he will teach the boy "all the one hundred and eight names of Krishna." This will make Satyaki aware of the rich tradition of Indian mythology, which the Westernized *bhadraloks* seem to have either forgotten or abandoned.

He does not want Satyaki to grow up to be "a *kupa-munduk*," a frog who lives exclusively in a well: Since the frog never leaves the well, it is the only reality he knows. He wants Satyaki to liberate himself from the *bhadralok* center and experience the wonders that lie at the margins as well. Against the tiny image of a man hang-gliding over a metropolitan skyline of tall buildings, Ray frames the uncle at a public park telling Satyaki and his friends marvelous tales of his visit to Machu Picchu, the richness of the Incan civilization, and the wonders of the universe. In an earlier scene, the uncle draws Satyaki's attention to the wit of the adman who has left out the "b" from the THUMS UP drink, and is delighted when

Satyaki raises his thumb to signal what this appropriated word stands for – namely, satisfaction!

In his dealings with adults, however, the uncle cunningly switches to the linguistic practice of "abrogation." This involves a complete rejection of the urban *bhadralok* culture's "aesthetic and illusory standards of normative or 'correct' usages and assumptions of traditional and fixed meanings 'inscribed' in its words."[11] He begins the abrogation process by first explaining to his niece (and Satyaki) his reasons for rejecting the Bengali *bhadralok* center and the "civilization" for which it stands. Many years earlier he had wanted to enroll in an art college in Calcutta; but then there fell into his hands the picture of a bison painted twenty thousand years ago by a cave dweller. The picture revealed to him a completeness and mastery of artistic execution that no art school in the world could have ever taught. It was this event that led him to explore the mystery that lies at "the heart of such savagery and primitivity." In order to be faithful to his resolve, however, he had to abdicate his own position within the *bhadralok* center and abandon all links that kept him tied to it.

The first time Manmohan Mitra meets Sudhendu, Anila's husband, he admonishes him not to mime the *bhadralok* practice of touching a familial elder's feet: "Don't touch my feet till you are free of doubt." This telling remark criticizes very accurately Sudhendu's pretense in offering this stranger, his wife's assumed uncle, the obligatory respectful gesture of *bhadralok* welcome while bad-mouthing him to his wife and his other *bhadralok* friends behind the uncle's back. He continues to disarm Sudhendu by throwing his passport at him, insisting that he examine the document to verify his globe-trotting credentials. Sudhendu does so sheepishly, because earlier in the day he had in fact expressly telephoned his wife to demand that she check the anthropologist's passport while he was in the shower!

When news of the alleged uncle's sudden arrival spreads among the Bose's *bhadralok* friends, they decide to come over and inspect him personally. This in itself is unethical, for what gives these civilized *bhadraloks* the right to impose their privileged gazes on him? The first to arrive are the Rakhits. When Mr. Rakhit chooses to define Manmohan's reentry into the *bhadralok* center as a "return of the prodigal," the uncle punctures his judgmental categorization by exploding the normative and fixed meanings that have accumulated around the word "prodigal." He informs Mr. Rakhit that, from a *bhadralok* perspective, "prodigal means that either one is *wasteful* or one is *repentant*." Since as an outsider he has neither been wasteful nor repentant, the word does not apply to him. He then

proceeds to declare that there has been method to his nomadic wander-
ings. He has lived with tribes all over the world and has dutifully record-
ed their culture and civilization in his notebooks. He has, in fact, just returned after studying the lives of forty-three Native American tribes. His
writings about them are soon going to be published in America. Here is
a man who has devoted his entire life to justifying the validity of people
who have been politically, historically, racially, and socially marginalized
by the determined centrists of their own cultures; and here are the Boses
and the Rakhits – Bengal's civilized *bhadraloks* – imposing Hamlet's dilemma of "to be or not to be" uncle on a man who chooses to play the
more exciting marginal role of "nuncle"!

The next *bhadralok* who is summoned by the Boses to expose their
mysterious visitor's spurious identity is Pritish Dasgupta, a highly polished
and skillful lawyer who is very clever with words. He begins his inquisi-
tion by formulating an argument around the Hindu concept of *dharma*
or duty. Since the Boses are performing their *dharma* in looking after
their guest – even though he is a man of highly questionable means who
does not cater to the dictates of Hinduism – Pritish wants to know the
uncle's own definition of *dharma*. Manmohan Mitra answers obliquely by
asking Anila to sing one of his favorite Bengali songs. Anila's song, which
within the narrative prepares her for her inclusion into the tribal dance
at the end of the film, celebrates all the values by which her uncle has lived
his life. The words of her song answer Pritish's queries and express the
uncle's *dharma* only for the authentic moment whenever, wherever, and
with whomever it may occur. It does not need or care for any institution-
alized space or support. "When the *veena* plays dulcet tones in a house,"
the song informs Pritish, "then grace and beauty awaken" and "a fresh
breeze blows from the outside" "reaching the inner depths of being." The
authentic moment created by the pure resolve of the song itself silences
Pritish.

Nettled by the anthropologist's glowing accounts of tribal cultures, Pritish counters with his own lofty paeans directed at the "progress" created
by "modern man's" invention, daring, and his skills in "technology." The
uncle is quick to remind him that progress and technology are not exclusive creations of the center: A lot of progress and technology has been
achieved at the margins, but the center has always refused to acknowledge
or validate it. He gives Pritish an example of the Eskimo's engineering
skills at creating an igloo out of two kinds of ice – opaque and transparent; and yet this principle of architectural construction is never recognized
by the urbanized, who refer to the Eskimo as "a wild man." (I would en-

dorse this valorization of Eskimos further by urging our conceited prosecutor to see Robert Flaherty's *Nanook of the North*, a film Ray might have had at the back of his mind when he put the Eskimo argument in Manmohan's mouth.) The shaman, the uncle continues, has no knowledge of Western medicine, and yet he has five hundred herbal remedies at his fingertips to offer the *bhadralok* if the latter would care to accept them; but most *bhadraloks* would not, since the shaman does not wear a stethoscope around his neck.

"Man's civilization," the uncle reminds Pritish, "has acquired such an arrogance that he can destroy the very world in which he has ushered in so much progress." If that is progress, he proclaims, then "it is my greatest regret that I am not a savage even though I have Shakespeare, Tagore, Marx and Freud in my bloodstream." What made these thinkers and artists so "savage" was their courage to expose and challenge the deficiencies they found at the centers of their own cultures. After exposing the mess man's rationality had created at the center, these individuals boldly went on to show how a blind adherence to such fundamental centers divided the haves from the have-nots and created unbridgeable schisms between the home and the world. They questioned the very being and nothingness of a paltry insignificant creature called humanity, and demonstrated how such creatures hid in the unconscious what they dared not recognize consciously.

"I am Nemo – a no one" – the uncle declares to his *bhadralok* opponents, who are submerged twenty thousand leagues in their own pettiness. Unable to rise to any kind of awareness or recognition of his *no-oneness,* the angry Pritish storms out of the house demanding, "either you declare who you really are or clear out" of the Bose household. The uncle chooses to leave rather than assert definitively his *some-oneness.*

The Burden(s) of Mise-en-Scène: Ray's 1990s Filmic Style

The style, or rather the lack of it, in Ray's final films summons up the image of an exhausted filmmaker directing from the confines of a large and comfortable easy chair. Missing are Ray's customary eye for detail; his meaningfully orchestrated camera movements and editing patterns; the finely executed passages of "silences" counterpointed and punctuated by revealing musical moments. The style is simplified to a mathematical exactness that doesn't leave much to the imagination. One is surprised by the obviousness of meanings conveyed through mise-en-scène. Again and again, nuance is sacrificed for outright statement.

Take the opening and closing scenes of *Ganashatru:* The film begins with the camera lingering over a stethoscope on a table. Then it pans over a quivering telephone wire till it arrives at the telephone. As it pulls back, the speaker – Dr. Gupta – is revealed relating his suspicions to the editor of a "progressive" newspaper.

The stethoscope, the instrument that probes the causes of disease within the bodies of stricken patients, is contrasted by Ray to the telephone, an instrument that conveys the effects of disease to the editor, and via his newspaper, to all the citizens of Chandipur. Both instruments personify Ashoke Gupta as a concerned doctor and an exemplary citizen. Listening to the alarming "noises" of sickness through his stethoscope, he chooses to make his own "voice" heard over the telephone to prevent a dangerous epidemic.

The film ends with Ray once again panning to the stethoscope on the table, the phone, and a small vial of the "polluted" temple water the laboratory has sent back after testing. This time, the doctor doesn't talk on the phone. Instead, we hear his off-screen voice calmly announcing to his family and supporters, "We've won." To confirm this, Ray adds a chorus of voices chanting "Long live Dr. Gupta!" from the street. The stethoscope and telephone have finally defeated the deadly "holy" water standing beside them on the table. The revelations, however, seem hopelessly forced and obvious.

At other moments in the film, too, the mise-en-scène is so obviously manipulated by Ray that one can often find oneself recoiling in disbelief. When Nisith, for example, asks Ranen to explain the leftist thrust of his literary journal *The Torch,* Ray shoots the entire conversation from Nisith's perspective. We thus see Ranen trying to explain his journal's liberal views to this conservative through a wall of hazy smoke from the latter's cigarillo. Not only does the smoke corroborate the name of the journal, but it foreshadows Nisith's mendacious views and actions, which will be "torched" by Ranen when he publishes Dr. Gupta's findings. In another scene, Nisith's Machiavellian intent is revealed via a close-up of his profile, silently smoking and witnessing the "fire" he has just created in the editor's office. In the background, we see the turncoat Haridas refusing to publish Dr. Gupta's controversial findings. (Nothing about the editor's office suggests that it is a space where progressive ideas and ideologies are either discussed or disseminated.) While Nisith is contemplating a long brown cigarillo, the dumbfounded doctor behind him rants like a bemused schoolboy, and the editor sits facing him looking thoroughly bored by both brothers' actions.

In Ray's final three films, dramatic action is shown occurring in spaces designated as "home"; but whereas in earlier films the characters' rooms became marvelous sites of their thoughts and their desires, "home" in his last three films fails to be an interesting place. In *Ganashatru,* "home" is reduced to an empty space through which countless entrances and exits are made; Ray makes no effort to particularize this domestic space, or show how it might be sacrosanct to the persons inhabiting it. In *Agantuk,* the action consigned to the Bose "home" is mostly presented in a visually uninspiring way. Only in the first dining-table sequence, the last bedroom scene between the Bose couple, or the outdoor scenes shot in the tribal village of Baner Pukar do we witness Ray making some effort to break away from the monotonous visuals that express the *bhadralok* vision. In *Shakha Proshaka,* however, Ray shakes off his stylistic lethargy to some extent and does manage to elevate his presentation of the Majumdar "home" through the four signifiers of *music, meals, mirrors,* and *nature.*

Proshanto's *music* in *Shakha Proshaka,* while soothing his disturbed mind, has the added function of disturbing his brothers: It constantly invades the privacy of each brother's room, thereby forcing some kind of suggestive response. While Ashoke grumbles that it prevents him from sleeping, Tapti keeps her husband Probir from arriving at the same conclusion by informing him that it is Bach, and he should listen to it with reverence. He smiles and does, even going to the extent of complimenting her on her musical knowledge. It is on Protap, however, that Bach has the most salutary effect. Protap has known Tapti since their college days, and when she enters his room to ask after his welfare, Bach's harmonies move him to lay his emotional turmoil at Tapti's (and the composer's) feet. While she gives him her firm approval, Bach's music seems to strengthen Protap inwardly. It enables him to regain the confidence he will need for that moment when he will have to confront his three elder brothers and tell them of his resignation without feeling either threatened by them or ashamed of his own actions.

It is at the Majumdar dining table, however, that the skeletons of the two elder brothers are dragged out of their *bhadralok almiarahs* (cupboards) and circulated for critical scrutiny along with the *meal.* Replying to critic Jayanti Sen's observation that dining-table sequences occur in many of Ray's films, the filmmaker explained, "they offer the opportunity of bringing together a number of people. One can read their subtle interactions. They are also an excellent way of showing different lifestyles."[12] Grouped around the table are Ashoke, Proshanto, Protap, and

Probir. Also present are Uma, the elder sister-in-law, eight-year-old Dingo, and his mother, Tapti. While the women, Proshanto, and Protap maintain a reluctant silence as they dine, the two elder brothers commence a game of sibling rivalry by bragging about the devious stratagems that have garnered them so much success and status in their life in metropolitan Calcutta. The silent witnesses first learn from Probir the rudiments of "long-distance betting" on horse races. He insists on justifying his compulsion to gamble as "a primal urge" and demands appreciation for "honestly" acknowledging his "vice." The only family member he seems to impress is his son Dingo, who declares between mouthfuls, "When I grow up I want to be a gambler, too." When the eldest brother tries to upstage Probir by declaring that he has no such compulsion to squander his hard-earned money, Probir turns the tables by uncovering his brother's under-the-table bribes, graft, and tax evasions. He reels off facts and figures, causing Proshanto to bang the aforementioned moral gavel, equating both men's "success" to a "zero."

When both brothers and their wives sheepishly retreat to their respective rooms, Ray first shows the shocked Uma stricken with guilt, submitting to her husband's stubborn sanctimonious insistence that "corruption is an accepted way of life in India" and "in spite of it, I consider myself successful." Ray registers the fact, however, that neither Uma nor her husband is comfortable with this corruption by making Ashoke constantly and fastidiously clean his spectacles as he tries to come to terms with his success. This *glass* motif is cleverly reprised when Ray's filmic gaze leaves this couple and focuses next on Tapti and Probir. Ray seats Tapti before her dressing table *mirror*, in which she and Probir are continuously reflected [Fig. 21]. As she gradually overwhelms Probir's resistance to recognizing his multitudinous moral lapses, she forces him to examine his own image. Blaming his excesses on his father, who always favored the other sons over him, he confesses to his numerous affairs and, like the repentant husband of *Kanchanjunga*, he promises to reform, if not for her sake, then definitely for their son, Dingo. Probir has seen himself in Tapti's mirror, and has not liked what has been thrown back at him.

What brings about a conclusive clearing of the air is the "picnic" sequence at Mungari. Venturing into *nature*, the two couples and Protap, who accompanies them, abruptly stop arguing. Against the stunning backdrop of trees, grass, and river, Tapti bursts into song. The two husbands, who had earlier drawn blood like fighting cocks, now become giggling schoolboys sharing memories of a term's-end picnic. Soon they begin to play an engaging game of "tongue twisters" with their wives. Dingo wan-

Figure 21. Tapti (Mamata Shankar) forcing Probir (Dipankar Dey) to examine his own image in her "mirror" in Shakha Proshaka (Branches of the Tree, *1990*). *(Photo courtesy the Ray Archives, University of California at Santa Cruz)*

ders away from the adults to investigate the wonders of the insect kingdom. Protap's tongue, still twisted by anger at what he has witnessed at the dining table, refuses to answer any question flung at him; he stands brooding silently on the edge of the wood. Probir, enraged by Protap's withdrawal, begins to taunt him to speak. With nature providing the appropriate stage setting, and with Proshanto's and Tapti's earlier affirmations flowing in his blood along with Bach's religious musical strains, Protap finally bursts into voice. He speaks passionately of his resignation and his resolve "to stay as far away as possible from you and your business worlds." As a struggling and poorly paid theater artist, he proclaims, he will try to "reclaim a little of our father's greatness." "We're all mediocrities in relation to father," he concludes, a claim that is accepted by his two stunned brothers and their grateful wives, and seconded later by Probir, who says to Tapti, "He really cut us down to size, didn't he?" Admiring his youngest brother, Probir promises to emulate Protap by correcting his own waywardness. "I'm trying, I'm trying," he pleads with his wife, assuring her that from now on ethical principles will replace all excesses in his life.

In *Agantuk*, Ray's style suddenly flares to life in three sequences. The first deals with the prominent *bhadralok* concern of eating. When Anila starts getting her home ready for the uncle, one of her main worries revolves around food. "Who knows what kind of food he likes to eat," she complains to her husband. "If he is vegetarian, that would mean making five different dishes every day." What prompts this *bhadralok* concern is the rigid convention of Bengali hospitality, which "decrees what is food and what is not food and what kinds of food should be eaten and on what occasions."[13] Food is given a specific significance in an Indian household, and *bhadralok* culture

sorts out its foodstuffs . . . and applies status distinctions of comparable sorts. Some foods are appropriate only to men, some only to women; some foods are forbidden to children, some can be eaten only on ceremonial occasions.[14]

When the uncle sits down for his first meal, he cheerfully announces to Anila, "I'm omnivorous and a small eater"; but Anila insists that he "must not skip any item" prepared by her. The celebrated *mashi,* or specially prepared Bengali fish, is placed by her at the center of the table. This must be eaten first, along with the "fancy crisp" that she is famous for preparing in a certain way. The uncle deliberately ignores the fish and starts his meal by choosing the less favored dish of lentils and rice. The curried spinach, not given pride of place on the dining table because it is a vegetarian item not popular with men and children, is the next item he hugely enjoys. He also insists that Satyaki have "more spinach than fish" so that he will be "as strong as Popeye." By ignoring the fish, the uncle empties it of all its prestige. The humble vegetable spinach and the cheap lentils that lower-class Indians normally consume are preferred over an upper-class delicacy like the specially made *mashi* or fish. Later, in his debate with Pritish, the uncle informs him gleefully that "I've eaten all kinds of meat: rat meat, snake meat, I've even eaten bat meat. The only meat I've yet to taste is human meat. I'm told it's quite tasty." He does not, like the *bhadralok,* attach prestige to particular categories of food: The forbidden (human meat) and the ceremonial (*mashi*), the raw and the cooked, have the same value to him. He enjoys all food without distinction as long as it is edible.

After the uncle chooses "to clear out," as Pritish put it, his niece and her husband, conspicuously etched in dark silhouettes, confess to each other the shameful parts they played in forcing their uncle to leave their *bhadralok* home. They are ashamed to put on the bedroom light and face each other. The entire scene is played out in darkness, and conveys their shame quite evocatively.

Unsatisfactory and Satisfactory Endings

One would have liked Dr. Gupta still to have triumphed in *Ganashatru* but in a different way. Sacred waters, even when they are not polluted, have drowned a lot of idealists in the past. What makes Dr. Gupta an exception? That small vial of polluted water has the power to topple the doctor's stethoscope from the table. The optimism generated by Ray at the end lasts only as long as the voices praising Dr. Gupta as a "champion of the people"; once they are switched off, life's brutal realities will take over. The optimistic ending materializes when Ranen and Biresh (the assistant editor of the allegedly "progressive" newspaper, who abruptly resigns and resolves to publish the doctor's controversial findings in most of Calcutta's major newspapers) arrive on cue as the narrative's two dei ex machina to extricate the Gupta family from eviction and dishonor.

The antagonistic climate, however, is not going to going to subside as quickly as Ray's ending suggests: Dr. Gupta's opponents are not going to take things lying down. Had the film ended with his supporters readying themselves for a long hard struggle, one would have understood their resolution to walk bravely upon a path studded with land mines. Instead, Ray has Dr. Gupta confidently declaring, "We have won." In the historical context of today's violent India, such an assertion is absurd. Surely Ray knows enough of Indian history to ascertain what really happens to the nonreligious when they dare to close sanctified places of worship.

The recuperating heart patient's proclamation "shanti! shanti!" ends *Shakha Proshaka;* but this cry of "peace! peace!" becomes very problematic when placed in the overall context of the film. Ray offers it as a prophetic utterance by Ananda Majumdar after his grandson Dingo's innocent revelation of his father's and elder uncle's nefarious business deals. The grieving patriarch hopes to set things right in his own mind by offering these apparently useless *shanti*s to the purest of his sons, Proshanto, while clutching his hands. "You're all that I need," Ananda finally murmurs, in the same breath banishing the three remaining sons from his presence. However, this is not fair: It is Protap, not Proshanto, who is most deserving. In resolving to remain pure, Protap shows more courage than

Proshanto, since his resolve is going to be tested daily in a brutal world where existence has to be chiseled out through compromise. Proshanto's life is noble but empty, whereas Protap faces risks and is constantly exposed to "zeroes" who are intent on dragging him down. Protap will have to fight every day for his *shanti*, whereas Proshanto only has to put Bach on the turntable.

After all this heartache, a nagging question raises its head: Why does the father choose *shanti* as some kind of panacea? Does he choose one "S" word to defeat another – "success" – for which his citified sons have sacrificed their morality? Or does Ray offer *shanti* in T. S. Eliot's ironic vein as an exhausted word whispered by a defeated father whose eyes have been finally opened to the noxious reality around him? But how can the father not have *seen* India's devastating deterioration all around him, when even the reclusive son, Proshanto, has felt and acknowledged it? We remember most vividly when Proshanto tells Protap, "I am alone in spite of the bottomlessness into which humanity has sunk." In the final analysis, though, it is good that the father's eyes have been opened. Perhaps, as he recovers, he will ultimately learn the inappropriateness of that word *shanti* and how conclusively it has lost *all* meaning in the India of today.

The final scenes of *Agantuk* significantly move the narrative outdoors and physically take the "repentant" Bose family (it isn't the "prodigal uncle," we are made to realize, who had to prove his repentance in order to enter the *bhadralok* center) far away from their metropolitan suburb to the marginalized tribal village of Baner Pukar. This is where their insulted uncle has gone to after his rude expulsion from their living room.

When they finally catch up with him, he is sprawled on the ground. In the tribal Kol tongue (which he speaks fluently), he asks a native Kol woman to fetch a cot when he sees his *bhadralok* relatives approaching. Even here, the distance between himself and them is scrupulously maintained: These are city folk who will not sprawl like him on the ground and sully their expensive attire [Fig. 22]. The young boy who follows his parents has a long way to go before he can muster sufficient courage and swing crazily on the aerial roots, as a Kol boy is shown doing from the nearby trees.

It is Anila, however, who makes the first move to cross that dividing line, abandon her customary position at the center, and take up a place on the margins where her uncle and these Kol tribes are located; and it is her uncle who gives her the opportunity to do so by requesting the Kols to perform their traditional ceremonial dance for these city-bred folk before the family all leave for the metropolis.

Figure 22. The distance between the "repentant" city folk Anila (Mamata Shan-kar), Sudhendu (Dipankar Dey), and Satyaki (Bikram Banerjee) at the "margins" and the insulted uncle, Manmohan Mitra's (Utpal Dutt) "center" in Agantuk (The Stranger, *1991). (Photo courtesy the Ray Archives, University of California at Santa Cruz)*

As the Kols dance in the noble spirit of their ancestors, Anila – keeping time to their rhythm and beat in her own *bhadralok* space comprising her husband and her son – is told by Sudhendu to "join the dancers." She does so to the silent approval of her uncle, whose smile signifies his victory.

When, finally, Manmohan Mitra bequeaths his entire inheritance (the real reason he had come to Calcutta) to the Bose family, money, which is so important to the *bhadralok* sensibility, is given to the metaphorical SOMEONES by a NO ONE. The uncle leaves, with very little in his pockets, to live with the aborigines in Australia. All he carries with him in the end are the precious notebooks in which he documents his tribal experiences – ironically, packed by Anila in a "civilized" suitcase.

On Ray – The Final Epitaph

Had Ray lived to make films after *Agantuk,* he may have continued to dismantle contemporary Bengal *bhadralok* culture. His last three films showed that he had made a new beginning in disrupting the "classical" in his own oeuvre and gradually replacing it with the "marginal" – proving that Ray was not completely out of step with contemporary India, as had unfairly been claimed.

The final triad may well be found wanting cinematically, when judged by the "classical" standards upheld by the vast body of Ray's films that precedes it. Its place in the rich tradition of Ray's cinema is vital, however: These are three fruitful branches of the Ray film tree, and they demonstrate (as I have tried to show in this chapter) that Ray was a director who refused to be isolated either by his ill-health, his classical sensibility, or by an India or a Bengal that had become only "imaginary homelands" for him. He was a filmmaker trying to discover cinema all over again, this time from the margins, not the center. He did not know where this road would take him, but like an *agantuk* artist, he was determined to follow this *pather panchali* wherever it might have led him.

Notes

Introduction

1. Satyajit Ray, *Our Films, Their Films* (Bombay: Orient Longman, 1976), 152.
2. Ibid., 156.
3. Robin Wood, *The Apu Trilogy* (New York: Praeger, 1971), 7.
4. Ibid., 10.
5. Ashish Rajadhyaksha, "Satyajit Ray, Ray's Films, and Ray-Movie," *Journal of Arts and Ideas* 23–4 (January 1993): 7–16, at 11.
6. Geeta Kapur, "Cultural Creativity in the First Decade: The Example of Satyajit Ray," *Journal of Arts and Ideas*, 23–4 (January 1993): 17–49, at 24.
7. Ray, *Our Films, Their Films*, 33.
8. Ibid., 36.
9. A. K. Ramanujan's "An Overview" on Indian poetics in Edward C. Dimock Jr. et al., eds., *The Literatures of India: An Introduction* (Chicago: University of Chicago Press, 1978), 115–18, at 117.
10. Ray, *Our Films, Their Films*, 33.
11. Ibid.
12. Ibid., 52.
13. For a complete list of all these awards refer to Ray's filmography in Chidananda Das Gupta, ed., *Film India – Satyajit Ray: An Anthology of Statements on Ray and by Ray* (New Delhi: Directorate of Film Festival Publications, 1981), 147–9.
14. Kapur, "Cultural Creativity," 39.
15. Ray, *Our Films, Their Films*, 41.
16. Gautum Kundu, "Satyajit Ray as Auteur: A Neglected Perspective," *Quarterly Review of Film Studies* 8(4) (Fall 1983): 85–8, at 86.
17. Rajadhyaksha, "Satyajit Ray, Ray's Films," 13.
18. Ibid., 15.
19. Ibid.
20. Ibid., 16.
21. Eric Rhode, "Satyajit Ray: A Study," *Sight and Sound* 30(3) (Summer 1961): 132–6; reprinted in Julius Bellone, ed., *Renaissance of the Film* (London: Collier–Macmillan, 1970), 9–23, at 21.
22. Ben Nyce, *Satyajit Ray: A Study of His Films* (New York: Praeger, 1988), 30.

23. Wood, *Apu Trilogy*, 39.
24. Ibid.
25. Pauline Kael, "The Home and the World," in *State of the Art* (New York: E. P. Dutton, 1985), 380–2, at 382.
26. Marie Seton, *Portrait of a Director: Satyajit Ray* (London: Dobson Books, 1971), 146.
27. Andrew Robinson, *Satyajit Ray: The Inner Eye* (Calcutta: Rupa & Co., 1990), 91.
28. Ibid., 118.
29. Ibid., 95.
30. Erik Barnouw and S. Krishnaswamy, *Indian Film*, 2d ed. (New York: Oxford University Press, 1980), 234–5.
31. Ibid., 239–40.
32. Kundu, "Satyajit Ray as Auteur," 86.
33. Ibid., 87.
34. Chidananda Das Gupta, *The Cinema of Satyajit Ray* (New Delhi: Vikas Publishing House, 1980), 50.
35. Ibid., 48.
36. Ibid., xii.
37. As quoted by Rajadhyaksha, "Satyajit Ray, Ray's Films," 16.
38. Suresh Chabria, "Satyajit Ray," *Cinema in India*, Annual '91, "Focus on Directors" (special issue): 89–92, at 91.

Chapter 1. Between Wonder, Intuition, and Suggestion: *Rasa* in Satyajit Ray's *The Apu Trilogy* and *Jalsaghar*

1. Chidananda Das Gupta, ed., *Film India – Satyajit Ray: An Anthology of Statements on Ray and by Ray* (New Delhi: Directorate of Film Festival Publications, 1981), 138.
2. Edwin Gerow, "The Persistence of Classical, Esthetic Categories in Contemporary Indian Literature: *Three Bengali Novels*," in Edward C. Dimock Jr. et al., eds., *The Literatures of India: An Introduction* (Chicago: University of Chicago Press, 1978), 212–38, at 212.
3. Ibid., 216.
4. V. K. Chari, *Sanskrit Criticism* (Honolulu: University of Hawaii Press, 1990), 231.
5. Rosie Thomas, "Indian Cinema: Pleasure and Popularity – An Introduction," *Screen* 26(3–4) (May–August 1985): 116–31.
6. Cited in Chari, *Sanskrit Criticism*, 239–40.
7. Raniero Gnoli, *The Aesthetic Experience According to Abhinavagupta* (Rome, Italy: MEO, 1956), xix.
8. J. L. Masson and M. V. Patwardhan, *Aesthetic Rapture*, vol. 1: *Text* (Poona: Deccan College Publications, 1970), 33.
9. Cited in Chari, *Sanskrit Criticism*, 241.
10. Ibid., 242.
11. Gnoli, *Aesthetic Experience*, 72.
12. From "Kavikanthābharana," verses 10–11, in W. S. Merwin and J. Mous-

saieff Masson, trans., *Sanskrit Love Poetry* (New York: Columbia University Press, 1977), 5–6.

13. Cited in Jaya Wadiyar Bahadur, *An Aspect of Indian Aesthetics* (Madras: University of Madras Press, 1956), 18–19.

14. Gnoli, *Aesthetic Experience,* xxvii–xxviii.

15. Masson and Patwardhan, *Aesthetic Rapture,* 1: 16–17.

16. Chari, *Sanskrit Criticism,* 245.

17. Bahadur, *Aspect of Indian Aesthetics,* 40.

18. Chari, *Sanskrit Criticism,* 245–6.

19. Ibid., 17–18.

20. Eliot Deutsch, "Reflections on Some Aspects of the Theory of Rasa," in Rachel Baumer and James R. Brandon, eds., *Sanskrit Drama in Performance* (Honolulu: University Press of Hawaii, 1981), 214–25, at 217.

21. R. A. Scott-James, *The Making of Literature* (London: Mercury Books, 1963), 69.

22. All references are from Kalidasa, *Sakuntala,* trans. Arthur W. Ryder (New York: E. P. Dutton & Co., 1959), 5.

23. All references from Humphrey House, *Aristotle's Poetics: A Course of Eight Lectures* (London: Rupert Hart-Davis, 1961), 101.

24. Ibid., 102.

25. Ibid., 109.

26. Ibid., 110 (emphasis added).

27. Ludovico Castelvetro's translation and interpretation of "Poetics" in Hazard Adams, ed., *Critical Theory since Plato* (New York: Harcourt Brace Jovanovich, 1971), 144–53, at 152 (emphasis added).

28. Chari, *Sanskrit Criticism,* 59.

29. Ibid., 60–1.

30. Ibid., 64.

31. Ibid., 70–1.

32. Gnoli, *Aesthetic Experience,* 73–4.

33. Gerow, "Persistence of Classical, Esthetic Categories," in Dimock et al., *Literatures of India,* 212–38, at 218.

34. Ibid., 219.

35. V. Raghavan, "Sanskrit Drama in Performance," in Baumer and Brandon, *Sanskrit Drama in Performance,* 9–44, at 22–3.

36. Sudhir Kakar, *The Inner World* (Delhi: Oxford University Press, 1978), 105.

37. James Joyce, *Portrait of the Artist as a Young Man* (New York: Viking Press, 1968), 212–13.

38. Ibid., 213.

39. Ibid.

40. Masson and Patwardhan, *Aesthetic Rapture,* 1: 53.

41. Kakar, *Inner World,* 57–8.

42. Ibid., 58.

43. Bibhuti Bhusan Banerji [Banerjee], *Pather Panchali (Song of the Road),* trans. T. W. Clark and Tarapada Mukherjee (Bloomington: Indiana University Press, 1968), 66.

44. Satyajit Ray, *The Apu Trilogy,* trans. Shampa Banerjee (Calcutta: Seagull Books, 1985), 22–3.
45. Ibid., 83.
46. Ibid., 117–18.
47. Kakar, *Inner World,*140–1.
48. Masson and Patwardhan, *Aesthetic Rapture,* 1: 23.
49. Ibid., 52.
50. A. K. Ramanujan and Edwin Gerow, "Dramatic Criticism" (on Indian poetics) in Dimock et al., *Literatures of India,* 128–36, at 133.
51. Ibid., 135.
52. Ibid.
53. Edwin Gerow, "*Rasa* as a Category of Literary Criticism," in Baumel and Brandon, *Sanskrit Drama in Performance,* 226–57, at 247.
54. Ibid., 248.
55. Robin Wood, *The Apu Trilogy* (New York: Praeger, 1971), 7.
56. Ibid., 13 (emphasis added).

Chapter 2. From Gazes to Threat: The Odyssean *Yatra* (Journey) of the Ray Woman

1. National Committee on the Status of Women, *Status of Women in India* (a synopsis of the "Report of the National Committee on the Status of Women" [1971–4]) (New Delhi: Allied Publishers, 1975), 13.
2. Sudhir Kakar, *The Inner World* (Delhi: Oxford University Press, 1978), 56–7.
3. A. R. Gupta, *Women in Hindu Society* (Delhi: Jyotsna Prakashan, 1982), 6.
4. Sudhir Kakar, *Intimate Relations* (Delhi: Penguin Books, 1990), 66–7.
5. Gupta, *Women in Hindu Society,* 7.
6. Ibid.
7. Ibid., 23.
8. Ibid., 21.
9. Ibid., 174.   10.
Rhoda Lois Blumberg and Leela Dwarki, *India's Educated Women: Options and Constraints* (Delhi: Hindusthan Public Corporation of India, 1980), 4.
11. Ibid., 63.
12. Ashis Nandy, "Woman versus Womanliness in India," in *At the Edge of Psychology* (Delhi: Oxford University Press, 1980), 32–46, at 40.
13. Ibid., 40–1.
14. Ibid., 42–3.
15. Rabindranath Tagore, "*Mashi*" *and Other Stories* (Bombay: Macmillan Pocket Edition, 1971), 167–8.
16. Mary Lago, "Introduction," in Rabindranath Tagore, *Nashtanir (The Broken Nest)* (Bombay: Macmillan Pocket Edition, 1983), 1–21, at 14–16.
17. Gilles Deleuze, *Cinema One: Movement–Image,* trans. Hugh Tomlinson and Barbara Habberjam (Minneapolis: University of Minnesota Press, 1986), 75.
18. Kakar, *Intimate Relations,* 83.
19. Ibid.
20. Lago, "Introduction," 11.

21. Kakar, *Inner World*, 70.

22. Sylvia Harvey, "Woman's Place: The Absent Family of Film Noir," in E. Ann Kaplan, ed., *Women in Noir* (London: BFI Publications, 1987), 22–34, at 25.

23. Pam Cook, "Duplicity in *Mildred Pierce*," in Kaplan, *Women in Noir*, 68–82, at 78.

24. I am borrowing in this paragraph many of Pam Cook's critical terminologies from her aforementioned essay's section entitled "Melodrama," 75–7, at 75.

25. Satyajit Ray's script, *Nayak (The Hero)*, in *Montage* (5/6) (July 1966): n.p.

26. Personal interview, *Montage* (5/6) (July 1966): n.p.

27. Richard Lannoy, *The Speaking Tree* (London: Oxford University Press, 1974), 99.

28. Geeta Kapur, "Mythic Material in Indian Cinema," *Journal of Arts and Ideas* 14–15 (July–December 1987): 79–108, at 98.

29. Nirad C. Chaudhuri, *Hinduism* (London: Oxford University Press, 1979), 14.

30. Kapur, "Mythic Material," 98.

31. Ibid., 101.

32. Lannoy, *Speaking Tree*, 101.

33. E. Ann Kaplan, "Mothers and Daughters in Two Recent Women's Films: Mulvey/Wollen's *Riddle of the Sphinx* (1976) and Michelle Citron's *Daughter-Rite* (1978)," in *Women & Film: Both Sides of the Camera* (New York & London: Methuen, 1983), 171–88, at 173.

34. Kakar, *Intimate Relations*, 56–60.

35. Gilles Deleuze, *Cinema II: The Time Image* (Minneapolis: University of Minnesota Press, 1989), 68–70.

36. Deleuze, *Cinema II*, 71.

37. Ibid.

38. Duras, as cited by E. Ann Kaplan, in "Silence as Female Resistance in Marguerite Duras's *Nathalie Granger* (1972)," in *Women & Film*, 91–103, at 94.

39. Kaplan, *Women & Film*, 95.

40. Kakar, *Inner World*, 93.

41. Toril Moi, *Sexual Textual Politics* (London: Methuen, 1985), 67–8.

42. Quoted in ibid., 111.

43. Quoted in ibid., 112.

44. Ibid.

Chapter 3. The Responses, Trauma, and Subjectivity of the Ray *Purush* (Man)

1. Nirad C. Chaudhuri, *The Continent of Circe* (Bombay: Jaico Publishing House, 1966), 169.

2. Ibid., 169, 170.

3. Ibid., 171.

4. Ibid., 268 (emphasis added).

5. Ibid., 273.

6. Kaja Silverman, "Historical Trauma and Male Subjectivity," in E. Ann Kaplan, ed., *Psychoanalysis and Cinema* (New York: Routledge, 1990), 110–27, at 114.
7. Silverman, "Historical Trauma," 113.
8. Chaudhuri, *Continent of Circe*, 268.
9. Northrop Frye, "Theory of Modes," in *The Anatomy of Criticism: Four Essays* (Princeton: Princeton University Press, 1957), 33–67, at 34.
10. Chidananda Das Gupta, ed., *Film India – Satyajit Ray: An Anthology of Statements on Ray and by Ray* (New Delhi: Directorate of Film Festival Publications, 1981), 38.
11. Ibid., 90.
12. Ibid.
13. Gilles Deleuze, *Cinema II: The Time Image* (Minneapolis: University of Minnesota Press, 1989), 15.
14. Frye, "Theory of Modes," 34.
15. Ibid., 41–2.
16. Das Gupta, *Film India*, 109.
17. Niccolò Machiavelli, "The Qualities of a Prince," in Lee A. Jacobus, ed., *The World of Ideas* (New York: St. Martin's Press, 1986), 35–51, at 46.
18. Frye, "Theory of Modes," 41.
19. Chaudhuri, *Continent of Circe*, 338, 341.
20. Ibid., 348.
21. Ibid., 348, 353.
22. Ibid., 355.
23. John Fiske, *Reading the Popular* (Boston: Unwin Hyman, 1989), 201.
24. Ibid., 206.
25. Ibid., 212.
26. Sankar, *Company Ltd.* (Calcutta: Sangam Books, 1977), 14.
27. Ibid., 8.
28. Ibid., 67.
29. Das Gupta, *Film India*, 93.
30. Richard Lannoy, *The Speaking Tree* (London: Oxford University Press, 1974), 35.
31. Ibid., 36.
32. Ibid., 183.
33. Gary Saul Morson and Caryl Emerson, "Penultimate Words," in Clayton Koelb and Virgil Lokke, eds., *The Current in Criticism* (Lafayette, Ind.: Purdue University Press, 1987), 43–64, at 55.
34. Morson and Emerson, "Penultimate Words," 55.
35. Mikhail Bakhtin, "Laughter and Freedom," in Dan Latimer, ed., *Contemporary Critical Theory* (San Diego: Harcourt Brace Jovanovich, 1989), 300–7, at 302.
36. Ibid.
37. Ibid., 303.
38. Ibid., 306.
39. Morson and Emerson, "Penultimate Words," 56.

40. Bakhtin, "Laughter and Freedom," 307.
41. Lannoy, *Speaking Tree*, 99.
42. Ibid., 100.
43. Sudhir Kakar, *The Inner World* (Delhi: Oxford University Press, 1978), 127.
44. Ibid., 126–7.
45. Ibid., 130.
46. Ibid., 131.
47. Ravi Vasudevan, "The Melodramatic Mode and the Commercial Hindi Cinema." *Screen* 30(3) (Summer 1989): 29–50, at 33.
48. Geeta Kapur, "Mythic Material in Indian Cinema," *Journal of Arts and Ideas* 14–15 (July–December 1987): 79–108, at 100.
49. Frye, "Theory of Modes," 38.
50. Ibid.
51. Deleuze, *Cinema II*, 140.
52. I am using some of the critical categories here stressed by Claire Johnson in her excellent essay *"Double Indemnity,"* in E. Ann Kaplan, ed., *Women in Noir* (London: BFI Publications, 1987), 100–11, at 102.
53. Chaudhuri, *Continent of Circe*, 355, 358.

Chapter 4. Satyajit Ray's Political Vision of the Doubly Colonized

1. Chidananda Das Gupta, ed., *Film India – Satyajit Ray: An Anthology of Statements on Ray and by Ray* (New Delhi: Directorate of Film Festival Publications, 1981), 138.
2. Richard Lannoy, *The Speaking Tree* (London: Oxford University Press, 1974), 11–12.
3. Ibid., 149.
4. Ibid., 158–9.
5. Govind Narain, *Munshi Premchand* (Boston: Twayne, 1978), 31.
6. Ibid., 42.
7. All references are to the story "Deliverance" in *The World of Premchand*, trans. David Rubin (Bloomington: Indiana University Press, 1964), 195–203.
8. Ibid., 195.
9. Ibid., 196.
10. Ashis Nandy, *The Intimate Enemy* (Delhi: Oxford University Press, 1983), 40.
11. Premchand, "Deliverance," 196.
12. Ibid. (all of the quotes cited are on the same page).
13. Ibid., 197.
14. Nandy, *Intimate Enemy*, 40.
15. Frantz Fanon, *The Wretched of the Earth* (New York: Grove Press, 1968), 250.
16. Premchand, "Deliverance," 198.
17. Ibid., 199.
18. Ibid., 201.
19. Ibid., 202.

20. Fanon, *Wretched of the Earth*, 41.
21. Premchand, "Deliverance," 203.
22. Bill Ashcroft, Gareth Griffiths, and Helen Tiffin, *The Empire Writes Back* (London/New York: Routledge, 1989), 103.
23. Narain, *Munshi Premchand*, 30.
24. All references to Premchand's story "Shatranj-ke-Khilari" ("The Chess Players") are from *Twenty-Four Stories from Premchand*, trans. Nandini Nopan and P. Lal (New Delhi: Vikas Publishing House, 1980), 78–86.
25. Ibid., 78, 79.
26. Ibid., 80.
27. Ibid., 81.
28. Ibid., 82–3.
29. Ibid., 83.
30. Ibid., 84.
31. Ibid., 86.
32. Sudhir Kakar, *The Inner World* (Delhi: Oxford University Press, 1978), 37.
33. Ibid., 40–1.
34. Ibid., 16.
35. Ibid., 17.
36. Ibid., 37.
37. John Dawson, *The Classical Dictionary of Hinduism* (London: Routledge and Kegan Paul, 1957), 264.
38. Kakar, *Inner World*, 37.
39. Fanon, *Wretched of the Earth*, 54.
40. Ibid., 210.
41. Kakar, *Inner World*, 19–20.
42. Lannoy, *Speaking Tree*, 151.
43. Kakar, *Inner World*, 37–8.
44. Ranajit Guha in "On Some Aspects of Historiography of Colonial India," in Ranajit Guha and Gayatri C. Spivak, eds., *Selected Subaltern Studies* (New York: Oxford University Press, 1988), 37–44, at 38.
45. Satyajit Ray, "Preface," in *"The Chess Players" and Other Screenplays*, ed. Andrew Robinson (London: Faber & Faber, 1989), vii–viii, at vii.
46. Ibid., vii.
47. Excerpted from Andrew Robinson, "Introduction," in Ray, *"Chess Players" and Other Screenplays*, 3–12, at 5–6, wherein they are properly cited. I have listed here only those sources relevant to this critical scrutiny.
48. Ibid., 7.
49. Quoted in Seymour Chatman, *Story and Discourse: Narrative Structure in Fiction and Film* (Ithaca: Cornell University Press, 1978), 132.
50. Ibid.
51. Ibid., 132–3.
52. E. M. Forster, *A Passage to India* (New York: Harcourt, Brace, & World, 1952), 195.
53. Ashis Nandy, "Beyond Orientalism Despotism: Politics and Femininity in Satyajit Ray," *Deep Focus* 1(2) (June 1988): 53–60.
54. Das Gupta, ed., *Film India*, 121.

Chapter 5. From Newly Discovered Margins: Ray's Responses to the Center

1. Asoke S. Viswanathan, "Crash of the Titans," *Calcutta Skyline*, March 1990, 42–4.
2. Ashis Nandy, *The Savage Freud* (Delhi: Oxford University Press, 1995), 262.
3. Richard Lannoy, *The Speaking Tree* (London: Oxford University Press, 1974), 169.
4. Quoted in ibid., 180.
5. Bill Ashcroft, Gareth Griffiths, and Helen Tiffin, *The Empire Writes Back* (London/New York: Routledge, 1989), 104.
6. The original short story that Ray vastly extended as *Agantuk* is entitled "The Guest"; it has been recently translated into English by Gopa Majumdar and included in Satyajit Ray, *Twenty Stories* (Delhi: Penguin Books India, 1992), 30–40.
7. Lannoy, *Speaking Tree*, 64.
8. Jayanti Sen, "A New Feather in Ray's Crown," *Cinema India – International*, 1 (1989), 26–8.
9. Ashcroft et al., *Empire Writes Back*, 171.
10. Ibid., 30.
11. Ibid., 38.
12. Jayanti Sen, "New Feather," 38.
13. Edmund Leach, *Lévi-Strauss* (Great Britain: Fontana/Collins, 1974), 32.
14. Ibid., 33.

Selected Bibliography

Adams, Hazard, ed. *Critical Theory since Plato*. New York: Harcourt Brace Jovanovich, 1971.

Ashcroft, Bill, Gareth Griffiths, and Helen Tiffin, eds. *The Empire Writes Back*. London/New York: Routledge, 1989.

Bahadur, Jaya Wadiyar. *An Aspect of Indian Aesthetics*. Madras: Madras University Press, 1956.

Bakhtin, Mikhail. "Laughter and Freedom." In Dan Latimer, ed., *Contemporary Critical Theory*, 300–7. San Diego: Harcourt Brace Jovanovich, 1989.

Banerji [Banerjee], Bhibhuti Bhusan. *Pather Panchali (Song of the Road)*. Trans. T. W. Clark and Tarapada Mukherjee. Bloomington: Indiana University Press, 1968.

Barnouw, Erik, and S. Krishnaswamy. *Indian Film*, 2d ed. New York: Oxford University Press, 1980.

Baumer, Rachel, and James R. Brandon, eds. *Sanskrit Drama in Performance*. Honolulu: University Press of Hawaii, 1981.

Blumberg, Rhoda Lois, and Leela Dwarki. *India's Educated Women: Opinions and Constraints*. Delhi: Hindusthan Public Corporation of India, 1980.

Castelvetro, Ludovico. "Aristotle's Poetics." In Adams, *Critical Theory since Plato*, 144–53.

Chari, V. K. *Sanskrit Criticism*. Honolulu: University of Hawaii Press, 1990.

Chatman, Seymour. *Story and Discourse: Narrative Structure in Fiction and Film*. Ithaca: Cornell University Press, 1978.

Chaudhuri, Nirad C. *The Continent of Circe*. Bombay: Jaico Publishing House, 1966.

Cook, Pam. "Duplicity in *Mildred Pierce*." In Kaplan, *Women in Noir*, 68–82.

Das Gupta, Chidananda, ed. *The Cinema of Satyajit Ray*. New Delhi: Vikas Publishing House, 1980.

____ ed. *Film India – Satyajit Ray: An Anthology of Statements on Ray and by Ray*. New Delhi: Directorate of Film Festival Publications, 1981.

Dawson, John. *The Classical Dictionary of Hinduism*. London: Routledge & Kegan Paul, 1957.

Deleuze, Gilles. *Cinema One: Movement–Image*. Trans. Hugh Tomlinson and Barbara Habberjam. Minneapolis: University of Minnesota Press, 1986.

____ *Cinema II: The Time Image*. Minneapolis: University of Minnesota Press, 1989.

245

Deutsch, Eliot. "Reflections on Some Aspects of the Theory of *Rasa.*" In Baumer and Brandon, *Sanskrit Drama in Performance,* 214–25.

Dimock, Edward C., Jr. et al., eds. *The Literatures of India: An Introduction.* Chicago: University of Chicago Press, 1978.

Doane, Mary Anne, Patricia Millencamp, and Linda Williams, eds. *Re-Vision: Essays in Feminist Film Criticism.* Los Angeles: American Film Institute, 1984.

Fanon, Frantz. *The Wretched of the Earth.* New York: Grove Press, 1968.

Fiske, John. *Reading the Popular.* Boston: Unwin Hyman, 1989.

Forster, E. M. *A Passage to India.* New York: Harcourt, Brace, & World, 1952.

Frye, Northrop. "Theory of Modes." In *The Anatomy of Criticism: Four Essays,* 33–67. Princeton: Princeton University Press, 1957.

Gerow, Edwin. "The Persistence of Classical, Esthetic Categories in Contemporary Indian Literature: *Three Bengali Novels.*" In Dimock et al., *Literatures of India,* 212–38.

"*Rasa* as a Category of Literary Criticism." In Baumer and Brandon, *Sanskrit Drama in Performance,* 226–57.

Gnoli, Raniero. *The Aesthetic Appearance According to Abhinavagupta.* Rome: MEO, 1956.

Guha, Ranajit. "On Some Aspects of Historiography of Colonial India." In Guha and Spivak, *Selected Subaltern Studies,* 37–44.

Guha, Ranajit, and Gayatri C. Spivak, eds. *Selected Subaltern Studies.* New York: Oxford University Press, 1988.

Gupta, A. R. *Women in Hindu Society.* Delhi: Jyotsna Prakashan, 1982.

Harvey, Sylvia. "Woman's Place: The Absent Film of Film Noir." In Kaplan, *Women in Noir,* 22–34.

House, Humphrey. *Aristotle's Poetics: A Course of Eight Lectures.* London: Rupert Hart-Davis, 1961.

Jacobus, Lee A., ed. *The World of Ideas.* New York: St. Martin's Press, 1986.

Joyce, James. *The Portrait of an Artist as a Young Man.* New York: Viking Press, 1968.

Kael, Pauline. "The Home and the World." In *State of the Art,* 380–2. New York: E. P. Dutton, 1985.

Kakar, Sudhir. *The Inner World.* Delhi: Oxford University Press, 1978.

Intimate Relations. Delhi: Penguin Books, 1990.

Kalidasa. *Sakuntala.* Trans. Arthur W. Ryder. New York: E. P. Dutton & Co., 1959.

Kaplan, E. Ann. *Psychoanalysis and Cinema.* New York: Routledge, 1990.

Women & Film: Both Sides of the Camera. New York & London: Methuen, 1983.

Women in Noir. London: BFI Publications, 1987.

Kapur, Geeta. "Cultural Creativity in the First Decade: The Example of Satyajit Ray." *Journal of Arts and Ideas* 23–4 (January 1993): 17–49.

"Mythic Material in Indian Cinema." *Journal of Arts and Ideas* 14–15 (July–December 1987): 79–108.

Koelb, Clayton, and Virgil Lokke, eds. *The Current in Criticism.* Lafayette, Ind.: Purdue University Press, 1987.

Krupanidhi, Uma, ed. "Satyajit Ray." Special issue, *Montage* 5–6 (July 1966).
Kundu, Gautam. "Satyajit Ray as Auteur: A Neglected Perspective." *Quarterly Review of Film Studies* 8(4) (Fall 1983): 85–8.
Lannoy, Richard. *The Speaking Tree*. London: Oxford University Press, 1974.
Machiavelli, Niccolò. "The Qualities of a Prince." In Jacobus, *World of Ideas*, 35–51.
Masson, J. L., and M. V. Patwardhan. *Aesthetic Rapture*, vol. 1: *Text*. Poona: Deccan College Publications, 1970.
Masson, J. Moussaieff, and W. S. Merwin. *Sanskrit Love Poetry*. New York: Columbia University Press, 1977.
Moi, Toril. *Sexual Textual Politics*. London: Methuen, 1985.
Morson, Gary Saul, and Caryl Emerson. "Penultimate Words." In Koelb and Lokke, *Current in Criticism*, 43–64.
Nandy, Ashis. *At the Edge of Psychology*. Delhi: Oxford University Press, 1980.
   "Beyond Orientalism Despotism: Politics and Femininity in Satyajit Ray." *Deep Focus* 1(2) (June 1988): 53–60.
The Intimate Enemy. Delhi: Oxford University Press, 1983.
The Savage Freud. Delhi: Oxford University Press, 1995.
Narain, Govind. *Munshi Premchand*. Boston: Twayne, 1978.
National Committee on the Status of Women. *Status of Women in India*. New Delhi: Allied Publishers, 1975.
Nyce, Ben. *Satyajit Ray: A Study of His Films*. New York: Praeger, 1988.
Premchand. "Chess Players." In *Twenty-Four Stories from Premchand*, 78–86. Trans. Nadini Nopan and P. Lal. New Delhi: Vikas Publishing House, 1980.
   "Deliverance." In *The World of Premchand*, 195–203. Trans. David Rubin. Bloomington: Indiana University Press, 1964.
Raghavan, V. "Sanskrit Drama in Performance." In Baumer and Brandon, *Sanskrit Drama in Performance*, 9–44.
Rajadhyaksha, Ashish. "Satyajit Ray, Ray's Films and Ray-Movie." *Journal of Arts and Ideas*, 23–4 (January 1993): 7–16.
Ramanujan, A. K., and Edwin Gerow. "Dramatic Criticism." In Dimock et al., *Literatures of India*, 128–36.
Ray, Satyajit. *The Apu Trilogy*. Trans. Shampa Banerjee. Calcutta: Seagull Books, 1985.
Nayak (The Hero). *Montage* (5/6) (July 1966), n.p.
Our Films, Their Films. Bombay: Orient Longman Ltd. 1976.
Shantranj-ke-Khilari (screenplay). In *"The Chess Players" and Other Screenplays*. Ed. Andrew Robinson. London: Faber & Faber, 1989.
Rhode, Eric. "Satyajit Ray: A Study." *Sight and Sound* 30(3) (Summer 1961): 132–6. Reprinted in Julius Bellone, ed., *Renaissance of the Film* (London: Collier–Macmillan Ltd., 1970), 9–23.
Robinson, Andrew. *Satyajit Ray: The Inner Eye*. Calcutta: Rupa & Co., 1990.
Sankar. *Company Ltd*. Calcutta: Sangam Books, 1977.
Scott-James, R. A. *The Making of Literature*. London: Mercury Books, 1963.
Seton, Marie. *Portrait of a Director: Satyajit Ray*. London: Dobson Books, 1971.
Silverman, Kaja. "Historical Trauma and Male Subjectivity." In Kaplan, *Psychoanalysis and Cinema*, 110–27.

Tagore, Rabindranath. *The Home and the World*. London: Macmillan & Co., 1919.

"Mashi" and Other Stories. Bombay: Macmillan Pocket Edition, 1971.

Nashtanir (The Broken Nest). Bombay: Macmillan Pocket Edition, 1983.

Thomas, Rosie. "Indian Cinema: Pleasure and Popularity – An Introduction." *Screen* 26(3–4) (May–August 1985): 116–31.

Vasudevan, Ravi. "The Melodramatic Mode and the Commercial Hindi Cinema." *Screen* 30(3) (Summer 1989): 29–50.

Wood, Robin. *The Apu Trilogy*. New York: Praeger, 1971.

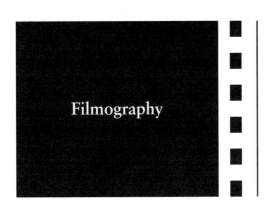

Filmography

Abbreviations: D, director; P, producer; S, screenplay; Ph, cinematography; E, editor; AD, art director; M, music; C, principal cast; N, narration; Aw, awards.

Pather Panchali (Song of the Little Road) (first in *The Apu Trilogy*). 1955. D, S, Satyajit Ray, after the novel by Bibhuti Bhusan Banerjee; P, Government of West Bengal; Ph, Subrata Mitra; E, Dulal Dutta; AD, Bansi Chandragupta; M, Ravi Shankar; C, Kanu Banerjee (Harihar Ray), Karuna Banerjee (Sarbojaya), Subir Banerjee (Apu), Runki Banerjee (Durga at six years old), Uma Das Gupta (Durga at twelve years old), Chunibala Devi (Indir [Granny]), Reba Devi (Sejothakrun); 115 min, b&w; Aw, Best Human Document, Cannes, 1956.

Aparajito (The Unvanquished) (second in *The Apu Trilogy*). 1956. D, S, Satyajit Ray, after the novel by Bibhuti Bhusan Banerjee. P, Epic Films; Ph, Subrata Mitra; E, Dulal Dutta; AD, Bansi Chandragupta; M, Ravi Shankar; C, Kanu Banerjee (Harihar Ray), Karuna Banerjee (Sarbojaya), Pinaki Sen Gupta (Apu as a child), Smaran Ghosal (Apu as an adolescent), Subodh Ganguly (headmaster), Charuprakash Ghosh (Nanda-*babu*), Kali Charan Ray (press owner), Ramani Sen Gupta (uncle), Anil Mukherjee (Shbunath); 113 min, b&w; Aw, Golden Lion, Venice, 1957.

Parash Pather (The Philosopher's Stone). 1957. D, S, Satyajit Ray, after a short story by Parasuram; P, L. B. Films International; Ph, Subrata Mitra; E, Dulal Dutta; AD, Bansi Chandragupta; M, Ravi Shankar; C, Tulsi Chakravarty (Paresh Dutta), Ranibala Devi (Giribala Dutta), Kali Banerjee (Priyatosh Biswas), Gangapada Basu (businessman), Haridhan Chatterjee (police inspector); 111 min, b&w.

Jalsaghar (The Music Room). 1958. D, S, Satyajit Ray, after a short story by Tarashankar Banerjee; P, Satyajit Ray Productions; Ph, Subrata Mitra; E, Dulal Dutta; AD, Bansi Chandragupta; M, Vilayat Khan; C, Chhabi Biswas (Biswambhar Roy), Padma Devi (Roy's wife), Pinaki Sen Gupta (Bireswar, Roy's son), Ganapada Basu (Mahim Ganguly), Kali Sarkar (Ananta, the head servant), Tulsi Lahiri (Taraprasanna), Begum Akhtar (singer), Ustad Wahid Khan (singer), Roshan Kumari (dancer); 100 min, b&w.

Apur Sansar (The World of Apu) (third in *The Apu Trilogy*). 1959. D, S, Satyajit Ray, after the novel by Bibhuti Bhusan Banerjee; P, Satyajit Ray Productions; Ph, Subrata Mitra; E, Dulal Dutta; AD, Bansi Chandragupta; M, Ravi Shankar; C, Soumitra Chatterjee (Apu), Sharmila Tagore (Aparna), Swapan Mukherjee (Pulu), Aloke Chakravarty (Kajal); 106 min, b&w; Aw, Best Original and Imaginative Film, London, 1960.

Devi (The Goddess). 1960. D, S, Satyajit Ray, after the story by Prabhat Mukherjee; P, Satyajit Ray Productions; Ph, Subrata Mitra; E, Dulal Dutta; AD, Bansi Chandragupta; M, Ali Akbar Khan; C, Chhabi Biswas (Kalikinkar Roy), Soumitra Chatterjee (Umaprasad [Uma]), Sharmila Tagore (Doyamoyee [Doya]), Karuna Banerjee (Harisundari), Purnendu Mukherjee (Tarapada), Arpan Choudhury (Khoka), Anil Chatterjee (Bhudib), Kali Sarkar (Professor Sarkar); 93 min, b&w.

Rabindranath Tagore (documentary). 1961. D, S, N, Satyajit Ray; P, Films Division, government of India; Ph, Soumendu Roy; E, Dulal Dutta; AD, Bansi Chandragupta; M, Jyotirindra Moitra; C, Smaran Ghosal (Tagore as an adolescent), Raya Chatterjee, Shovanlal Gangopadhyaya, Purnendu Mukherjee, Kalol Bose; 54 min, b&w.

Teen Kanya (Three Daughters; a.k.a. Two Daughters). 1961. D, S, M, Satyajit Ray, after three short stories by Rabindranath Tagore ("Monihara" is omitted from most foreign-release prints; hence the variant release titles); P, Satyajit Ray Productions; Ph, Soumendu Roy; E, Dulal Dutta; AD, Bansi Chandragupta; C, "The Postmaster," Anil Chatterjee (Nandalal), Chandana Banerjee (Ratan), Nriparti Chatterjee (Bisay), Khagen Pathak (Khagen), Gopal Roy (Bilash); "Monihara" ("The Lost Jewel"), Kali Banerjee (Phanibhusan Shaha), Kanika Mazumdar (Monimalika), Kumar Roy (Madhusudan), Gobina Chakravarty (schoolmaster/narrator); "Samapti" ("The Conclusion"), Soumitra Chatterjee (Amulya), Aparna Das Gupta (Mrinmoyee), Sita Mukherjee (Jogmaya), Gita Dey (Nistarini), Santosh Dutta (Kisori), Mihir Chakravarty (Rakhal); 171 min for *Three Daughters*, 114 min for *Two Daughters*; b&w.

Kanchanjungha. 1962. D, S, M, Satyajit Ray (his first original screenplay); P, NCA Productions; Ph, Subrata Mitra; E, Dulal Dutta; AD, Bansi Chandragupta; C, Chhabi Biswas (Indranath Choudhury), Karuna Banerjee (Labanya), Anubha Gupta (Anima), Pahari Sanyal (Jagadish), Alakananda Roy (Monisha), Subrata Sen (Shankar), Arun Mukherjee (Ashok), Anil Chatterjee (Anil), N. Viswanathan (Pranab Banerjee), Sibani Singh (Tuklu); 102 min, color.

Abhijan (The Expedition). 1962. D, S, M, Satyajit Ray, after the novel by Tarashankar Banerjee; P, Abhijatrik Calcutta; Ph, Soumendu Roy; E, Dulal Dutta; AD, Bansi Chandragupta; C, Soumitra Chatterjee (Narsingh), Waheeda Rehman (Gulabi), Robi Ghosh (Rama), Ruma Guha Thakurta (Mary Neelima), Gyanesh Mukherjee (Joseph), Charuprakash Ghosh (Sukhanram); 150 min, b&w.

Mahanagar (The Big City). 1963. D, S, M, Satyajit Ray, after the short story "Abataranika" by Narendranath Mitra; P, R. D. Bansal; Ph, Soumendu Roy;

E, Dulal Dutta; **AD,** Bansi Chandragupta; **C,** Madhabi Mukherjee (Arati Mazumdar), Anil Chatterjee (Subrata), Haren Chatterjee (Priyogopal), Haradhan
Banerjee (Mr. Mukherjee), Vicky Redwood (Edith), Jaya Bhaduri (Bani); 131
min, b&w.

Charulata (*The Lonely Wife*). 1964. D, S, M, Satyajit Ray, after the novella
Nashtanir (*The Broken Nest*) by Rabindranath Tagore. P, R. D. Bansal; **Ph,** Su-
brata Mitra; **E,** Dulal Dutta; **AD,** Bansi Chandragupta; **C,** Madhabi Mukherjee
(Charulata), Soumitra Chatterjee (Amal), Sailen Mukherjee (Bhupati), Shyamal
Ghosal (Umapada), Geetali Roy (Mandakini); 117 min, b&w; **Aw,** Best Direc-
tion, Berlin, 1965.

Two (a.k.a. *The Parable of Two*). 1964. D, S, M, Satyajit Ray; P, Esso; **Ph,** Soumendu Roy; **E,** Dulal Dutta; **C,** Rabi Kiron; 15 min, b&w (short).

Kapurush-o-Mahapurush (*The Coward and the Holy Man, a.k.a. The Coward
and the Saint*). 1965. D, S, M, Satyajit Ray, after the short stories "Janaiko
Kapuruser Kahini" by Premendra Mitra and "Birinchi Baba" by Parasuram;
P, R. D. Bansal; **Ph,** Soumendu Roy; **E,** Dulal Dutta; **AD,** Bansi Chandragupta;
C, "Kapurush," Madhabi Mukherjee (Karuna), Soumitra Chatterjee (Amita-
bha Roy), Haradhan Banerjee (Bimal Gupta); "Mahapurush," Charuprakash
Ghosh (Birinchi), Robi Ghosh (the assistant); 139 min, b&w.

Nayak (*The Hero*). 1966. D, S, M, Satyajit Ray; P, R. D. Bansal; **Ph,** Subrata
Mitra; **E,** Dulal Dutta; **AD,** Bansi Chandragupta; **C,** Uttam Kumar (Arindam
Mukherjee), Sharmila Tagore (Aditi Sengupta), Sumita Sanyal (Promilla Chat-
terjee), Bharati Devi (Manorama Bose), Ranjit Sen (Haren Bose), Kanu Mukher-
jee (Pritish Sakar), Nirmal Ghosh (Jyoti), Somen Bose (Shankarda), Bireswar
Sen (Mukanda Lahiri), Premangsu Bose (Biresh), Lali Choudhury (Bulbul Bose),
Subrata Sen Sharma (Ajoy), Jamuna Sinha (Shefali); 120 min, b&w.

Chiriakhana (*The Zoo*). 1967. D, S, M, Satyajit Ray, after the novel by Saradin-
du Banerjee; P, Star Productions; **Ph,** Soumendu Roy; **E,** Dulal Dutta; **AD,** Bansi
Chandragupta; **C,** Uttam Kumar (Byomkesh Bakshi), Sailen Mukherjee (Ajit),
Sushil Mazumdar (Nisanath Sen); 125 min, b&w. (This film is included for
completeness, although Ray did not consider it part of his oeuvre. It was a project generated by some of his assistants; he took it over at a backer's insistence.)

Goopy Gyne Bagha Byne (*The Adventures of Goopy and Bagha; a.k.a. Goopy
and Bagha*). 1968. D, S, M, Satyajit Ray, after the story by Upendrakishore Ray-
choudhury; P, Purmina Pictures; **Ph,** Soumendu Roy; **E,** Dulal Dutta; **AD,** Bansi
Chandragupta; **C,** Tapen Chatterjee (Goopy), Robi Ghosh (Bagha), Santosh
Dutta (King of Shundi, King of Halla), Jahar Roy (prime minister), Harindranath Chattopadhyaya (magician); 132 min, b&w/color; **Aw,** Best Film, Melbourne, 1970.

Aranyer Din Ratri (*Days and Nights in the Forest*). 1970. D, S, M, Satyajit
Ray, after the novel by Sunil Ganguly; P, Priya Films; **Ph,** Soumendu Roy; **E,**
Dulal Dutta; **AD,** Bansi Chandragupta; **C,** Soumitra Chatterjee (Ashim), Shar-

mila Tagore (Aparna), Shubhendu Chatterjee (Sanjoy), Robi Ghosh (Shekar), Samit Bhanja (Hari), Simi Garewal (Duli), Pahari Sanyal (Sadasiv Tripathi), Kaberi Bose (Jaya), Aparna Sen (Atasi), Noni Ganguly (Lokha); 115 min, b&w.

Pratidwandi (*The Adversary*, a.k.a. *Siddhartha and the City*) (first film in the City trilogy). 1970. D, S, M, Satyajit Ray, after the novel by Sunil Ganguly; P, Priya Films; Ph, Soumendu Roy; E, Dulal Dutta; AD, Bansi Chandragupta; C, Dhritiman Chatterjee (Siddhartha Choudhury), Debraj Roy (Tunu), Krishna Bose (Sutapa), Jayashree Roy (Keya), Kalyan Choudhury (Siben), Soven Lahiri (Ananta Sanyal), Sefali (Latika); 110 min, b&w.

Sikkim (documentary). 1971. D, S, M, N, Satyajit Ray; P, Government of Sikkim; Ph, Soumendu Roy; E, Dulal Dutta; ~50 min, color.

Seemabaddha (*Company Limited*) (second film in the City trilogy). 1971. D, S, M, Satyajit Ray, after the novel by Sankar; P, Chitranjali (Bharat Shamsher Jung Bhadur Rana); Ph, Soumendu Roy; E, Dulal Dutta; AD, Ashoke Bose; C, Barun Chanda (Shyamalendu Chatterjee), Sharmila Tagore (Sudharshana [Tutul]), Parumita Choudhury (Dolan), Harindranath Chattopadhyaya (Sir Biren Roy), Haradhan Banerjee (Talukdar); 112 min, b&w.

The Inner Eye (documentary on blind artist Binod Behari Mukherjee). 1972. D, S, M, N, Satyajit Ray; P, Films Division, Government of India; Ph, Soumendu Roy; E, Dulal Dutta; 20 min, color.

Ashani Sanket (*Distant Thunder*). 1973. D, S, M, Satyajit Ray, after the novel by Bibhuti Bhusan Banerjee; P, Balaka Movies (Sarbani Bhattacharya); Ph, Soumendu Roy; E, Dulal Dutta; AD, Ashoke Bose; C, Soumitra Chatterjee (Gangacharan), Babita (Ananga), Sandhya Roy (Chutki), Ramesh Mukherjee (Biswas), Chitra Banerjee (Moti), Seli Pal (Bhattacharjee), Noni Ganguly (Jadu); 101 min, color; Aw, Golden Bear, Berlin, 1974.

Sonar Kella (*The Golden Fortress*). 1974. D, S, M, Satyajit Ray, after a story of his for the children's magazine *Sandesh* (founded by his grandfather and revived in 1961); P, Ministry of Information, Government of Bengal; Ph, Soumendu Roy; E, Dulal Dutta; AD, Ashoke Bose; C, Soumitra Chatterjee (Felu), Santosh Dutta (Lalmohan Ganguly), Kushal Chakravarty (Mukul), Kamu Mukherjee (Mandar Bose), Ajoy Banerjee (Amityanath Burman); 120 min, color.

Jana Aranya (*The Middleman*) (third film in the City trilogy). 1975. D, S, M, Satyajit Ray, after the novel by Shankar; P, Indus Films; Ph, Soumendu Roy; E, Dulal Dutta; AD, Ashoke Bose; C, Pradip Mukherjee (Somnath), Satya Bandopadhyaya (his father), Dipankar Dey (Bhombol), Lili Chakravarty (Kamala), Utpal Dutt (Bishuda [Bishu]), Robi Ghosh (Natabar Mitter), Soven Lahiri (Goenka), Aparna Sen (Somnath's girlfriend); 131 min, b&w (Ray's last film in black and white).

Bala (documentary on dance). 1976. D, S, N, Satyajit Ray; P, National Center for Performing Arts and Government of Tamil Nadu; Ph, Soumendu Roy; E, Dulal Dutta; 33 min, color (short).

Shatranj-ke-Khilari (The Chess Players). 1977. D, S, M, Satyajit Ray, after the 1924 short story by Munshi Premchand; P, Devki Chitra Productions; Ph, Soumendu Roy; E, Dulal Dutta; AD, Bansi Chandragupta; **Songs**, Reba Muhuri, Birjir Maharaj; **Choreography**, Birjir Maharaj; C, Amjad Khan (Wajid Ali Shah), Sanjeev Kumar (Mirza Sajjad Ali), Saeed Jaffrey (Mir Roshan Ali), Richard Attenborough (General Outram), Shabana Azmi (Mirza's wife [Khurshid]), Farida Jalal (Mir's wife [Nafeesa]), Victor Banerjee (Prime Minister Ali Naqui), Tom Alter (Outram's aide-de-camp [Weston]), Farooq Shaikh (Aquil), David Abraham (*munshi*), Leela Mishra (Hiria), Samarth Narain (Kaloo), Barry John (Dr. Joseph Fayrer); 113 min, color (Ray's first film in Hindi).

Joi Baba Felunath (The Elephant God). 1978. D, S, M, Satyajit Ray, after another of his children's detective stories; P, R. D. Bansal; Ph, Soumendu Roy; E, Dulal Dutta; AD, Ashoke Bose; C, Soumitra Chatterjee (Felu), Santosh Dutta (Lalmohan Ganguly), Siddhartha Chatterjee (Tapesh), Utpal Dutt (Maganlal), Jit Bose (Ruku), Manu Mukherjee (Machli Baba); 112 min, color.

Hirok Rajar Deshe (The Kingdom of Diamonds). 1980. D, S, M, Satyajit Ray; P, Ministry of Information, Government of Bengal; Ph, Soumendu Roy; E, Dulal Dutta; AD, Ashoke Bose; C, Soumitra Chatterjee (Udayan), Utpal Dutt (King of Hirok), Robi Ghosh (Bagha), Tapen Chatterjee (Goopy), Santosh Dutta (scientist); 118 min, color (sequel to *The Adventures of Goopy and Bagha*).

Pikoo (a.k.a. Pikoo's Day). 1981. D, S, M, Satyajit Ray, after his story "Pikur Diary"; P, Henri Fraise; Ph, Soumendu Roy; E, Dulal Dutta; C, Arjun Guha Thakurta (Pikoo), Aparn Sen (his mother), Victor Banerjee (lover), Promod Ganguly (grandfather); 26 min, color (short, commissioned for French TV by ORTF).

Sadgati (Deliverance). 1981. D, S, M, Satyajit Ray, after the 1931 short story by Munshi Premchand; P, Doordarshan Television; Ph, Soumendu Roy; E, Dulal Dutta; C, Om Puri (Dukhi), Smita Patil (Jhuriya, his wife), Mohan Agashe (Ghasiram [Baba, Panditji]), Gita Siddharth (Panditayin); 52 min, color (TV film) (Ray's second film in Hindi).

Ghare-Baire (The Home and the World). 1984. D, S, M, Satyajit Ray (filming completed by Sandip Ray, due to his father's ill health), after the novel by Rabindranath Tagore; P, National Film Development Corporation of India; Ph, Soumendu Roy; E, Dulal Dutta; AD, Ashoke Bose; C, Soumitra Chatterjee (Sandip), Victor Banerjee (Nikhil), Swatilekha Chatterjee (Bimala), Gopa Aich (sister-in-law), Manoj Mitra (headmaster), Indrapramit Roy (Amulya), Jennifer Kapoor (Miss Gilby); 140 min, color.

Sukumar Ray (documentary). 1987. D, S, M, Satyajit Ray; P, Government of West Bengal; N, Soumitra Chatterjee; Ph, Barun Raha; E, Dulal Dutta; AD, Ashoke Bose; C, Soumitra Chatterjee, Utpal Dutt, Santosh Dutta, Tapen Chatterjee; 30 min, color.

Ganashatru (*An Enemy of the People*). 1989. **D, S, M,** Satyajit Ray, after the 1882 play *En folkefiende* by Henrik Ibsen; **P,** National Film Development Corporation of India; **Ph,** Barun Raha; **E,** Dulal Dutta; **AD,** Ashoke Bose; **C,** Soumitra Chatterjee (Dr. Ashoke Gupta), Ruma Guha Thakurta (Maya), Mamata Shankar (Indrani), Dhritiman Chatterjee (Nisith), Dipankar Dey (Haridas Bagchi), Subhendu Chatterjee (Biresh), Manoj Mitra (Adhir), Viswa Guha Thakurta (Ranen Halder), Rajaram Yagnik (Bhargava), Satya Banerjee (Manmatha), Gobinda Mukherjee (Chandan); 100 min, color.

Shakha Proshaka (*Branches of the Tree*). 1990. **D, S, M,** Satyajit Ray; **P,** D. D. Productions, Erato Films and Satyajit Ray, and Soprofilms, Paris; **Ph,** Barun Raha; **E,** Dulal Dutta; **AD,** Ashoke Bose; **C,** Soumitra Chatterjee (Proshanto Majumdar), Haradhan Banerjee (Ashoke Majumdar), Ajit Banerjee (Ananda Majumdar), Dipankar Dey (Probir Majumdar), Ranjit Mullick (Protap Majumdar), Promod Ganguly (Ananda's father), Ruma Guha Thakurta (Uma), Mamata Shankar (Tapti), Sohan (Dingo); 130 min, color.

Agantuk (*The Stranger*). 1991. **D, S, M,** Satyajit Ray; **P,** National Film Development Corporation of India, Erato Films and Satyajit Ray, D. D. Productions, and Soprofilms, Paris; **Ph,** Barun Raha; **E,** Dulal Dutta; **AD,** Ashoke Bose; **C,** Utpal Dutt (Manmohan Mitra), Dipankar Dey (Sudhendu Bose), Mamata Shankar (Anila Bose), Dhritiman Chatterjee (Pritish Dasgupta), Robi Ghosh (Mr. Rakhit), Bikram Banerjee (Satyaki Bose); 120 min, color.

Additional Films Cited

Glengarry Glen Ross, dir. James Foley (Tokofsky/Zupnik, USA, 1992)

Journal d'un curé de campagne (*Diary of a Country Priest*), dir. Robert Bresson (France, 1950)

Mildred Pierce, dir. Michael Curtiz (Warner Bros., USA, 1945)

Nanook of the North, dir. Robert Flaherty (Revillon Frères, Canada, 1922)

North by Northwest, dir. Alfred Hitchcock (Hitchcock/MGM, USA, 1959)

Rashomon, dir. Akira Kurosawa (Japan, 1950)

Silence, The (*Tystnaden*), dir. Ingmar Bergman (Sweden, 1963)

Vertigo, dir. Alfred Hitchcock (Hitchcock/Paramount, USA, 1958)

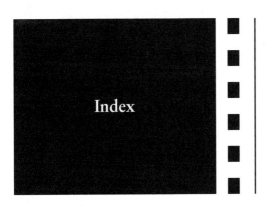

Index

Note: Pages in bold italics denote illustrations.

255